LEWIS & CLARK

The Journey of
the Corps of Discovery

LEWIS &
CLARK

AN ILLUSTRATED HISTORY

BY DAYTON DUNCAN

*Based on a documentary film
by Ken Burns, written by Dayton Duncan*

WITH A PREFACE BY KEN BURNS
AND CONTRIBUTIONS BY
STEPHEN E. AMBROSE,
ERICA FUNKHOUSER,
WILLIAM LEAST HEAT-MOON

Alfred A. Knopf   NEW YORK   2018

THIS IS A BORZOI BOOK
PUBLISHED BY ALFRED A. KNOPF

ISBN 0-679-45450-0
ISBN 0-375-70652-6 (pbk)
LC 97-73823

Manufactured in China
Hardcover edition published October 8, 1997
Reprinted five times
Seventh printing, May 2004
Paperback edition published September 3, 1999
Reprinted Four Times
Sixth Printing, February 2018

Contents

—

Come Up Me

F OR THE RIVER TRAVELER of any century, the Missouri is a beast, a long, dangerous, wildly beautiful snake of a thing. It feels alive. Its cottonwoods groan and snap and explode in the frigid winters of the northern Plains, its banks and breaks hide needle-sharp prickly pears and chiggers by the trillions, and its vast prairies and distant mountains and seemingly limitless length test one's comprehension at every turn. Its weather changes in an instant: broiling sun gives way to hailstones the size of baseballs and then to idyllic sunsets of startling majesty, what Emily Dickinson once called the "far theatricals of day." Its muddy current brings relentless news from its headwaters: tree trunks and snags and carcasses of unlucky bison or antelope. Its stunning cataracts and waterfalls, its breathtaking mountain views, its high cliffs and the intricately carved architecture of its palisades constantly echo a higher intelligence. It *is* alive.

"It's a river that says: 'I am a grandfather spirit. I have a life,' " the writer William Least Heat-Moon told us. On a boat trip he recently took up the Missouri, covering much of the same route that the Lewis and Clark expedition had nearly two hundred years before, Heat-Moon recalled that the river seemed to tease him, to threaten him, to toy with him, as if it was some great spirit. Despite the obstacles, he said, "I never once felt that that river wanted to kill me." Instead, as it had for Lewis and Clark, the river drew him on, beckoning him: "You're going against the snags and the sawyers and the sandbars.

You're going against the treachery of the river," he said. "But you are also going against this river which seems to say to the traveler, 'Come up me.'"

In May 1804 Meriwether Lewis and William Clark, traveling with nearly four dozen other men and calling themselves the Corps of Discovery, heard that voice and set off up the great Missouri River. They were journeying for their President, Thomas Jefferson, for whom Lewis had once worked as secretary, but they were also the vanguard of a brand-new country eager to expand its borders and catalogue the many mysteries of a western land they saw as "a treasure house of the unprecedented." What drew them up the river was an unformed and unarticulated sense that their country's destiny lay that way.

This book was born in the midst of producing a documentary film history of the Lewis and Clark journey. That film is part of a broader series of biographies of noteworthy Americans that will be shown from time to time on public television, which in turn adds to a body of films on American history that has consumed all of my adult life. Looking back over these projects, and looking ahead to the new ones, it is clear that in many ways I have made the same film over and over again. Each production asks one deceptively simple question: Who are we? That is to say, Who are we Americans as a people? What does an investigation of the past tell us about who we were and what we have become? Each film (and book) offers an opportunity to pursue this question in a new way, and while never answering it fully, nevertheless deepens the question with each successive project.

For the documentary maker (both film and book), Lewis and Clark present special problems. There is not a schoolchild in America who does not know that the explorers made it back safely. We realized, therefore, that in order for our narrative to be a dramatic and compelling one we must endeavor at every juncture to place the viewer or reader in the moment, to make the past somehow come alive. The expedition's tense confrontation with the Teton Sioux along the lower Missouri, their freezing-cold first winter in North Dakota, Lewis's anxiety at the difficult birth of Sacagawea's son, their wonder at the beauty of the White Cliffs and Great Falls in Montana, their nightmarish trip over the Rockies, their first joyful glimpse of the Pacific, their desperate fight with the Blackfeet Indians on the return, and their ecstatic welcome home as heroes—every scene must be endowed with the possibility that these familiar events might not turn out the way we all know that they did.

This is a difficult but not impossible task with an abundance of photographic material, as we had for our film and book on the Civil War, but the story of Lewis and Clark took place many years before the advent of photography and there are only a handful of relevant contemporary paintings. We were therefore forced, in both the film and the book, to take significant poetic license. Photographs of Indian tribes taken many years after their encounter with Lewis and Clark are used throughout, as are paintings made on later expeditions by other explorers. Each lends a sense of what the Corps of Discovery might have seen without violating too severely our own insistence on a faithful reconstruction of the past. The astute reader and viewer will undoubtedly come across a few temporal inconsistencies.

To our great delight, we found the journals the explorers kept to be a vivid and thrilling visual resource. Just to hold them in our hands in the safety of the American Philosophical Society in Philadelphia and imagine what it was like *out there* was a great gift. There, in incredibly accessible handwriting, are their poignant, indeed heroic, descriptions of natural wonders never before seen by white men, their hastily scribbled maps, their simple but accurate drawings of birds and fish and native people. Our lenses moved in and almost microscopically surveyed the landscape of their recorded experience, picking out single words and phrases: "my friend," "Hungery Creek," "scens of visionary inchantment," "O! the joy," "troublesome," and "We proceeded on."

As filmmakers, though, we knew that precious journals and "borrowed" photographs or paintings would not give an accurate sense of the explorers' difficult and exhilarating push up the Missouri. What we needed to do was to retrace the Corps of Discovery's steps, to film live modern cinematography of what they saw when they saw it. So for the next three years, we froze on riverbanks, slogged through mud, endured temperatures in the nineties, and faced physical demands we had not experienced in twenty years of making historical documentaries. We filmed at every time of day and night, in every season, and from every conceivable vantage—looking, straining, insisting on bringing back a reality as close to the expedition's as was humanly possible.

To our great disappointment, much of what Lewis and Clark saw we can no longer see. Progress has eliminated or diminished or obscured many of the pristine views that had challenged the vocabularies of the awestruck explorers as they struggled to describe the sublime works of nature they stumbled across at every bend in the river. We were forced to shoot around a hydroelectric dam that blocked a clean view of the Great Falls of the Missouri. We found, to our dismay, that a carefully composed shot would sometimes contain a power line or a fence line or the ruins of a later homesteader's attempt at Manifest Destiny. Or a highway. Often our only company out on the dusty dirt tracks of the prairie were the ominous black vehicles of the military men who service the hundreds of missile sites now dotting the land Lewis and Clark had first claimed for the United States. Where the Corps had observed huge herds of

A Herd of Bison Crossing the Missouri River, by William Jacob Hays, Sr., 1863

buffalo stretching to the horizon, we saw only a few head of cattle, tagged and lowing comfortably in their fields.

But somehow, as we worked beside the Missouri (and later its sister the Columbia), the grandfather spirit pulled us along and gave us images of great beauty and experiences and emotions we will never forget. We saw a mountain goat and her kid hiking up the steep sides of the Gates of the Mountains in Montana as a dark rain and mist swirled above *and* below them. We braved a squall in an enclosed crab-boat at the mouth of the Columbia and wondered how the narrow open canoes of the expedition ever made it down and across that treacherous river. We saw a magnificent rainbow at the Great Falls just as Meriwether Lewis had, and we all stopped and thought about his and our inability to describe it. We greeted a hundred dawns and witnessed just as many sunsets—big, wide dramatic affairs that went on, in summer months, until way past ten in the evening. We watched lightning from fifty miles away and cowered, rain-soaked, near the White Cliffs as it exploded just overhead. We saw lots of bald eagles.

We argued land use and western politics and big government with a river guide who was just as much a Jeffersonian as we thought we were. We delighted in the machine-gun staccato of Stephen Ambrose's gruff voice as he made the story of Lewis and Clark come alive. We spent two days at the Lower Brule Sioux Reservation in South Dakota shooting a small cluster of authentic tepees by the Missouri River—just down the road from a nearly

Come Up Me

empty, down-on-its-luck casino, where we later ate buffalo. We spoke to Gerard Baker, a Hidatsa Indian and superintendent of the Little Bighorn Battlefield National Monument, and saw the "discoveries" of the expedition from a different, decidedly bittersweet, perspective.

At every step, whether near Kansas City or Bismarck or Helena, Stevenson, Washington, or Geraldine, Montana, or Monowi, Nebraska, the grandfather spirit that was and is the Missouri called us. Soon it became clear that the real "star" of our film and book was not these two very interesting, nearly opposite, explorers and their brave crew, but the magnificent land itself and the many promises it held. And the Missouri, that great highway into the unknown, had brought both the Corps of Discovery and now us to that realization.

Lewis and Clark first became more than just a blip on my historical radar screen—that is to say, more than just a piece of required but hardly interesting grade school history—in the fall of 1984. *American Heritage* magazine was celebrating its thirtieth anniversary and had just sent out a questionnaire to several hundred noted historians asking them which moment in American history they would most like to have witnessed, at which event they would like to have been that proverbial fly on the wall. The best replies would be arranged chronologically and published in the year-end issue—a wonderful, eclectic "survey" of our country's past.

The editor of the magazine, Byron Dobell, was my friend, and one day over lunch he mentioned the developing article and asked which event I thought had elicited the most responses. In a flash I said the Civil War, the great traumatic event at the heart of our nation's history and the subject of a film I was planning to make. No. Philadelphia, 1776? No. World War II? No. The Depression? No. Men on the moon? No, more important than men on the moon, Dobell said. I gave up. It was Lewis and Clark. Some historians had wanted to be with the two explorers as Jefferson gave them their marching orders; some wanted to be with them the afternoon they set off from their base camp across the Mississippi from St. Louis in 1804. Others wanted to straddle the Continental Divide and look into Lewis's eyes and see reflected the difficult passage he knew lay ahead. One man wanted to see the Pacific with them, and another wanted to be with them on the return as they passed the first wave of new settlers heading west up the Missouri in the wake of the Corps's discoveries. I was stunned, and I needed to know more.

A few years later, I met a writer named Dayton Duncan who had just published an extraordinary book retracing the expedition's footsteps called *Out West*. It was a masterpiece, beautifully written and unusually moving. It interwove the experiences of Lewis and Clark with Duncan's own journey with humor and deep understanding. It seemed to me when I finished the book that no one loved his country more than Dayton Duncan. It was also clear that I wanted to do a film on Lewis and Clark.

To my great good fortune, Dayton became a close friend, eventually moving his family to the small New Hampshire village where I have lived for nearly twenty years. Here, we conspired to make a film together about the Corps of Discovery. Without a doubt, it has been one of the most satisfying collaborations I have ever had. Like the two completely different explorers, each of us brought different skills and sensibilities to the project, complementing each other in the best sense of that word. And like Lewis and Clark's, our bond of friendship strengthened as we worked, my confidence in him complete.

This wonderful book, entirely Dayton's, grew out of our film and his previous work on the Corps of Discovery. There is something about the journey of Lewis and Clark that you can't let go of once it gets under your skin. Something about the painful combination of triumph and tragedy, of loss and spectacular gain, of progress and its cost. Something about the promise of our democratic ideals, a promise put to the test in the wilderness just beyond what was then our country. Something about friendship and trust and love. Something about a beginning and an ending all at the same time. Lewis and Clark get under your skin. Dayton Duncan can't let go. I've felt it, too. It's a palpable tug, a wanderlust not just for the experience of a new unknown place but for the abiding wisdom and meaning that issue from the questions these sacred places insist we ask. As one travels the Missouri and its environs, the ghosts and echoes of an almost inexpressibly wise past rise up and envelop you. The river beckons, calling everyone who comes near: "Come up me. Come up me."

———

One evening, in the summer of 1995, my assistant cameraman Roger Haydock and I were racing along in our Chevy Suburban trying to get from the small town of Big Sandy, Montana, to a bridge over the Missouri at the mouth of the Judith River (named for the woman William Clark would later marry). We were trying to get to a bluff overlooking the south side of the big river before the sunset quit, and I had accelerated the car to well over seventy on the deeply rutted dirt road that led from Big Sandy. We were then to drive on to Winifred, Montana, where we would hook up with Dayton and another crew member.

Big Sandy is in Chouteau County, a county more than three times the size of Rhode Island and one of the biggest producers of wheat and barley in the entire United States. It has a population of only 5,452 souls and fewer than 850 of them live in Big Sandy. Big Sandy is forty-five long miles from the Judith Landing bridge. It's another twenty-five miles to Winifred from there—most of it dirt. Winifred, Montana, is a beautiful, run-down wheat town with no more than 175 people on a high, windswept plain south of the Missouri.

Even at seventy miles an hour the seventy-plus miles between the two towns seemed enormous, stupefying, outrageous. Who could live there? How did Lewis and Clark, fighting against the river's swift current and sometimes making only a handful of miles a day, do it? Stand it? The bigness of the sky and the silence were immense and troubling. As Roger and I sped along, we began to notice tiny farmhouses, sitting isolated on barren hills high above the road. Trees had been planted around each tidy home, as much, we said to ourselves, to relieve the loneliness as to break the fierce winds that roar down from Canada in the winter and provide shade from a sweltering sun in July.

Now, lights began to come on in each house. We could see them for ten miles as we approached. Lives were lived there; here was the proof. Lives as important as ours, we knew. But how did they do it? How did one survive the savageness of isolation? Even when we were traveling at high speeds, there was a kind of ancient fear that arose in us, a kind of agoraphobia, even though we knew that within an hour or so we would meet our companions, have a meal together, and sleep in a comfortable motel. As the daylight faded, it was clear we would miss the shoot; clouds had long since moved in and hidden whatever "far theatricals" had been planned. A blue-gray, gunmetal evening was upon us. I eased up on the accelerator and Roger and I began to talk.

We spoke about Lewis and Clark and our profound admiration for them— for simply getting through this unrelenting landscape. What did they think about lying out under the stars? Roger wondered. What would the next day bring for them? My question, as a filmmaker, had always been "Who are we?" Here, in a country ruled by the tyranny of distance, that question seemed simplistic, superficial, not quite to the point. A few bright stars now poked out among the clouds, blending completely in the horizonless night with the twinkling farmhouse lights.

For all our proud pronouncements about political freedom, America, I suddenly blurted out to Roger, has been as much about spiritual search, about the survival of the soul, as anything. And here on the frontier, surrounded by that awful silence, where paradoxically one's physical existence is most threatened, the question of the soul's survival is the loudest. It was true for the Shakers and the Mormons; they thrived on the frontier, I told him. What was it about this severe land that brought these questions to the fore? For the native people who had lived here for hundreds of generations, for Lewis, for Clark, for those who followed them, for us? Something had called us all.

The huge canopy overhead shone with even more stars and planets, and as the lights around the bridge at Judith Landing became visible down in the river's dark valley, Roger and I grew silent again. Then, a curious feeling arose in me, true, honest, and as uncomplicated as anything I had ever felt. For just a moment, I *knew* why Jefferson needed this land, why the Corps of Discovery had followed the siren song of the Missouri so consciously, so purposefully, so relentlessly, why these people needed to live here, what I was doing here. In that instant, my old question changed. It was no longer "Who are we?" that was animating my work, but "Who am I?" And that question went out and boomed across the valley and the night sky, shot up the near-silent river, resounded in the canyons and the breaks, and spread out across the endless prairie. It mixed with everyone else's question and then stole back quietly to our car, settling peacefully among us. Following the dirt trail, with Lewis and Clark's sky above us, we crossed the inky Missouri and made our way up to Winifred.

———

"There are grave doubts at the hugeness of the land," Henry Adams once wrote many years after Lewis and Clark had completed their celebrated journey, whether "one government can *comprehend* the whole." Adams was expressing perfectly his country's profound anxiety over the growing sectional discord that many thought would eventually bring civil war, and the underlying issues of race that taunted the American ideal of equality, magnifying its obvious and monumental hypocrisy for all to see. But in a more direct way he was confessing an utterly American fear that somehow we might have outgrown ourselves, that the seaboard collection of former colonies that had once *been* the nation had indeed stretched beyond our comprehension, straining both the promise and the possibilities of our fledgling experiment. In short, Adams was asking: Had we simply gotten too big to go on?

Civil war did come and race would remain the central fault line in American society. The continent was quickly tamed—was "comprehended"—in just a few short generations. But the question of national meaning and unity, inherent in Adams's anguished words, the search for a uniquely American identity, the sense that our vast and exquisite geography might lead to some sense of self-definition and sustaining national purpose, also continued and grew. We *did* go on, "puzzled and prospering," as the expedition's mentor, Thomas Jef-

Lewis and Clark, 1804,
by L. Edward Fisher

ferson, put it, "beyond example in the history of man." Somehow the tension and dialogue and negotiation between our exterior natural landscape and the interior landscape of our ideals has been at the heart of who we are, the dynamo of our national progress.

"America is the land of zero," the philosopher Jacob Needleman said. "We start from zero. We start from nothing. We start only from our own reason, our own longing, our own search." In a way, this challenging documentary film project and companion book have been a search, too: to learn about the mysterious inner workings of this remarkable republic and those strange and complicated people who like to call themselves Americans. Eventually, we begin to see that this very process of self-examination is it; discovery is not so much about the thing discovered but about discovery itself. The Corps of Discovery discovered nothing *but* themselves. In so doing, they discovered us.

KEN BURNS
Walpole, New Hampshire

Honored Parence.

I now embrace this oppertunity of writing . . . to let you know where I am and where I am going. I am well, thank God, and in high Spirits. I am now on an expidition to the westward, with Capt. Lewis and Capt. Clark, who are appointed by the President of the united States to go . . . through the interior parts of North America. We are to ascend the Missouri River with a boat as far as it is navigable and then go by land, to the western ocean, if nothing prevents. . . .

We expect to be gone 18 months or two years. We are to Receive a great Reward for this expidition, when we Return. I am to Receive 15 dollars pr. month and at least 400 ackers of first Rate land, and if we make Great Discoveries as we expect, the united States has promised to make us Great Rewards. . . . For fear of exidants I wish to inform you that I left 200 dollars in cash, at Kaskaskias . . . and if I Should not live to return, my heirs can git that and all the pay Due me from the U.S. . . . Government.

I . . . will write next winter if I have a chance.

SERGEANT JOHN ORDWAY

Introduction

ONE AFTERNOON in the spring of 1804, in a heavily loaded keelboat and two oversized canoes, nearly four dozen men crossed the Mississippi River and started up the Missouri, struggling against its thick, muddy current.

They were on the most important expedition in American history—the United States' first official exploration into unknown spaces, and a glimpse into their young nation's future.

They would become the first United States citizens to experience the Great Plains: the immensity of its skies, the rich splendor of its wildlife, the harsh rigors of its winters.

They would be the first American citizens to see the daunting peaks of the Rocky Mountains, the first to struggle over them, the first to cross the Continental Divide to where the rivers flow west.

And—after encountering cold, hunger, danger, and wonders beyond belief—they would become the first of their nation to reach the Pacific Ocean by land.

It would be the greatest adventure of their lives.

The best authenticated accounts informed us, that we were to pass through a country possessed by numerous, powerful and warlike nations of savages, of gigantic stature, fierce, treacherous and cruel; and particularly hostile to white men.

SERGEANT PATRICK GASS

They carried the most modern weapons of their time, but in their two moments of greatest need, women would intervene on their behalf; and time and time again, they would be saved by the kindness of strangers.

They told people who had been occupying the land for hundreds of generations that the West now belonged to someone else; yet they would meet more friends than enemies, and only once fire their guns in anger.

They were led by two utterly different men, who, representing a new nation that celebrated individual achievement, would rely instead on cooperation and teamwork.

They called themselves the Corps of Discovery, yet they would fail to find the thing they had been sent most of all to discover. Their real discovery would be the land itself—and the promises it held.

It was the first report on the West, on the United States over the hill and beyond the sunset, on the province of the American future. There has never been another so excellent and so influential. . . . It satisfied desire and it created desire: the desire of a westering nation.

BERNARD DeVOTO

LEWIS & CLARK

CHAPTER 1

*Look
Forward
to Distant
Times*

However our present interests may restrain us within our own limits, it is impossible not to look forward to distant times, when our rapid multiplication will expand itself beyond those limits and cover the whole . . . continent, with a people speaking the same language, governed in similar forms and by similar laws.

THOMAS JEFFERSON

WHEN THOMAS JEFFERSON became President in 1801, two out of every three Americans lived within fifty miles of the Atlantic Ocean. Only four roads crossed the Allegheny Mountains. The United States ended on the eastern banks of the Mississippi River.

To the southwest, stretching from Texas to California, lay New Spain. England controlled Canada; its traders were expanding southward into what is now Minnesota and the Dakotas for valuable furs, and its ships were dominating the Pacific Northwest. Russia, with outposts in Alaska, would soon erect a fort on the northern coast of California. And from the Mississippi to the Rocky Mountains was the vast French territory called Louisiana, where Napoleon Bonaparte hoped to reestablish an empire in the New World.

But while many nations dreamed of controlling the West's destiny, they still knew very little about the place itself. Spanish conquistadors had explored the Southwest. French and Spanish fur traders had ventured partway up the Missouri River, and the British had visited the Mandan Indians in what is now North Dakota. Ships from various countries were plying the northern coast of the Pacific to trade for sea otter pelts, which commanded exorbitant prices in China. Robert Gray, an American sea captain, had discovered and mapped the mouth of the Columbia River in 1792, followed by his English counterpart George Vancouver. And in 1793 the Scotsman Alexander Mackenzie had crossed Canada by land, and then had urged Great Britain to take over the entire North American fur business by establishing a string of forts and trading posts across the continent.

The west side of Thomas Jefferson's home at Monticello. Even though he never traveled much farther west than the Shenandoah Valley, to Lewis he was "the author of our enterprize," and Clark called him "that great Chaructor the Main Spring of the action."

For those who coveted its fabled treasures, however, the bulk of the West remained an immense blank—a void on their maps and an awesome gap in their knowledge, filled only by rumor and conjecture.

No one was more anxious to change that than the new President, Thomas Jefferson. Though he had never traveled more than fifty miles west of Virginia's Shenandoah Valley, Jefferson had always been fascinated by the West. His personal library at Monticello contained more books about the region than any other library in the world.

Some of them told him that woolly mammoths and other prehistoric animals still roamed there. Others described erupting volcanoes and a mountain of pure salt, 180 miles long and 45 miles wide. On the basis of his reading, Jefferson believed that Virginia's Blue Ridge Mountains might be the continent's highest and that somewhere in the West was a tribe of blue-eyed Indians who spoke Welsh, descendants of a fabled Prince Madoc who supposedly had settled in the New World three centuries before Columbus.

Above all, like everyone else at the time, Jefferson believed in the Northwest Passage—a river, or a series of rivers connected by a short portage, that would cross the western mountains, make direct trade with the Orient easier and more profitable, and unlock the wealth of North America. Whichever nation discovered the Northwest Passage, and then controlled it, Jefferson believed, would control the destiny of the continent.

For more than a century, the Spanish, French, and British had been searching for the Passage. Three times, Jefferson himself had tried to organize American expeditions to find it—each time in vain. In 1783 he had attempted to interest George Rogers Clark, the revolutionary war hero, in a privately financed exploration. Nothing came of it. Three years later, as minister to France, Jefferson had met John Ledyard, a Connecticut Yankee who dreamed of achieving fame and wealth by being the first to cross the continent. Ledyard's plan was to go through Russia to Alaska, then walk from the Pacific Coast to the Mississippi, taking with him only two huntings dogs, an Indian peace pipe, and a hatchet to chop firewood. "He is a person of ingenuity and information," Jefferson wrote at the time. "Unfortunately, he has too much imagination." Nonetheless, Jefferson lent his name and some money, and Ledyard set out. But the adventure ended abruptly when Catherine the Great had him arrested in Siberia.

As Secretary of State under President George Washington, Jefferson and the members of the American Philosophical Society had contracted the French

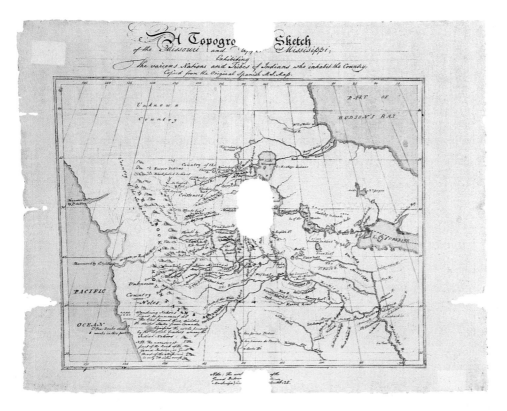

When Jefferson became President, most of the West was still a great unknown, as demonstrated by this map by Antoine Soulard, circa 1802. The Missouri River appears to flow from a gap in the Rocky Mountains, which themselves seem to form a narrow, unintimidating barrier. Almost everything farther west is a blank.

botanist André Michaux in 1793 for an expedition to "seek for and pursue that route which shall form the shortest and most convenient communication between the higher parts of the Missouri and the Pacific Ocean." Only $128.50 was raised (Washington donated $25.00 and Jefferson $12.50), and Michaux never made it past the Ohio River.

Now, as President, Jefferson decided to try once more.

January 18th, 1803. Confidential. Gentlemen of the Senate and of the House of Representatives.

The river Missouri, & the Indians inhabiting it, are not as well known as is rendered desireable. . . . It is however understood that the country on that river is inhabited by numerous tribes, who furnish great supplies of furs. . . .

An intelligent officer with ten or twelve chosen men . . . might explore the whole line, even to the Western ocean. . . . The appropriation of two thousand five hundred dollars . . . would cover the undertaking.

THOMAS JEFFERSON

In a secret message to Congress to win its support, Jefferson emphasized the potential *commercial* benefits of the expedition. But he told the ambassadors from France, Spain, and England—whose territories would be crossed—that it would be a purely *scientific* expedition. The British and French ambassadors wrote out passports assuring safe conduct. Distrustful of American motives, the Spanish declined, but Jefferson simply ignored their objections.

At last, in early 1803, Jefferson's persistent dream of exploring the West—for the sake of science, commerce, *and* the national interest—seemed about to be fulfilled.

———

Capt. Lewis is brave, prudent, habituated to the woods, & familiar with Indian manners & character. He is not regularly educated, but he possesses a great mass of accurate observation on all the subjects of nature which present themselves.

THOMAS JEFFERSON
to Dr. Benjamin Rush
February 28, 1803

To lead what he called his Corps of Discovery, the President turned to his personal secretary, Meriwether Lewis. Lewis had grown up in Jefferson's own

Albemarle County, the serious-minded son of a planter who had died during the Revolution, when Lewis was only five. By age sixteen, he was responsible for the welfare of his mother, brothers, and sisters. At eighteen, he eagerly volunteered for Jefferson's ill-fated Michaux expedition, but was turned down.

Instead, the young Lewis had joined the regular army on the frontiers of western Pennsylvania and Ohio and made a name for himself as a promising officer before Jefferson brought him to Washington in 1801. There, as the new President's sole aide, he drew up a list of army commanders who could be expected to be loyal to the new administration, copied presidential documents, ran errands, and set up residence in what is now the East Room of the White House, the building the two men occupied, Jefferson wrote a daughter, "like two mice in a church."

During his two years of daily association with Jefferson, Lewis had also become intimately acquainted with the President's far-ranging interests in the West—its geography, its plants and animals, its people and their habits, and its potential for the young republic.

Meriwether Lewis, painted by Charles Willson Peale. Although Jefferson had noticed what he called "depressions of the mind" in his young protégé, he also considered Lewis "brave, prudent, habituated to the woods, & familiar with Indian manners & character."

Some considered Lewis an unlikely choice to command such an important expedition. "Stiff and without grace," an acquaintance called him, "bowlegged, awkward, formal, almost without flexibility." Levi Lincoln, the Attorney General, worried that the twenty-eight-year-old Lewis might be too impulsive, take too many risks, and endanger this "enterprise of national consequence." Jefferson himself had noted occasional "depressions of the mind" in Lewis (inherited, the President speculated, from his father) but still considered him the best man for the job.

To prepare for the long journey, Lewis was dispatched that spring to Philadelphia, the home of the American Philosophical Society and the young nation's center of scientific learning. On his way, he stopped at the arsenal in Harpers Ferry for a supply of tomahawks and knives and fifteen of the newest weapons being produced there: prototypes of a short-barreled, .54-caliber rifle that was soon to be standard issue for the army. For nearly three weeks, he studied celestial observations in Lancaster, Pennsylvania, under Andrew Ellicott, an eminent astronomer-surveyor.

In Philadelphia, another month was consumed while Lewis was tutored by four scientists at the University of Pennsylvania. Benjamin Smith Barton

Supplies for the unknown. Lewis wrote out list after list of provisions the expedition would need to accomplish its multiple missions—from guns, ammunition, and medical supplies (above) to scientific instruments (opposite). Still on the East Coast, he amassed nearly two tons of goods and quickly spent the $2,500 Congress had authorized for the entire exploration.

instructed him on describing and preserving botanical specimens; Robert Patterson added more lessons in determining latitude and longitude; Caspar Wistar, an anatomist and the foremost authority on fossils, explained how to search for signs of ancient beasts, some of which were believed to still be living in the West. And for advice on medicine, Lewis turned to the nation's most esteemed physician, Dr. Benjamin Rush. The doctor assembled a medical kit for the explorer and lectured him on its uses, with heavy emphasis on the preferred treatment for most ills of the time: bloodletting, which Rush favored for everything from fevers to dislocated bones.

Besides these crash courses in science, Lewis spent his time in Philadelphia acquiring supplies—and going through most of the $2,500 Congress had appropriated. He bought compasses, quadrants, a telescope, and a chronometer (costing $250) needed to calculate longitude. For camp supplies, he purchased 150 yards of cloth to be oiled and sewn into tents and sheets; pliers, chisels, handsaws, hatchets, and whetstones; an iron corn mill and two dozen tablespoons; mosquito curtains, 10½ pounds of fishing hooks and fishing lines, 12 pounds of soap—and 193 pounds of "portable soup," a thick paste concocted by boiling down beef, eggs, and vegetables, to be used if no other food was available on the trail.

Some $669.50 went for presents for the Indians he expected to encounter:

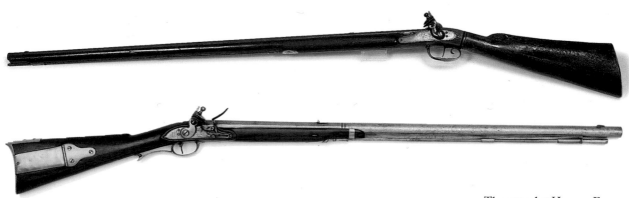

twelve dozen pocket mirrors, 4,600 sewing needles, silk ribbons, ivory combs, handkerchiefs, yards of bright-colored cloth, 130 rolls of tobacco, tomahawks that doubled as pipes, 8 brass kettles, vermilion face paint, 33 pounds of tiny beads of assorted colors, plus much more.

For the men he expected to accompany him, Lewis bought 45 flannel shirts for $71.10; coats, frocks, shoes, woolen pants, blankets, knapsacks, and stockings; powder horns, knives, 500 rifle flints, 420 pounds of sheet lead for bullets, and 176 pounds of gunpowder packed in 52 lead canisters that themselves could be melted down into bullets when empty. With his own money, he purchased a novelty item to impress the Indians he might meet: a long-barreled rifle that fired its bullet by compressed air (like a BB gun) rather than by flint, spark, and powder.

By mid-June, as the army began transporting the 3,500 pounds of supplies to the Ohio River, Lewis was ready to return to Washington. He had decided he needed a co-commander, and he knew exactly which one he wanted.

June 19th, 1803
Dear Clark,

My friend . . . If there is anything in this enterprise, which would induce you to participate with me in it's fatiegues, it's dangers and it's honors, believe me there is no man on earth with whom I should feel equal pleasure in sharing them as with yourself.

MERIWETHER LEWIS

The arsenal at Harpers Ferry provided Lewis with fifteen of its newest rifles, prototypes of the Model 1803 (above, bottom) that became the United States Army's first standard issue. With his own funds, Lewis bought an air rifle—believed to be the one shown here (above, top)—that fired without spark or powder and would amaze every Indian tribe the expedition met.

Mathematical Instruments

1 Hadley's Quadrant
1 Mariner's Compass & 2 pole chain
1 Sett of plotting instruments
3 Thermometers
1 Cheap portable Microscope
1 Pocket Compass
1 brass Scale one foot in length
6 Magnetic needles in small straight
   Silver or brass cases opening on the side
   with hinges.
1 Instrument for measuring made of tape
   with feet & inches marked on it, confined
   within a circular lether box of sufficient
   thickness to admit the width of the tape
   which has one of its ends confined to an axis
   of metal passing through the center of the box,
   around which and within the box it steadily
   wound by means of a small crank on the outer
   side of the box which forms a part of the axis,
   the tape when necessary is drawn out with
   the same facility & ease with which it is
   wound up

A Secret Code and a Blank Check

In planning the Lewis and Clark expedition, Thomas Jefferson tried to leave nothing to chance. Two documents show how far he would go to help guarantee a successful mission.

To ensure that sensitive messages from Lewis could not be read by the wrong people, Jefferson taught his protégé a special code. A desire for such secrecy was nothing new to the President. In 1790, as Secretary of State, he had invented a complicated cipher machine for diplomatic communications. But since Lewis couldn't carry the machine with him into the wilderness, Jefferson had him memorize a different method, relying on an alphabetical matrix.

As a way of demonstrating the code to Lewis, Jefferson encrypted a sample—and hopeful—message: "I am at the head of the Missouri. All well, and the Indians so far friendly." Deciphering the code matrix required both parties to remember a key word. Jefferson chose "artichokes."

No "artichoke" messages are known to have been sent between Lewis and Jefferson during the expedition—although, given the President's penchant for secrecy, who is to say that Jefferson didn't receive some and then destroyed the evidence?

The other document is a letter from Jefferson to Lewis, written on July 4, 1803, the same day the news of the Louisiana Purchase was announced. It is one of the most extraordinary papers any President has ever signed.

The one-page letter summarized Lewis's mission and suggested that if he actually reached the Pacific by land, it might be safer and quicker to return by sea "in such vessels as you may find on the Western coast." But he wouldn't have any money to pay for passage or buy supplies.

Jefferson's letter supplied the answer. The President "solemnly pledge[d] the faith of the United States" to reimburse anyone for any service or goods that Lewis wanted, adding that the explorer should simply show the letter to any sea captain, merchant, foreign consul, or citizen of any nation he encountered anywhere in the world on a sea voyage back to Washington.

"And to give more entire satisfaction & confidence to those who may be disposed to aid you," he concluded, "I, Thomas Jefferson, President of the United States of America, have written this letter of general credit for you with my own hand, and signed it with my name." It was, in effect, a credit card without limits.

As things turned out, however, Lewis never encountered a ship on the Pacific coast. And when the expedition ran out of trade goods but needed food and supplies from local Indians, the clothes on Lewis's back proved far more valuable than Jefferson's remarkable blank check. Among the receipts Lewis submitted to the government upon his return was a bill for $135 as reimbursement for "one Uniform Laced Coat, one silver Epaulet, one Dirk & belt, one hanger & belt, one pistol & one fowling piece, all private property, given in exchange for Canoe, Horses &c. for public service during the expedition."

Even without using the letter of credit, the Corps of Discovery overspent its budget. In authorizing the expedition, Congress had appropriated the $2,500 that Jefferson and Lewis had estimated it would cost. But by the time all the bills were paid, the total was more than fifteen times larger: $38,722.35.

William Clark, born in Virginia, had spent most of his life on the Kentucky and Ohio frontiers, where he had learned both to fight and to negotiate with Indians, to build forts in the wilderness, and to find his way through unknown territory. He was, one acquaintance said, "of solid and promising parts, and as brave as Caesar."

He was four years older than Lewis, whom he had once commanded in the army; less formally educated, but with more practical experience and a steadier yet more outgoing personality—a friend, but also a perfect complement in both training and temperament to the man who was inviting Clark to make history with him.

In 1783 his older brother had reluctantly turned down Jefferson's *first* proposal to explore the West. Now William Clark was being offered the same opportunity, and he leapt at the chance.

Dear Lewis,
This is an undertaking fraited with many difeculties, but My friend
I do assure you that no man lives whith whome I would perfur to
undertake Such a Trip.

WILLIAM CLARK

In his own hand, President Jefferson wrote and signed this letter of unlimited credit, promising the full faith of the United States government for any expenses Lewis might incur. Jefferson also drew up this code matrix, whereby secret messages could be deciphered if both he and Lewis remembered the key word, "artichokes."

Lewis's invitation broke with all military protocol by proposing a dual command of the expedition and promising Clark a captain's commission, the same as his own. The War Department refused, and when Jefferson—who always considered it *Lewis's* expedition—did not intervene, Clark swallowed his disappointment and agreed to continue.

But Lewis insisted that he and Clark keep the matter secret, and for the next two and a half years Second Lieutenant Clark would be referred to as "captain" and would share every decision equally with his younger but higher-ranking friend.

To Captain Meriwether Lewis.

The object of your mission is to explore the Missouri river, & such principal stream of it, as, by it's course and communication with the waters of the Pacific ocean . . . may offer the most direct & practicable water communication across this continent for the purposes of commerce.

THOMAS JEFFERSON

William Clark, painted by Charles Willson Peale. Four years older, steadier, and more experienced than Lewis, he was officially only a second lieutenant during the expedition. But Lewis always referred to Clark as "captain" and disregarded military tradition by sharing the command with him.

While Lewis had been studying science, buying supplies, and recruiting Clark, Thomas Jefferson had also been busy preparing for the start of his pet project. He drafted and signed an extraordinary letter of credit for Lewis to carry along, promising the full faith of the government to repay anyone whose goods or services might be needed in an emergency. Concerned about the possibility of the wrong people intercepting Lewis's reports from territory claimed by foreign powers, Jefferson devised a complicated, secret code for him to use.

And the President also wrote out page after page of precise instructions for the expedition "after your departure from the United States": Find the Northwest Passage and the most direct route to the Pacific; draw maps; make detailed observations of the soils, minerals, crops, animals, and weather; meet the Indians and record their languages, populations, religions, customs, food, clothing, and willingness to trade with the Americans. In his lengthy directions, Jefferson overlooked nothing. He even suggested that one copy of Lewis's notes be kept on birch bark "as less liable to injury from the damp than common paper"—an instruction apparently never followed, since birch was not common along the route the explorers would take.

But on July 4, 1803, the day before Lewis left Washington for the West, news from Europe was proclaimed that dramatically expanded the expedition's importance, adding to its already long list of duties and making any secrecy unnecessary.

> *Washington City. Monday, July 4. OFFICIAL. The Executive have received official information that a Treaty was signed on the 30th of April, between the ministers . . . of the United States and . . . the French, by which the United States have obtained full right to and sovereignty over New Orleans, and the whole of Louisiana.*
>
> *National Intelligencer*

In 1802 Jefferson had sent ministers to France, offering to buy New Orleans, the vital port at the mouth of the Mississippi River. But instead, Napoleon Bonaparte, preparing for another war with England, had made a surprising counteroffer: he would sell the entire Louisiana Territory, all 820,000 square miles, to the United States for $15 million. It was a sum nearly twice the federal budget, and although he questioned his own constitutional authority in doing so, Jefferson readily agreed. For just three cents an acre, the President more than doubled the size of his country with a single stroke of his pen.

Not everyone—particularly Jefferson's political opponents—considered the Louisiana Purchase much of a bargain. "A great waste, a wilderness unpeopled with any beings except wolves and wandering Indians," said the Boston *Columbian Centinel*. "We are to give money of which we have too little, for land of which we already have too much." Federalist Joshua Green called it a "shameful gross speculation, pretending to bring we knew not what, situated we knew not where, and [with] no more right to it than . . . to land in the moon."

In Paris, however, Napoleon predicted that the lands west of the

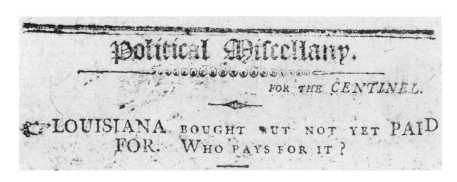

Political Miscellany.

FOR THE *CENTINEL.*

LOUISIANA BOUGHT BUT NOT YET PAID FOR. WHO PAYS FOR IT?

Not everyone believed that purchasing the Louisiana Territory was a good idea, particularly newspapers in New England. Boston's *Columbian Centinel* (left) considered it a waste of money, while the *New Hampshire Sentinel* of Keene (above) called it a "dire portent" for democracy and predicted that Jefferson had forsaken the "plaudits of posterity."

Mississippi would "strengthen forever" the young United States. "I have just given to England," he added, a "rival that will sooner or later humble her pride."

At least on paper, half of the West now belonged to the United States. But as Lewis left Washington on July 5 to join Clark and proceed to the eastern shore of the Mississippi to make final preparations for their long journey, no one knew for sure what Thomas Jefferson had just bought.

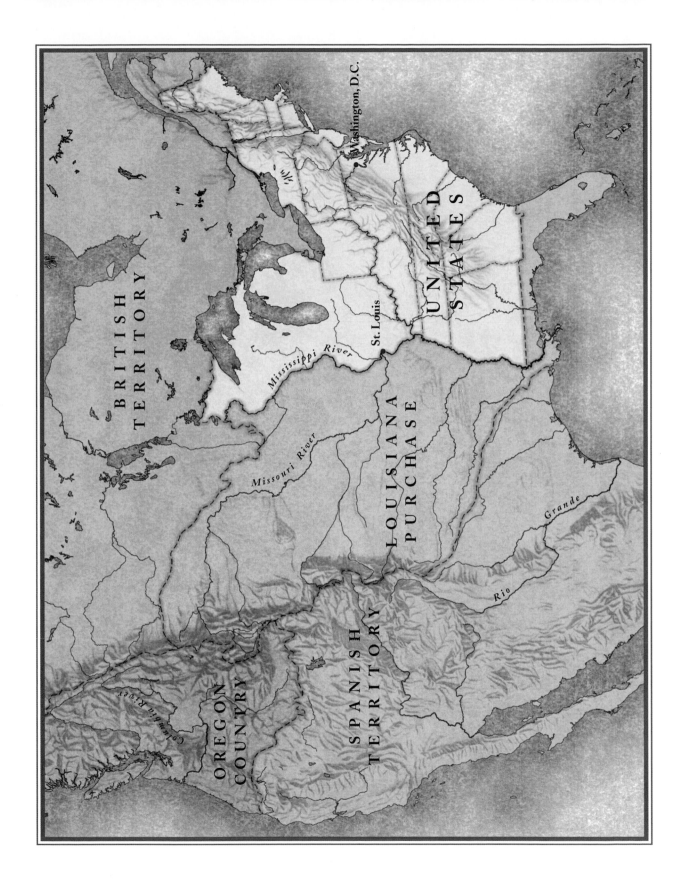

CHAPTER 2

*Floyd's
Bluff*

Washington
Dear Captain Lewis,

The acquisition of the country through which you are to pass has inspired the public generally with a great deal of interest in your enterprize. [But my political opponents] would rejoice in it's failure. . . . I hope you will take care of yourself, and be the living witness of their malice and folly. Present my salutations to Mr. Clarke, assure all your party that we have our eyes turned on them with anxiety for their safety.

THOMAS JEFFERSON

WITH THE nearly four dozen men they had recruited on their way, Lewis and Clark spent the winter of 1803–4 at Camp Dubois, a collection of huts they built on the Illinois side of the Mississippi, upstream from St. Louis. They bided their time drilling the men, gathering information from fur traders about the route ahead, and purchasing final supplies, including nearly two tons each of flour and salt pork, fifty pounds of coffee, and one hundred gallons of whiskey.

Because of the Louisiana Purchase, their duties were now diplomatic as well as exploratory. On March 10 the two captains attended formal ceremonies in St. Louis officially transferring upper Louisiana from France to the United States, and in April they delayed their departure to arrange for a delegation of Osage chiefs to travel to Washington and meet with President Jefferson.

Finally, on May 14, 1804, at four o'clock in the afternoon, the Corps of Discovery set off from Camp Dubois—"under a jentle brease," Clark wrote—and sailed across the Mississippi and four and a half miles up the Missouri. They stopped for several days at the town of St. Charles, whose citizens staged a ball in their honor, and stopped again at Femme Osage, not far from where the legendary frontiersman Daniel Boone had built his final home.

The captains' compass. Clark used it to compile the expedition's daily courses and distances for the map he would make for Jefferson.

A Day on the River

For the Corps of Discovery, every day on the Missouri River was a mixture of both routine and surprise. Breakfast each morning consisted of cold leftovers from dinner the night before (lunch would be the same), because of the captains' order that "no cooking will be allowed in the day while on the march," since it would take too much time and delay their progress.

As most of the men broke camp, loaded the boats, and pushed off once more against the Big Muddy's current, George Drouillard and a small hunting party would set out overland in search of fresh meat. Drouillard was half Shawnee and had been hired as an interpreter because of his skills at sign language, but his abilities with a rifle were equally important. "I scarcely know how we should subsist," Lewis wrote later in the journey, "were it not for the exertions of this excellent hunter."

Out on the river, eight French *engagés* were responsible for the red pirogue; a detachment of six soldiers manned the white pirogue. The members of the "permanent party" managed the big keelboat. Each of the three sergeants had specific duties at the front, middle, and back of the boat. The two most experienced rivermen, Privates Pierre Cruzatte and François Labiche, both half Omaha, alternated between the front oar on the left side (setting the pace for the other oarsmen) and the bow (guiding the boat among the snags, sandbars, and other obstacles).

Of the two captains, Clark spent the most time on the keelboat—managing the men, taking constant compass readings, and using "dead reckoning" (estimating distances from bend to bend) for the map he hoped to produce. Lewis often walked or rode on shore, helping with the hunting, noting likely sites for future settlements and forts, or performing his scientific duties by gathering plants, taking soil samples, or making celestial observations at the meridian to plot the longitude of prominent spots. Most likely, Lewis's Newfoundland dog went with his master.

At day's end, camp would be established. The permanent party was divided into three squads, or "messes," each one led by a sergeant. John Ordway would distribute the daily ration of cornmeal or flour or salt pork to each mess, divide whatever fresh meat the hunters had brought in, and pour each man a four-ounce "gill of ardent spirits," the whiskey that was their reward for a hard day. As the tents were set up and firewood gathered, the cooks—who were exempted from the other duties—prepared the one big meal of the day.

At night, guards were posted (Drouillard and the cooks exempted), and Cruzatte might break out his fiddle to entertain the men around the campfire. But before they went to sleep, there was one more duty awaiting some of the men: recording the day's events in their journals.

Jefferson had insisted on detailed—and multiple—records. Lewis and Clark, in turn, ordered the sergeants "to keep a seperate journal from day to day of all passing occurences, and such other observations on the country &c. as shall appear to them worthy of notice." Privates were apparently encouraged to do the same. Strangely, the one person who seems to have been the least rigorous in his journal keeping was Lewis. Despite Jefferson's instructions—and for reasons not entirely known—there are long lapses in which no daily entries can be found for him. It is a great loss, since Lewis was the best-educated member of the expedition and a fine, descriptive writer when he set his mind to it.

Fortunately, there were several reporters on the epic journey, which not only fills in the gaps in Lewis's entries but helps round out the picture of even the most routine days. June 15, 1804, for example.

All of the writers note an early start, but Patrick Gass and Charles Floyd specify 5:00 a.m., with Floyd commenting that they were "much Feteaged of yesterdays worke." John Ordway calls the weather fair. Joseph Whitehouse adds that the wind was from the southeast and "fresh," so that they sailed the keelboat for a while—surely a welcome relief to exhausted men, since the current was swift ("strong water," says Floyd; "exceedingly rapid," according to Ordway). From Gass we learn of "mulberries in great abundance." Whitehouse comments that during the day "the party drank a Drachm of whisky and Roe on." Floyd writes that the hunters killed four bears and three deer for dinner.

Clark has the fullest account of the day. The river was rising, he wrote, and early on the keelboat struck a submerged tree, "which was near injuring us Verry much." After passing a number of islands, they became temporarily stuck in shallows where the current was too strong for sailing and rowing, and "we were Compelled to pass under a bank which was falling in, and use the Toe rope occasionally." (Undoubtedly, it was after this that the captains allowed the men a shot of whiskey.)

The expedition covered twelve and a quarter miles that day, according to Clark's calculations. Camp was made on the north side of the river across from a bend (three miles wide, says Floyd), offering a view of two abandoned Indian villages. Ordway calls one village "Lapero" and Whitehouse calls one "little Zoe

[Sioux]," but Clark again provides a fuller account, no doubt based on information the veteran boatmen of the lower river had given him. One village had contained the Little Osage, with "an ellegent bottom Plain which extends Several miles in length," where the Indians once grew corn. A band of Missouri Indians had lived in the other village. Then war had broken out with the Sauks. "The war was So hot & both nations becom So reduced," Clark wrote, that the Little Osages and some of the Missouris fled to the protection of the Grand Osage village farther south; the rest of the Missouris migrated upriver to live with the Otos near the mouth of the Platte.

Despite the grueling day, all five of the journalists felt compelled to describe the beauty of their surroundings that evening: "the pleasantest place I have ever seen," according to Ordway, whose assessment was then trumped by Floyd's "handsom a prarie as ever eney man saw."

Had Lewis been the only journal keeper, none of these details would be known. His only notation for June 15, 1804, is brief and technical: a celestial reading at noon with his octant from a spot he designated as "Point of Observation No. 9."

Clark sometimes wrote his field notes on scraps of paper or in this journal bound in rough elkskin, opened here to his recordings of October 26, 1805.

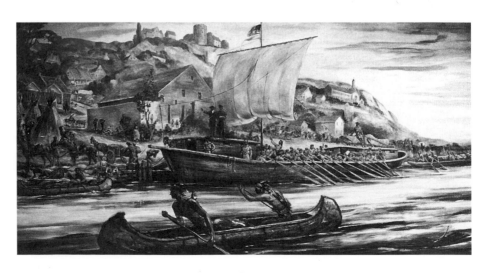

As he waited for the expedition to begin in earnest, William Clark wrote out "A Memorandum of Articles in Readiness for the Voyage," which included 50 kegs of salt pork, 7 barrels of salt, 600 pounds of grease, and 3,400 pounds of flour.

On May 25 they reached La Charette, a cluster of seven dwellings less than sixty miles up the Missouri but, as Sergeant Charles Floyd noted in his journal that night, "the last settlement of whites on this river."

May 28th, 1804. Rained hard all last night. Some thunder and lightening . . . found Several articles Wet, Some Tobacco Spoiled.

May 29th. Rained last night. . . . The Musquetors are verry bad. Made 4 miles.

May 30th. Rained all last night. Set out at 6 o'clock after a heavy Shower and proceeded on. . . . A heavy wind accompanied with rain & hail. We Made 14 miles to day. The river Continue[d] to rise, the count[r]y on each Side appear[ed] full of Water.

May 31st. Rained the greater part of last night. The wind . . . blew with great force untile 5 oClock p.m. which obliged us to lay by.

William Clark

Bad weather greeted them nearly every morning. Mosquitoes—some as big as houseflies, according to Clark—swarmed around their faces; they were "so numerous," Lewis said, "that we frequently get them in our throats as we

When the expedition arrived at St. Charles, Missouri, Clark wrote, "a number of Spectators french & Indians flocked to the bank to See the party." He estimated the town had 450 inhabitants, "pore, polite & harmonious." After they held a festive ball to entertain the explorers, three of the men had to be court-martialed for bad behavior. This painting by Charles A. Morganthaler depicts the expedition's departure from the town on May 21, 1804.

breathe." (They covered their bodies with bear grease during the day, and at night were thankful for Lewis's foresight in purchasing mosquito netting.)

But their biggest obstacle was the Missouri itself—big, broad, choked with snags, and pushing relentlessly at more than five miles an hour in the opposite direction of their destination. The keelboat was fifty-five feet long and eight feet wide, capable of carrying ten tons of supplies. Maneuvering it against the insistent current was a constant challenge. Occasionally, when the wind was right, they could sail it up the river. More often, they had to use oars or setting poles, avoiding the main channel by moving slowly from eddy to eddy. Sometimes, the only way to proceed was cordelling—the men wading along the muddy banks and pulling the heavy boat forward with a rope. (The two smaller boats, called pirogues, also required sails, oars, and brute strength to be maneuvered upstream.)

Drifting logs rammed the boats. Cordelling ropes broke. The mast caught in an overhanging tree and snapped off, causing a day's delay to make a new one. The keelboat got stuck on sandbars and once was nearly swamped by a collapsing riverbank. "The base of the riverbanks being composed of a fine light sand, is easily removed by the water," Lewis explained. "It quickly undermines them

Along the Missouri. Thirty years after Lewis and Clark, the Swiss artist Karl Bodmer ascended the Missouri River and painted many of the same scenes the Corps of Discovery would have experienced. In his preliminary sketches, Bodmer showed the river choked with snags and driftwood, but only a few are evident in this painting.

Floyd's Bluff

"Very Active, Strong and Docile"

Meriwether Lewis's first partner on the Corps of Discovery was not William Clark but a dog named Seaman. He was, Lewis wrote, "of the newfoundland breed very active strong and docile."

The captain had paid twenty dollars for him somewhere in the East, and by mid-September of 1803—a full month before Lewis and the keelboat reached Clark on the Ohio River—Seaman was already proving his worth by catching squirrels on the river and bringing them back to his master, who found fried squirrel a "pleasant food." By the time Lewis (and now Clark) reached the Mississippi in November, the dog's position on the expedition was secure: when an admiring Shawnee Indian offered three beaver skins for the Newfoundland, "of course," Lewis scoffed in his journal, "there was no bargain."

Like everyone else on the Corps of Discovery, Seaman kept busy going up the Missouri. He retrieved a goose, ran down a deer that a hunter had wounded, and splashed after beaver (whose tails the men considered a delicacy), even diving into their lodges to roust them out. Near the mouth of the Yellowstone, he accomplished a feat that made snagging squirrels seem puny by comparison: he caught an antelope in midstream and dragged it to shore.

When a buffalo bull lurched out of the river in the middle of one night, threatening to trample the heads of the sleeping explorers, it was Seaman whose barking turned the bull from camp. And in the midst of grizzly country, where every day seemed to bring dangerously close encounters with the bears, at night the men were never attacked, Lewis noted, because "our dog gives us timely notice of their visits, he keeps constantly patroling all night."

Like everyone else on the expedition, Seaman also suffered. In what is now South Dakota, the summer heat nearly prostrated him. A wounded beaver bit his hind leg, cutting an artery so severely that Lewis feared

Lewis's constant companion on the expedition was a big Newfoundland dog, like this one, that he bought for twenty dollars and named Seaman. Seaman caught squirrels, beaver, and an antelope and was often plagued by cactus and mosquitoes.

for his companion's life. And, of course, the bugs and prickly pear cactus that Lewis called the expedition's greatest "curse" were as hard on the dog as they were on the men. Mosquitoes swarmed around his unprotected nose and eyes. Cactus barbs pierced the pads of his feet and made him bite and scratch himself, Lewis wrote, "as if in a rack of pain."

And like everyone else, he had a landmark named for him: Seaman Creek (now Monture Creek), a swift stream flowing into the Blackfoot River.

The journals do not mention what Seaman ate during the ordeal of near starvation in the Bitterroot Mountains. (Nor do they comment on whether any of the men ever contemplated making a meal out of the big Newfoundland, as they hungrily purchased dog after dog from the Indians along the Columbia River.) They do tell us that many tribes were impressed by the dog's size and intelligence, and that on the return trip three Indians attempted to steal Seaman. Lewis was incensed and sent some men in pursuit with orders to shoot, if necessary. If the Indians hadn't abandoned the dog and fled upon seeing the search party approach, Seaman would have been the cause of the first bloodshed on the expedition.

Seaman's last appearance in the journals is on July 15, 1806, during the trip home. Lewis and a number of the men were once again at the Great Falls—and once again complaining of mosquitoes that "continue to infest us in such manner that we can scarcely exist." Lewis could find some relief under his mosquito netting, he noted, but "my dog even howls with the torture he experiences."

With that image of howling from bug bites, Seaman disappears from the record. For the next two months, as the expedition hurried toward St. Louis, the dog is never mentioned, even in passing. It is possible that some tragedy befell him—an accident, a fatal sickness, being mistakenly left behind in the rush downstream—and that he never made it back to the wooded land where he once frolicked after squirrels.

But it is inconceivable to imagine something like that happening without Lewis or one of the other journalists making a note of it—no more likely, in fact, than if one of the men had been killed in the final leg of the journey and no one had recorded the event in a journal. For Seaman had long since ceased being merely Meriwether Lewis's pet. To the members of the expedition he had become, as Clark once called him, "our dog."

[and] the banks being unable to support themselves longer, tumble into the river with tremendious force, distroying every thing within their reach."

Fourteen miles was considered a good day's progress. After two long months, they were still in what is now Missouri.

The men suffered from snakebites, dislocated shoulders, sore joints, and occasional sunstroke. Others broke out in boils from a bad diet and spending so much time in damp clothing. Their drinking water came from the river: each cup, one man recorded, was half mud and ooze. Virtually all of them got dysentery.

Lewis, who had learned the rudiments of herbal healing from his mother, lanced the boils and applied a mixture of elm bark and cornmeal to the sores. He treated snakebites with a poultice of bark and gunpowder. Following Dr. Benjamin Rush's instructions, he bled his patients frequently. And he freely dispensed some of the six hundred pills the doctor had sold him: laxatives so powerful that the men called them "Rush's Thunderbolts."

July 4th. A Snake Bit Jo. Fields on the Side of the foot, which Sweled much; apply Barks to Coor [cure]. . . . Passed a Creek on the South Side about 15 yards wide Coming out of an extensive Prarie. As the Creek has no name and this Day is the 4th of July we name this Independance Creek.

July 11th and 12th. Set out errly this morning [and] proceeded on. . . . Came to about 12 oclock P.m. for the porpos of resting on[e] or two days. Ouer object in Delaying hear is to tak Some observations and rest the men who are much fategeued. Armes and amunition enspected [and] all in Good order. The men [are] all sick.

SERGEANT CHARLES FLOYD

The roster of the men of the Corps of Discovery, in William Clark's hand. The sergeants—John Ordway, Nathaniel Pryor, Charles Floyd, and Patrick Gass— top the list. Clark's slave, York, is not included.

Charles Floyd, one of the men in what was called the "permanent party," was twenty-two years old at the time, "a young man of much merit," Lewis noted. He was born in Kentucky and may have been a distant relative of Clark's.

Beyond that, not much is known about him—or the others: "stout, healthy, unmarried men," Lewis called them, "accustomed to the woods and capable of bearing bodily fatigue."

They came from every corner of the young nation. John Ordway was from Hebron, New Hampshire. Joseph Whitehouse was a Virginian. Patrick Gass came from Irish stock in Pennsylvania. One man had been born in Germany; several in Canada. Three were the sons of white fathers and Indian mothers. Reuben and Joseph Field were brothers. Clark brought along a black man named York, a slave he had owned since childhood.

There were nine French Canadian *engagés*— and Lewis's big Newfoundland dog, Seaman.

Some of the men had previously worked as gunsmiths, blacksmiths, carpenters, millers, and tailors. Many had been happily pawned off on the expedition by the frontier army, including one private, Clark said, who "never drinks water."

Orderly Book, May 17th. A Sergeant and four men of the Party . . . will convene at 11 oClock to day on the quarter Deck of the Boat, and form themselves into a Court martial to hear and determine the evidence . . . against William Werner & Hugh Hall . . . & John Collins. . . .

Orderly Book, June 29th . . . Ordered. A Court martial will set this day . . . for the trial of John Collins and Hugh Hall . . . charged with getting drunk on his post this morning. . . .

Orderly Book, Camp New Island, July 12th, 1804. A Court ma[r]tial consisting of the two commanding officers will convene this day at 1 OCk. P.M. for the trial of . . . such prisoners as are Guilty of Capatol Crimes, and under the rules and articles of War punishable by Death.

Alexander Willard . . . charged with lying down and sleeping on his post whilst a sentinel. . . . To this charge the prisoner pleads: Guilty of Lying Down; and not Guilty, of Going to Sleep.

. . . The court . . . are of oppinion that the Prisoner . . . is guilty [and] do Sentence him to receive One hundred lashes on his bear back, at four different times in equal proportion—and order that the punishment Commence this evening at Sunset.

WILLIAM CLARK
MERIWETHER LEWIS

The Corps of Discovery's keelboat, as sketched by William Clark in his field notes. With a broad sail and 20 oars, it could hold 10 tons of cargo and sometimes was propelled by setting poles or by men wading near shore and pulling it along with a cordelling rope.

They were undisciplined at first. During the winter in Illinois, there had been drunken brawls and open disobedience. At St. Charles, several of the men were absent without leave after one of the parties in town. At the mouth of the Kansas River, near what is now Kansas City, two men on night duty broke into the supply of whiskey. Along the lower Missouri that summer, the captains convened impromptu courts-martial five different times, for offenses ranging from talking back to officers to sleeping on guard duty and outright desertion.

Most offenders were given fifty to one hundred lashes. The deserter was forced to run a gauntlet between the men four times, while each one struck him with willow switches and the ramrods from their muskets.

Two gravesites. North of the Platte River, the expedition climbed a rounded knob (top) to visit the burial mound of Blackbird, a famous Omaha chief who had died of smallpox in 1800 and was buried sitting on his favorite horse. The captains left a white flag, bound with red, white, and blue, as a mark of respect. Nine days later and less than 50 miles upriver, the expedition held its own burial ceremony on August 20, 1804, when Sergeant Charles Floyd became the first United States soldier to die west of the Mississippi. The captains named Floyd's Bluff and Floyd's River in his honor. The American artist George Catlin went up the Missouri in 1832 and painted both landmarks. Floyd's grave, in Sioux City, Iowa, is now marked by a 100-foot obelisk.

By fall, there were no more serious breaches of discipline.

*July 31st. I am verry Sick and Has been for Somtime, but have Recoverd
my helth again.*

CHARLES FLOYD

*August 19th. This day sergeant Floyd became very sick and remained so all
night. He was seized with a complaint somewhat like a violent cholick.*

PATRICK GASS

*August 20th. Sergeant Floyd much weaker and no better . . . [N]o pulse
& nothing will stay a moment on his Stomach . . . Passed two Islands,
and at the first Bluff on the starboard side, Sgt. Floyd Died with a great
deal of composure; before his death he Said to me, "I am going away. I
want you to write me a letter."*

WILLIAM CLARK

Near what is now Sioux City, Iowa, the Corps of Discovery suffered its first
fatality when Floyd died from what Lewis diagnosed as "bilious cholic," but
which may have been a burst appendix. (There was nothing the captains could
have done to save him—appendectomies weren't practiced until the late 1800s.)

*He was layed out in the most decent manner possable. We . . . dug a
Grave on the top of a round knob & buried the De[cea]sed with the
honours of war. The funeral Serrymony performed &c. we named this
hill Sgt. Floyd's Bluff.*

PRIVATE JOSEPH WHITEHOUSE

*He was buried with the Honors of War, much lamented. A Seedar post
with [his] name was fixed at the head of his grave. This Man at all times
gave us proofs of his firmness and Determined resolution to doe Service to
his country and honor to himself. After paying all the honor to our
Decesed brother we camped in the Mouth of Floyds River about 30 yards
wide. A butifull evening.*

WILLIAM CLARK

Sergeant Charles Floyd had become the first United States soldier to die
west of the Mississippi.

CHAPTER 3

Land of Plenty

There is no timber in this part of the country; but continued prairie on both sides of the river. A person by going on one of the hills may have a view as far as the eye can reach without any obstruction; and enjoy the most delightful prospects.

PATRICK GASS

*A*S THEY MOVED farther north and west, the men noticed the landscape changing. Except along the riverbank, there were virtually no trees. The land seemed to unfold and roll on forever. They had emerged onto one of the world's largest grasslands—the Great Plains. They had never seen anything like it in their lives.

Having for many days past confined myself to the boat, I determined to devote this day to amuse myself on shore with my gun and view the interior of the country. . . . The shortness and [freshness] of grass gave the plain the appearance . . . of [a] beatifull bowling-green in fine order. . . . [T]his senery, already rich, pleasing and beatiful, was still farther hightened by immence herds of Buffaloe, deer, [and] Elk . . . which we saw in every direction feeding on the hills and plains. I do not think I exagerate when I estimate the number of Buffaloe which could be compre[hend]ed at one view to amount to 3,000.

MERIWETHER LEWIS

Small numbers of buffalo had appeared farther down the river. Now huge herds were commonplace, and for the first time the men shot and ate some. And they began to encounter other animals they had never seen before—new ones, it seemed, almost every day.

September 14th. John Shields . . . killed a verry large white rabbit or haire . . . of a different description of any one ever yet seen in the

"Curiousities"

Among the multiple missions Thomas Jefferson assigned to Meriwether Lewis, the one perhaps dearest to the President was his instruction that the expedition take careful note of the plants and animals of the West, "especially those not known in the United States."

From the age of twenty-three, Jefferson had maintained a "garden book," keeping track of the flowers and plants at Monticello, and much of his only published book, *Notes on the State of Virginia,* was devoted to describing the plants of his native state. "No occupation is so delightful to me," he once wrote, "as the culture of the earth." He was equally fascinated by the animal world. When a French naturalist theorized that animals in the New World were inferior to those of Europe, Jefferson sent him a huge, stuffed moose as proof to the contrary. And in 1797, when he arrived in Philadelphia (then the nation's capital) as Vice President, Jefferson brought along the fossilized bones of a ground sloth unearthed in Virginia and delivered a scientific paper about it to the American Philosophical Society, the country's preeminent scientific organization. (The ground sloth was later given the formal name *Megalonyx jeffersoni* in his honor.)

As President Jefferson's private secretary, young Meriwether Lewis would have had time to study those bones. They were kept, along with the rest of Jefferson's collection of fossils, in the East Room of the White House—the same room Lewis used as his quarters. Lewis also had available to him Jefferson's extensive library of books on natural science, not to mention opportunities to engage in extended conversations with the naturalist-President himself.

Nevertheless, before sending his protégé west, Jefferson dispatched him to Philadelphia for more extensive training. Lewis was not formally educated in the natural sciences, Jefferson seemingly apologized in a letter to Dr. Benjamin Smith Barton, one of the Philadelphia tutors, but "he possesses a remarkable store of accurate observations . . . and will therefore readily single out whatever presents itself new to him."

Jefferson's confidence in Lewis's talents turned out to be well placed.

Out on the trail, Lewis was soon devoting much of his time simply to recording his observations. Each day he (or Clark) wrote down the temperature and wind direction and weather conditions at sunrise and at four o'clock, noted whether the river was rising or falling, and added additional remarks. On September 19, 1804, for instance, he made this comment: "The leaves of Some of the Cottonwood begin to fade, yesterday saw the 1st brant passing from the N.W. to S.E." At important milestones, Lewis also took celestial

Two birds are named for the explorers: Lewis's woodpecker (*Melanerpes lewis,* top) and Clark's nutcracker (*Nucifraga columbiana*). Clark discovered his namesake in Idaho on August 22, 1805. Lewis first saw his woodpecker in Montana on July 20, 1805, during the westward journey, then shot one on the way home in 1806; its skin, still preserved, is in the Museum of Comparative Zoology at Harvard.

readings to determine latitude and longitude. And he did not ignore Jefferson's instruction to observe and collect interesting soils and minerals along the way.

But it was the plants and animals that kept him busiest. During just two weeks in early September 1804, as the expedition entered the High Plains, eight plants and eight animals were encountered that were unknown in the East and new to science. "Curiousities," the diarists often called them. More followed, throughout the long journey.

Lewis took pains to describe each of them as carefully as possible. (He had with him Barton's *Elements of Botany,* the nation's first botany textbook, and several other volumes of natural science to help with technical language.) Plants were collected, dried, pressed, and stored away to be brought back to Jefferson. Dead animals were measured, weighed, skinned, and dissected, and their hides, horns, and skeletons preserved. A few were stuffed, by means of taxidermy techniques recommended by the President. And some were captured and sent back alive. (Only a prairie dog and magpie survived, but they shared a rare distinction: they became undoubtedly the only animals in American history to have lived part of their lives in the White House, for Jefferson's personal study, and in Philadelphia's Independence Hall, where a natural science museum was temporarily located.)

In all, the Corps of Discovery recorded for science some 178 plants and 122 animals that previously had not been described. Among them were flora and fauna that have come to symbolize the West: the antelope, coyote, mountain goat, and bighorn sheep; the lodgepole and the ponderosa pine, the Pacific yew and the Sitka spruce; the steelhead and the cutthroat trout; the prairie dog and the grizzly bear.

Clark took part in the discoveries and descriptions— Clark's nutcracker still bears his name, as does the cutthroat trout *(Oncorhynchus clarki)*—but Lewis was without question the principal botanist and zoologist. Lewis's woodpecker *(Melanerpes lewis),* Lewis's wild flax, and the bitterroot *(Lewisia rediviva)* commemorate just a few of his many discoveries.

Even during some of the most unlikely times, he

The head of a pronghorn, as drawn by Karl Bodmer in the 1830s. Some expedition members called it a goat or cabre, but Lewis referred to it as an antelope, the name that persists even though technically it is a different species. "The superior fleetness of this anamal . . . was to me really astonishing," Lewis wrote. "It appeared reather the rappid flight of birds than the motion of quadrupeds. I think I can safely venture the asscertion that the speed of this anamal is equal if not superior to that of the finest blooded courser."

dutifully made his contributions to science. During the perilous ordeal in the Bitterroot Mountains, Lewis nonetheless observed and described the Oregon ruffed grouse and Franklin's grouse, the Sitka alder and the western red cedar, the orange honeysuckle, blue huckleberry, and common snowberry—all new to science. On the return trip, as he and three men galloped for their lives across the Plains to escape the Blackfeet, Lewis took time to note the white-margined spurge, a small plant never before described, yet easy to overlook in such a situation.

And on August 12, 1806, in his last journal entry of the entire journey, a wounded Lewis devoted only a few lines to describing his injuries. But he could not put down his pen before going into elaborate detail about a "singular Cherry" he had observed on the Missouri River bottomlands. "The pulp of this fruit is of an agreeable ascid flavor and is now ripe," he concluded. "I have never seen it in blume."

Of the two captains, Lewis was better at botany and zoology. His journals include these drawings of the head of a California condor (*Gymnogyps californianus,* top left), the pinecone of a Sitka spruce *(Picea sitchensis),* the swordlike leaf of a Christmas fern *(Polystichum munitum),* and the leaf of a vine maple *(Acer circinatum).* He and Clark recorded 178 plants and 122 animals that were new to science.

The same day that Lewis described the "cock of the plains," or sage grouse, in his journal, Clark sketched this portrait of the bird (above). Lewis said it was two-thirds the size of a turkey; Clark estimated it at three-quarters.

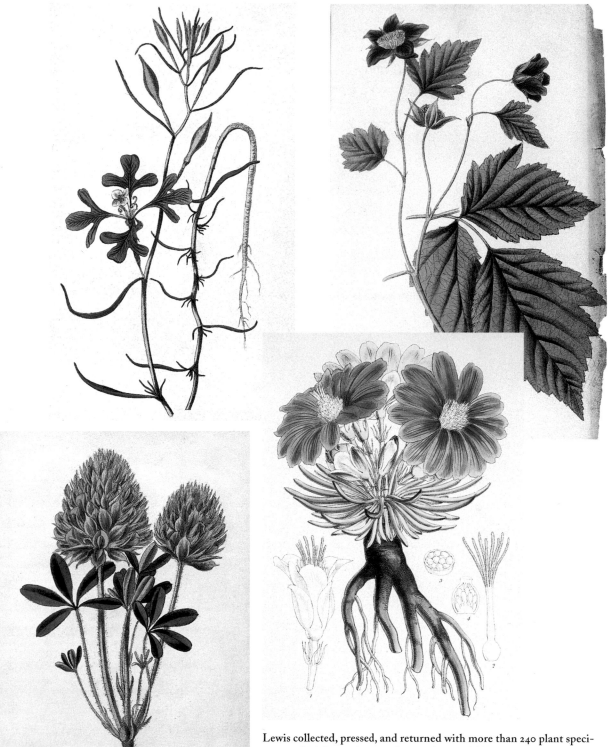

Lewis collected, pressed, and returned with more than 240 plant specimens, which later scientists drew and named. These early paintings show
the ragged robin (*Clarkia pulchella*, top left), prairie turnip (bottom left),
salmonberry (top right), and bitterroot *(Lewisia rediviva)*. Indians used
all but the ragged robin for food, but the men of the expedition generally
didn't like their taste. Lewis in particular found the boiled bitterroot
"naucious to my pallate." It is now Montana's state flower, and a
mountain chain and major river are named for it.

States. . . . Capt. Clark joined us. [He] had killed a curious annimil. . . . The legs like a Deer; feet like a Goat; horns like a Goat, only forked. . . . Such an animil was never yet known in [the] U.S. States. The Capt. had the Skins of the hair & Goat Stuffed in order to send back to the city of Washington. The bones and all.

JOHN ORDWAY

September 17th. Colter Killed a Goat like the one I killed and a curious kind of Deer of a Dark gray Colr. more so than common. . . . This Spec[i]es of Deer jumps like a goat or Sheep.

WILLIAM CLARK

September 18th. Yesterday captain Lewis while hunting killed a bird not common in the states: it is like a magpie and is a bird of prey.

PATRICK GASS

September 18th. George Drewyer [Drouillard] killed a prarie woolf. Some larger than a fox; long teeth & of a different description from any in the States. . . . The Bones of the woolf was taken apart and Saved, as well as the Skin . . . in order to send back to the States next Spring, with the other curiousities we have.

JOHN ORDWAY

The strange new animals were the jackrabbit, antelope, mule deer, black-billed magpie, and coyote. Native peoples of the Plains were well acquainted with them all, and a few Spanish, French, and British trappers had seen them before. But the detailed descriptions the captains wrote down in their notebooks were the first recorded for science.

Following Jefferson's instructions, the explorers took measurements of each new species, noted their habits, and placed their hides and skeletons in crates for shipment back to the White House.

On September 7 they encountered another new animal, which in their descriptions they called by a variety of names. John Ordway, however, called it by the name by which it is still known: the prairie dog. For the better part of a hot day, the expedition halted while everyone—except for a few guards left with the boat—busily struggled first to dig, then to flood one out of its burrowing hole so it could be captured alive as a present from the West for the President.

*Discovered a Village of Small animals that burrow in the gro[und]. . . .
[It] covers about 4 acrs of Ground . . . and Contains great numbers of
holes on the top of which those little animals Set erect, make a Whistleing
noise and whin allarmed Slip into their hole. . . . Those animals are
Called by the french* Petite Chien.

WILLIAM CLARK

*I have called [it] the barking squirrel. . . . It's form is that of the
squirrel . . . [but] they bark at you as you approach them, their note being
much that of little toy dogs; their yelps are in quick succession and at each
they [give] a motion to their tails upwards. . . . It is much more quick
active and fleet than it's form would indicate.*

MERIWETHER LEWIS

*We attempted to dig to the beds of one of those [ground rats]; [but] after diging
6 feet, found by running a pole down that we were not halfway to his Lodges.*
WILLIAM CLARK

*All of the party, except the guard, went to it; and [then] took all the
kettles and vessels for holding water, in order to drive the animals out of
their holes by pouring in water.*

PATRICK GASS

Of all the strange new animals the Corps of Discovery encountered, prairie dogs fascinated them the most. The animals lived in villages like this one, painted by William Jacob Hays, some of which covered up to 10 acres by Clark's estimate. Virtually every member of the expedition spent September 7, 1804, trying to flush one of the "barking squirrels" from its hole and capture it alive to send back to President Jefferson.

The sheer vastness of the Great Plains astonished the explorers as much as the animals living there. "This is the most open country I ever beheld, almost one continued prairie," wrote Patrick Gass. Clark called the area "void of every thing except grass." John Ordway marveled that "we could See all around for a long distance . . . as far as our eyes could behold."

They attempted to drown several of [these prairie dogs] out of their holes, but they caught but one, which they brought in alive. . . . Shields killed a prairie dog, which was cooked for the Capts dinner. . . . They are a curious animal.

JOHN ORDWAY

———

When the Corps of Discovery first entered the High Plains, George Shannon—at age nineteen the expedition's youngest member—went hunting one day and didn't return. Days passed. The captains grew worried and sent small groups out to find him. All returned empty-handed.

August 28th. J. Shields & J. Fields, who was Sent back to look for Shannon & the Horses, joined us & informed [us] that . . . they Could not over take him. . . . This man not being a first rate Hunter, we deturmined to Send one man in pursute of him with Some Provisions.

WILLIAM CLARK

September 6th. Colter came to the Boat; had not found Shannon.

JOHN ORDWAY

Then, sixteen days after his disappearance, Shannon suddenly showed up—thin, gaunt, and hungry. Somehow, he had gotten ahead of the boats, and in his desperation to find the main party had pushed on alone, farther and farther upriver.

His ammunition had given out, and he had killed one rabbit with a stick he shot from his rifle. Other than that, for nearly two weeks he had eaten nothing but wild grapes.

Relieved that the young man was still alive, Clark marveled in his journal: "Thus a man had like to have Starved to death in a land of Plenty for the want of Bullitts or Something to kill his meat."

CHAPTER 4

Children

My heart is gladder than it ever was before to see [a white man]. If you want to open the road, no one can prevent it. It will always be open to you.

KAKAWISSASSA,
LIGHTNING CROW

*L*EWIS AND CLARK WERE the first official representatives of the United States in the West. As such, they were under instructions from Jefferson to seek out as many Indian tribes as possible on their journey to the Pacific.

The President wanted the Corps of Discovery to establish friendly relations with the native peoples of this newest section of the nation—especially because of the lucrative fur trade that he hoped the Americans would soon dominate. But for purely scientific reasons, Jefferson was fascinated by Indian customs, and part of the captains' duties was to amass as much information as possible about the people they met.

Along the lower Missouri during the early summer of 1804, however, they found few Indians to negotiate with or to study. The Kansas Indians, who lived upstream from the mouth of the river bearing their name, were out hunting buffalo on the Plains when the expedition passed through their territory. Farther north, the captains traveled a short distance up the Platte River in hopes of meeting some Pawnees or Otos. They found no one. In late July, George Drouillard, the expedition's valued hunter and interpreter, finally came upon a lone Missouri Indian, who was persuaded to return to his village and bring back a handful of chiefs (including some Otos) for a daylong parley at a place on the west bank that Clark named "Council Bluff."

August 3rd. This morning the two Captains held a council with the [Oto] Indians & made 6 Chiefs under the american government. They all rec[eive]d their medel & other presents With Great kindness & thankful-

Chiefs of the lower Missouri. Charles Bird King painted a portrait of this delegation of Omaha, Kansas, Missouri, and Pawnee Indians when they visited the East in 1821. One of them is wearing a peace medal.

ness. . . . They made some verry sensable Speeches, Smoked and drank with us. Shook hands and parted.

JOHN ORDWAY

By mid-August they were passing through the land of the Omahas. Messengers were dispatched, and Lewis and Clark ordered prairie fires to be lit as a signal to the Indians to come to the river, but again none were found. Instead, the captains visited the gravesite of Blackbird, a famous Omaha chief who had died during a smallpox epidemic four years earlier and was buried, sitting astride his favorite horse, on a hill overlooking the river. Lewis and Clark left a red, white, and blue flag flying on the burial mound's ceremonial pole and pushed on up the Missouri.

Finally, at the end of August, the Yankton Sioux were contacted, and a large delegation came down from their villages on the James River to meet with the explorers, who had camped at a place they called Calumet Bluff. On the morning of the thirtieth, the Indians were ferried across the river for a council.

The captains followed the same routine they had used with the Otos and Missouris—and which they would repeat with every tribe they encountered for the next two years.

To impress the chiefs with American military power and technology, the captains paraded the men and displayed magnets, compasses, and spyglasses, and Lewis fired off his air gun. "They were all amazed at the curiosity," Joseph Whitehouse wrote, "and as Soon as he had Shot a fiew times they all ran hastily to See the Ball holes in the tree."

To display the wealth of the nation the Americans represented, they distributed gifts: beads, cloth, scissors, sewing needles, razors, combs, mirrors, tobacco, knives, tomahawks. They gave out medals embossed with Thomas Jefferson's likeness on one side, two hands clasped in friendship on the other; and they presented paper certificates that pronounced the chiefs to be special friends of the United States.

Then—referring to their country of seventeen states as "the seventeen great nations of America"—the captains gave a lengthy speech they had written in advance.

Children. Your old fathers the French and the Spaniards have gone beyond the great lake toward the rising sun, from whence they never intend returning to visit their former red children.

Children. The great chief of the seventeen great nations of America, impelled by his parental regard for his newly adopted children on the troubled waters, has sent us out to clear the road . . . and make it a road of peace.

The speech was intended to explain the new United States claim of sovereignty over the territory, to induce the tribes to trade with American fur companies that the captains promised would soon be showing up, and to persuade the Indians to be at peace not only with white people but with rival tribes. Whites had been trading along this part of the Missouri for nearly a century, and the tone of the captains' words—calling the Indians "children" and referring to a far-off but powerful "great father"—was nothing new to the Native Americans' ears.

Tokens of friendship. Chiefs were given these medals (opposite, bottom) showing Jefferson on one side and a handshake on the other; so-called "lesser chiefs" received paper certificates, signed by Jefferson, with blanks for filling in the chief's name. In his list of Indian presents (below), Lewis included colored beads, silk handkerchiefs, mirrors, scissors, and thimbles as just a few of the gifts meant to display the wealth and generosity of the Indians' new "great father."

"Make Yourself Acquainted"

Thomas Jefferson's instructions to Meriwether Lewis about the Indian tribes the Corps of Discovery would encounter were explicit—and far-reaching. "Endeavor to make yourself acquainted," the President wrote, "as far as a diligent pursuit of your journey shall admit," and then he rattled off a long list of topics to pursue: populations, languages, food, clothing, housing, laws, customs, trading practices, "their ordinary occupations in agriculture, fishing, hunting, war, arts, & the implements for these," physical appearance, diseases, "the state of morality, religion & information among them," and many more.

Lewis and Clark did their best to follow Jefferson's orders. With each tribe they met, they asked hundreds of questions, collected items of interest, and tried to observe as much as possible and write the information down in their journals.

Lewis excelled at describing the different objects in an Indian village. Pages of his journals were devoted to everything from cooking pots to moccasins. One long passage painstakingly described the way that the Arikaras made glass beads. "The art is kept a secret by the Indians among themselves," he noted, "and is yet known to but few of them." Another explained how the Lakotas constructed a tepee out of buffalo hides. Among the Mandans he described—and then sketched—their battle axes. "He did have the naturalist's ability to describe objects with almost photographic fidelity," according to historian James Ronda. "Lewis brought to ethnography the practiced eye of one who delighted in describing and cataloging the creatures of the natural world."

Clark was better at deciphering Indian customs, particularly the rituals associated with the meetings of chiefs. He noted what the leaders wore, where they sat in relation to one another, and what role tobacco and smoking a pipe played in any important council. He also discerned that in many tribes, a chief's authority often relied on persuasion, not arbitrary orders. "Power," he wrote, "is merely the acquiescence of the warriors in the superior merit of a chief."

Other expedition members added their own observations. John Ordway described the burial scaffolds used by the Mandans, the hoop and pole games Indian children played, and a local recipe for corn bread. Joseph Whitehouse struggled to explain the sound of the Salish language. Patrick Gass, a carpenter by trade, expounded on how an earth lodge was built.

Some of what they saw and recorded among the Indians the explorers viewed through their own cultural prism. Gass witnessed a Mandan offering food to a buffalo skull and scoffed: "Their superstitious credulity is so great, that they will believe by using the head well, the living buffalo will come and that they will get a supply of meat."

Prior to recrossing the fearful Bitterroot Mountains, Lewis described a ceremony conducted by the expedition's young Nez Percé guides: "Last evening the indians entertained us with seting the fir trees on fire," he wrote. "They have a great number of dry lims near their bodies which when set on fire creates a very suddon and immence blaze from bottom to top of those tall trees. . . . [T]he natives told us that their object in seting those trees on fire was to bring fair weather for our journey." For the Indians, it was ritual. For Lewis, "this exhibition reminded me of a display of fireworks." (His weather diary for the next five days, however, records generally fair skies.)

Over the course of the expedition, nearly fifty tribes were encountered, and the dizzying diversity of Native

American life is one of the clearest (though unspoken) images to emerge from the journals. The West through which the Corps of Discovery traveled was neither an "uninhabited wilderness" nor a single "Indian world." Indians thought of themselves as many different people, not as one monolithic group—and understandably so. They were as varied as the western landscape itself.

Lewis and Clark met people who roamed the Plains following the buffalo herds, living in tepees that could be moved at a minute's notice; people who were farmers and lived in permanent villages of rounded earth lodges; people who lived in stick wickiups and dug for roots; people who fished for their food and dwelled in large houses made of wooden planks. Some measured their wealth in horses; others had no horses at all. Some were predominantly tall, or wore the forelocks of their hair pushed upward as a sign of distinction. Others were shorter, stouter, and saw beauty in a forehead flattened by boards.

Though a handful of tribes had never seen white people before they met Lewis and Clark, all of them had already been affected by the three-hundred-year presence of Europeans on the continent. Still, the expedition's account stands, in effect, as an important ethnological benchmark of the many Indian cultures that existed prior to American expansion to the Pacific.

Using the Rocky Mountains as a dividing point, the captains eventually compiled an "Estimate of Eastern Indians" and an "Estimate of Western Indians," which attempted to name each of the tribes they met (and some they had only heard about), then listed at least nineteen items about every one. The word lists they so carefully compiled of Indian languages were either misplaced or lost at the end of the expedition.

But the daily journals themselves still provide rich, sometimes surprising details: a game played by the Chinooks that seemed to the Americans something like backgammon; how the Nez Percé gelded their horses;

the gambling habits of the Shoshones; a special ceremony of the Yankton Sioux in which honored guests were carried into the village on a buffalo robe, then treated to a feast of roast dog.

And, of course, there are the articles Lewis and Clark sent back to Jefferson, a man who was fascinated by everything associated with Indians. To satisfy the President's curiosity, they dispatched crate after crate of Indian artifacts: painted buffalo robes, a bow and quiver, a tobacco pouch made of otter skin, a Mandan clay pot, a conical Clatsop hat, a Chinook skirt, and much more.

They even sent Indians. The principal purpose of a chief's visit to the East was diplomacy, the notion being that Indians on their way to meet the President would be impressed by the size and power of the United States and therefore more willing to cooperate with American plans. But for Jefferson, the visits were also a chance to learn even more about the continent's first inhabitants, whose cultural objects soon decorated the foyer of Monticello.

"Tell my friend of Mandane . . . that I have already opened my arms to receive him," Jefferson enthusiastically wrote Lewis, when he learned that the captain had returned to St. Louis with Sheheke, a Mandan chief. "Perhaps while in our neighborhood it may be gratifying to him . . . to take a ride to Monticello and see in what manner I have arranged the tokens of friendship I have received from his country particularly, as well as from other Indian friends: that I am in fact preparing a kind of Indian Hall."

Exploration is a two-way street. Imagining Sheheke as the leader of a Mandan "corps of discovery" to the East, one wonders less what he reported home about Washington, D.C., and the cities along the way, than what he had to say, when he returned to his earth lodge village, about the house near Charlottesville and the various items in possession of the man who called himself the "great father."

Children. Know that the great chief who has . . . offered you the hand of unalterable friendship is the great Chief of the Seventeen Great Nations of America, whose cities are as numerous as the stars of the heavens, and whose people like the grass of your plains cover . . . the wide extended country . . . to where the land ends and the sun rises from the face of the great waters. . . . [H]e will serve you and not deceive you.

Children. . . . You are to live in peace with all the white men; neither wage war against the red men your neighbors. . . . Injure not the persons of any traders . . . who visit you under the protection of your great father's flag.

Children. Do these things which your great father advises and be happy . . . lest by one false step you should bring down upon your nation the displeasure of your great father . . . who could consume you as the fire consumes the grass of the plains.

Children. . . . Follow [his] counsels and you will have nothing to fear, because the Great Spirit will smile upon your nation and in future ages will make you outnumber the trees of the forest.

The Yanktons said they would respond the next morning. That evening, however, they performed ceremonies of their own for the newcomers—as an act of hospitality, but also to display their own power.

As Soon as it was dark a fire was made. A drum was repaired among them. The young men painted themselves different ways. Some with their

Following Jefferson's instructions, Lewis and Clark recorded the Indians' customs, languages, populations, and much more. Sometimes they added drawings to their observations. Among the Shoshones, Lewis drew a diagram (below, right) of a weir the Indians used for catching fish. On New Year's Day, 1806, he sketched two swords, a bludgeon, and a five-foot-long Clatsop paddle (below).

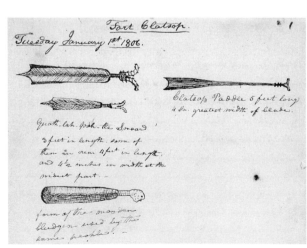

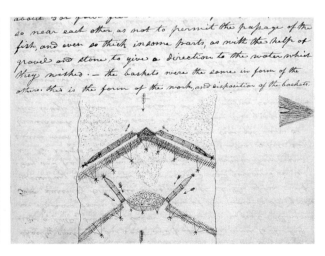

*faces all white, others with their faces part white round their forehead
and breasts etc. Then they commenced dancing in [a] curious manner to
us. Their was a party that Sung and kept time with the drumm. They all
danced or all their young men especially.*

*. . . They would dance around the fire for Some time and then houp,
& then rest a fiew minutes. One of the warriors would git up in the
centre with his arms & point towards the different nations, & make a
Speech, telling what he had done, how many he had killed & how many
horses he had Stole etc. All this make them Great men & fine
warriers. . . . The Bravest men & them that kills most gets the greatest
honoured among them.*

JOSEPH WHITEHOUSE

A century after Lewis and
Clark, the photographer
Edward S. Curtis traveled
throughout the West,
capturing on film many
members of the tribes the
Corps of Discovery described
in their journals. Bear's Belly
(middle) and the woman
gathering reeds are Arikaras.
Hollow Horn Bear (left) is
from the Brulé band of the
Teton Sioux.

Clark, who was more at ease among Indians than Lewis and seems to have
genuinely enjoyed their company in ways his co-commander never did, called
the Yanktons a "stout, bold looking people." He took down a vocabulary of their
language, enumerated the names and numbers of their various bands, described
the shape and decorations of their clothes and tepees, mentioned that the Yanktons presented a fat dog for roasting "as a mark of their great respect" for the expedition, discussed their trading relationship with the British, and wrote at
length about a warrior society of theirs whose members took solemn vows never
to retreat or seek shelter during battle. They were "brave, active young men,"
Clark wrote, and "likely fellows." In a recent fight with the Crows, he noted,
eighteen out of the twenty-two members of the society were killed; the remain-

ing four were saved only when other friends dragged them away. The Yanktons, John Ordway reported, "camped along side of us and behaved honestly."

The next morning after breakfast, the chiefs gathered with the captains, presented ceremonial pipes to smoke, and gave speeches of their own. One, named the Shake Hand, noted that he already had medals from the Spanish and English but was willing to travel to see the new "great father" if the Yanktons were given more presents and trade goods. "We wish to have a trader to stop among us," said another, named Tar-ro-mo-nee, who had been given an American flag as a present. "I would be very glad," he added, if "our two fathers would give us some powder and ball and some milk [whiskey] with the flag."

But a Yankton chief named Half Man also issued a warning. The next tribe they would encounter farther up the Missouri, he told the captains, "will not open their ears, and you cannot, I fear, open them." They were the Teton Sioux—the Lakotas—and their reputation reached all the way to Washington.

Scalp dance of the Teton Sioux. During the expedition's visit, the tribe celebrated a victory over the Omahas by dancing late into the night while displaying 65 Omaha scalps. George Catlin painted a similar scene 30 years later, when he camped with the tribe at the mouth of the Teton River.

You will probably meet with parties of [the Teton Sioux]. On that nation
we wish most particularly to make a friendly impression, because of
their immense power.

THOMAS JEFFERSON

The Lakotas had only recently migrated west onto the Great Plains, but they
were now the most powerful tribe in the region, intent on controlling the flow
of European trade goods along the Missouri. For years they had intimidated
French and Spanish boatmen—stopping some from continuing upriver, de-
manding tribute from others, even confiscating canoes and all their cargo.

At the mouth of the Bad River, near what is now Pierre, South Dakota, the
Corps of Discovery met them for the first time.

They are, or appear as yet, to be the most freendly people I ever Saw but
they will Steal and plunder if they can git an oppertunity. . . . About 15
days ago they had a battle with the Mahars [Omahas]. They killed 65 men
and took 25 women prisoners. They took the 65 . . . scalps and had them
hung on Small poles, which ther women held in their hands when they
danced.

We Saw them have one dance this evening. . . . They had drums and
whistles for musick. . . . They kept it up untill one oclock,
dancing . . . war dances round the fire, which was curious to us.

JOSEPH WHITEHOUSE

The two sides agreed to hold a council on a sandbar in the river on the
morning of September 25. A canvas awning was erected for protection against
the sun and the wind. Packages of gifts were prepared. An American flag was
unfurled and raised on a pole. The soldiers put on their dress uniforms.

Even William Clark seemed anxious. The expedition, he noted, "prepared
all things for action, in case of necessity." Still, the captains were confident of
success—and named a nearby island Good Humored Island.

At midmorning large numbers of Lakotas gathered on both riverbanks.
Chiefs named Black Buffalo, the Partisan, and Buffalo Medicine—along with
thirty warriors—came over for the ceremonies.

Gave the 3 Chiefs 3 niew meddals & 1 american flag. Some knives &
other Small articles of Goods. . . . Gave the head chief, the Black

*Buffalow, a red coat & a cocked hat & feather, etc.; likewise Some
Tobacco. . . . They did not appear to talk much untill they had got the
goods, and then they wanted more, and Said we must Stop with them or
leave one of the pearogues with them as that was what they expected.*

JOHN ORDWAY

Lewis and Clark tried to proceed with their usual display of military power—the parade and the air gun—but the Lakotas were not impressed. To them, the expedition represented a commercial threat. The new trading system being proposed by the captains would undermine Lakota influence.

Once again they demanded more goods and insisted that the expedition go no farther upriver. A quick tour of the keelboat for the three chiefs did nothing to ease the mounting tensions. Clark took them back to shore.

But when they landed, three warriors seized the canoe's tow rope, while another grabbed its mast. The Partisan began arguing hotly with Clark, who drew his sword. Along the bank, Lakota warriors notched their arrows.

Tatanka Witko, or Fool Bull, a medicine man of the Teton Sioux, photographed by John A. Anderson in 1900. "Those people have Some brave men which they make use of as Soldiers," Clark wrote of the tribe, whose confrontation with the explorers marked the tensest moment of the expedition's first year.

*Capt Clark Spoke to all the party to Stand to
their arms. Capt Lewis who was on board [the
keelboat] ordered every man to his arms. The
large Swivel [gun was] loaded immediately
with 16 Musquet balls in it, the 2 other Swivels
loaded well with Buck Shot [and] each of them
manned. Capt Clark . . . told them that we
must and would go on . . . that we were not
Squaws, but warriers.*

*The chief Sayed he had warriers too and if
we were to go on they would follow us and kill
and take the whole of us by degrees.*

JOHN ORDWAY

The fate of the entire expedition hung in the balance.

It was one of the chiefs, Black Buffalo, who defused what could have been a disaster for both sides. He intervened, changing the subject and saying his only request was that the women and children of his village be allowed to see the keelboat and meet the explorers before they moved on.

Along the Missouri River, some tribes lived in tepees and moved from place to place following the buffalo herds. Some, like these Pawnees photographed by William Henry Jackson, lived in permanent villages of earth lodges.

Clark quickly agreed, and for three more days—marked by both friendly celebration and occasional confrontation—the expedition stayed among the Lakotas. But they anchored the keelboat a mile away, near a willow-covered island, which Clark named Bad Humored Island to reflect his mood—and his opinion of the tribe.

> *These are the vilest miscreants of the savage race, and must ever remain the pirates of the Missouri, until such measures are pursued by our government as will make them feel a dependence on its will for their supply of merchandise.*
>
> WILLIAM CLARK

Early October was upon them. The weather was turning colder. As the expedition continued up the river, the men kept themselves on high alert, worried that the Lakotas might pursue them and attack. If so, one private wrote, "we were determined to fight or die."

Instead, on the riverbank, they began seeing abandoned villages of earth lodges. These had once been the homes of the Arikaras, a farming people who only twenty years earlier had numbered nearly thirty thousand and controlled the land along the Missouri for a hundred miles. Then, beginning in 1780, a series of smallpox epidemics had swept through. The Indians had no immunity against the disease. Nine out of ten Arikaras died.

On October 8 the explorers reached what was left of the tribe—three small villages. Here they received a much warmer welcome than they had from the Teton Sioux.

Can you think anyone [here will] dare put their hands on the rope of your boat? No. Not one. . . . When you return if I am living, you will see me again the same man. . . . We shall look at the river with impatience for your return.

KAKAWISSASSA, LIGHTNING CROW

The Sioux [have] not a good heart. . . . When I go to see my [great] father [in the east] I wish to return soon for fear of my people being uneasy. [But] I also wish to go. . . . When I return [it] will make my people glad.

PIAHITO, EAGLE'S FEATHER

The Arikara chiefs promised to attempt making peace with their enemies the Mandans and Hidatsas upriver, said they looked forward to increased trade with the Americans, and agreed to send a representative to join a delegation of Oto and Missouri chiefs whom Lewis and Clark had persuaded to go east to visit Jefferson.

Like all the Indians that Lewis and Clark met, the Arikaras struggled to understand precisely the expedition's mission. Despite their weapons and their keelboat loaded with goods, they were not a war party or fur traders, the captains explained. We are *explorers,* they said, embarked on a "long journey to the Great Lake of the West, where the land ends and the sun sets on the face of the great water." The Arikaras talked among themselves and finally concluded that the Corps of Discovery was on a vision quest.

For five days the expedition lingered among the Arikaras—unwinding from the tensions they had been through with the Lakotas and, in accordance with Jefferson's instructions, studying the customs of their hosts. When the captains offered some whiskey after the council meetings, the Arikaras declined. Why, they asked politely, would friends offer something that turns people into fools? And when the expedition held its last court-martial, sentencing John Newman to seventy-five lashes for "criminal and mutinous expression," an Arikara chief was shocked by the order. He was not against punishment for crimes, he told Clark, but "his nation never whipped even their children."

The true center of attention, however, was Clark's slave, York.

Those Indians wer much astonished at my Servent. They never Saw a black man before. All flocked around him & examind him from top to toe.

WILLIAM CLARK

All the nation made a great deal of him. The children would follow after him, & if he turned towards them, they would run from him & hollow as if they were terrefied, & afraid of him.

JOHN ORDWAY

York played along with the children, telling them he was a wild bear who had been caught and tamed but still occasionally ate human flesh. The adults

On the Banks of the Missouri. In this Edward S. Curtis photograph, a Mandan stands on a river bluff near the tribe's villages, the last fixed point on Lewis and Clark's map of the Missouri.

were equally fascinated. In York's color and strength they saw special spiritual power—even more than they ascribed to the other explorers, with their dazzling array of weapons and magical gadgets.

To the Americans, York was a slave. To the Arikaras, he was Big Medicine.

A curious custom with the Souixx as well as the [Arikaras] is to give handsom squars to those whome they wish to show some acknowledgements to. . . . 2 [handsome young] Squars were Sent by a man to follow us. They came up this evening, and pursisted in their civilities.

WILLIAM CLARK

Among the Arikaras—and many other northern Plains tribes—sexual relations were sometimes imbued with ritual meanings. Through sex with a young man's wife, the wisdom and special power, usually called "medicine," of older men in the tribe (or of important strangers) could be transferred to the younger husbands. Many tribes practiced polygamy, and the offer of a wife for an evening to a visitor was also a sign of hospitality.

The Arikaras, Patrick Gass noted, "are the best looking Indians I have ever seen . . . as well as the most friendly" and their women, according to Clark, were "very fond of caressing our men." While the journals offer no evidence that either of the captains ever accepted any of the offers of sexual favors they received throughout the long journey, there is no question but that the rest of the men did.

October 21st. We had a disagreeable night of sleet and hail. It snowed during the forenoon, but we proceeded early on our voyage.

PATRICK GASS

As the explorers pushed north, into what is now North Dakota, huge flocks of geese and other birds passed overhead, migrating south. There were frosts at night, even an occasional snow flurry, though it was still October. Clark was seized by rheumatism, which Lewis treated by applying a hot stone wrapped in flannel.

When they left St. Louis, the captains had hoped to reach the headwaters of the Missouri before stopping for the winter. That was clearly out of the question now.

By October 26, according to Clark's estimates, they had traveled sixteen hundred miles up the big river. But they were nowhere near its source—or the fabled Northwest Passage they believed would lead them through the western mountains to the sea.

Instead, after six months of hard travel, they were arriving at the last fixed point on their map of the Missouri, beyond which everything was only rumor and conjecture.

With winter coming on, the captains decided they would stop here, at the edge of the unknown.

VISION QUEST

WILLIAM LEAST HEAT-MOON

IN JUNE OF 1995 on my voyage through the American interior from New York City to the Pacific Ocean, I and three others were ascending the Missouri River from its mouth near St. Louis to its headwaters close to the Continental Divide in Montana; we were going twenty-five hundred miles against the springtime current, along the same route the Lewis and Clark expedition followed nearly two centuries earlier on their way to the great western sea. Over some stretches we traveled in a twenty-two-foot flat-hulled pocket cruiser called a C-Dory, and in others we had to take to a Grumman canoe with a minuscule four-horsepower motor. The long ascent was at times slow to the point of tedium as the current carried us back a portion of each mile we gained.

One afternoon in central North Dakota, we tried to ease our labored passage by pulling the C-Dory up alongside a makeshift dock so we could disembark and walk about and eat a sandwich. From a thick copse suddenly and quietly appeared five Indians: two men, a woman, and two children. They were solidly, broadly built, with large round heads like earthenware bowls, and unlike so many Indians one meets today—even in the Far West—they clearly

had no European ancestry. Physically, facially, they seemed to come from another time, in spite of their denims and T-shirts.

We were on Indian land so I assumed they were about to accost us for trespassing. Approaching the dock slowly, the adults holding cans of beer, they asked coolly where we had come from. At first they were incredulous that a boat from the Atlantic Ocean could reach the middle of the Great Plains, but their curiosity quickly overwhelmed their caution and suspicion. They wanted to step aboard. The stern of our little boat dipped deeply as they climbed over. The children jumped about in the cabin, and the men peered at the depth finder, turned the wheel, tapped the compass; then they asked for a ride. Our fuel was precariously low, with miles of isolated country between us and the next gasoline, so I had to decline. To temper their disappointment I pulled out T-shirts imprinted with our boat emblem and name— *Nikawa,* an Osage word meaning "river-horse." The people seemed pleased and, to my surprise, promised a shiny jacket lettered HUNKPAPA, their tribe, a division of the Teton Sioux. The Hunkpapa were formidable fighters who for years and years resisted

Skirting the Skyline, by Joseph Kossuth Dixon

white encroachment; in the middle of the nineteenth century, an Indian agent spoke of them as "now the most dreaded on the Missouri." Sitting Bull was a Hunkpapa.

I stood there, remembering Lewis and Clark: it was the Tetons, perhaps more than any other tribe, who threatened the passage of the Corps of Discovery in 1804. At a council between the Americans and Sioux that began well enough, the Indians grew dissatisfied with the gifts offered, finding them so insufficient the captains tried to defuse the tension by inviting several chiefs aboard the keelboat, where soldiers displayed "much curiosities as was strange to them." During the milling about, Lewis had some trade whiskey broken out, each chief receiving a modest fourth of a glass. Amid the tippling and hubbub, one Sioux, feigning drunkenness, turned "troublesome," and Clark began the delicate, difficult, and dangerous task of getting the Tetons back on the banks. Once there, the pretender deliberately staggered into Clark and spoke crudely in an attempt to intimidate the expedition into going back down the river. The captain drew his sword, Lewis ordered the swivel guns on the boat readied, and the soldiers picked up their muskets while the Sioux drew arrows from their quivers. Clark, through an inadequate interpreter, told the chiefs the expedition would continue upriver and to understand the white men "were not squaws but warriors," to which Chief Black Buffalo answered they, too, were warriors and could easily pursue the expedition and pick off the men "by degrees." Standing, staring, trying to face each other down, the two sides calmed, and eventually Lewis resolved the issue by inviting Black Buffalo and a pair of his men to reboard the keelboat and spend the night before sailing five miles upriver to a council feast the next morning. And so a politic conclusion to an issue that was, although driven by economic concerns, primarily at that moment one of pride and respect for passage through Indian land.

As my crew and I talked with the Hunkpapa aboard the *Nikawa*, I found it thrilling to look into the Teton Sioux faces and imagine how we had inadvertently almost re-created that episode from two centuries earlier, albeit with results, I hoped, less antagonistic. While things had changed over the last eight generations, still, the Lewis and Clark expedition seemed surprisingly, marvelously immediate. I could imagine a smiling Thomas Jefferson, whose policy of making a "friendly impression" on the native peoples and of bringing them into a new political and economic realm with the United States Lewis and Clark so patently failed to accomplish with the Teton Sioux. Recalling Clark's later description of the Tetons as "the vilest miscreants of the savage race [who] must ever remain the pirates of the Missouri," Jefferson might have been delighted indeed to see all of us soon laughing aboard our little boat.

Clark's severe expression here is unusual in the captains' journals, this sentence written a little farther upstream from us, in the log fort near the villages of the Knife River Mandan and Hidatsa, people who materially helped the expedition survive the difficult Great Plains winter. The five palisaded earth lodge settlements near the fort were a grand nexus of commerce among the two resident tribes and the Crow, Cheyenne, Arapaho, Kiowa, and Assiniboin as well as white traders; it was a place where the expedition could witness and share the splendid diversity of Indian life and culture existing across the northwest Plains.

With each new stretch of their ascent up the Missouri, Lewis and Clark encountered a different tribe whose distinctive culture and disposition toward them required changed responses and approaches, a necessity the captains came to grasp and practice more wisely as they "proceeded on." We must remember today that for most of the tribal peoples Lewis and Clark were not the first whites they had encountered; those living along the upper Missouri in central North Dakota, for example, had met Sieur de la Verendrye and his men in 1738, nearly three generations earlier. These Indians had rather well-formed notions about eastern strangers and their purposes, notions that varied as much as their histories of dealing with explorers and traders; it was up to Lewis and Clark to discover ways to overcome a negative or hostile response and encourage a warmer reception. The leaders could not, given the limited information they received before departure and their narrow understanding of the Indian trading network, immediately fathom the welter of economic and political presumptions and expectations the various tribes held, a complexity heightened by the differing languages and interpreters who often were less than fluent. And there was also the continual problem of conflicts among the tribes themselves. Just as the river presented new challenges with each riffle and wooded bend, every twisting league upstream, so did the native peoples.

The expedition, we must always keep in mind, was not simply one of pure exploration for the sake of scientific knowledge. Whether we like it or not, it was also one of imperialism: Thomas Jefferson and a majority of the Congress wanted to take unchallenged possession in all ways of the new and huge country just purchased from France. Among the various influences informing and shaping the goals of the Corps of Discovery were a certain chauvinism and presumption toward a people whom whites wanted to become, in Clark's words, "our Dutiful Children." Such attitudes and expressions sometimes gave offense. At Fort Mandan, according later to British Canadian trader Alexander Henry the Younger, Hidatsa chiefs did not take well to "the high-sounding language the American captains bestowed upon themselves and their nation, wishing to impress the Indians with an idea that they were great warriors and a powerful people, who, if exasperated, could crush all the nations of the earth."

Among its assignments, the expedition was to help establish an economic and political hegemony under the "great father in Washington" by lessening the influence of the Canadian traders and making St. Louis the economic capital of the upper Missouri River country. Like others of the time, Lewis and Clark believed political sovereignty and economic control would march west together, and that their mission would usher in the changes. They were right.

And the Indians? They had a difficult time seeing Lewis and Clark as other than some sort of new traders rather than as explorers conducting rudimentary scientific inquiries that would help open and hold the West for the young United States. The Corps of Discovery was primarily important to most of the tribes not because of its research but because it carried gifts and trade goods while promising enlarged bartering opportunities. To be sure, although the Indians were quite curious about the men (especially Clark's slave, York) and about their gadgets (Lewis's air rifle and spyglass, Clark's compass, even writing paper), their greatest interest was an economic one: how could they obtain goods like those? Remove this primitive form of consumerism from the expedition and one can only imagine how differently, perhaps calamitously, the journey might have gone.

Without doubt the surprisingly peaceful nature of those twenty-eight months of passage was much a result of immediate economic imperatives reason-

ably well comprehended by red and white alike with both sides wanting material gain, a process little different from international diplomacy today. That some tribe—or several in loose alliance—did not wipe out the little Corps in spite of its frequent displays of pomp and mostly bluffing military muscle reveals the Indian desire for material and economic gain. Indeed, as the affray with the Tetons shows, when gifts or the number of trade items fell short of Indian expectations, relationships became testy and occasionally dangerous.

The winter among the Mandan and Hidatsa villages gave the Corps a chance to slow down and observe two cultures closely to see how these people lived: their loves, quarrels, meals, beliefs, aspirations. During the nearly half year they laid over in North Dakota, the depth of the captains' understanding increased measurably. The men attended ceremonies and feasts, practiced intimacies with the women, traveled with the bison hunters, watched births and deaths, learned what made a Mandan laugh, a Hidatsa distrustful. The expedition at last had enough time and an excellent location to examine and record ways of living they had grasped only haphazardly months before; they had the chance to put aside eastern biases that could only hinder the knowledge necessary to fulfill their mission.

A thousand miles into the voyage, they would begin to answer questions about Indian life Jefferson laid out in his 1803 instructions that effectively turned formally uneducated soldiers into part-time ethnographers whose learning would soon carry tremendous economic import. The President wrote Lewis: "The commerce which may be carried on with the people inhabiting the line you will pursue, renders a knolege of those people important." Among other questions, he specified inquiries into native traditions, foods, clothing, dwellings, diseases, remedies, and "peculiarities in laws, customs & dispositions." The influen-

Class at Riverside Indian
School, Oklahoma, 1901

tial Philadelphia physi-
cian Benjamin Rush, an
adviser to the Corps, sent Lewis a more pointed list:
"How long do they suckle the Children? . . . At
what *time* do they rise—their Baths? . . . Is suicide
common among them?—ever from love? . . . How
do they dispose of their dead?"

This emphasis on research during the long Plains
winter helped educate Lewis and Clark and make
them more effective in dealing with Indians during
the remaining months of the trip. How much it really
did to open the way to a mutually enriching commercial relationship with the tribes is more dubious.
Nevertheless, that only two Indians died at the hands
of the Corps (Reuben Field stabbed one Piegan and
Lewis shot another when a Blackfeet raiding party
tried to steal guns and horses) is as remarkable as the

Corps's very survival (only Sergeant Charles Floyd
died, and he not from Indians but apparently from
appendicitis) and eventual safe return.

On the rest of their westward trip to the Pacific,
the explorers encountered more and more tribes that
had little experience with white men, so relations
and gaining safe passage through less than welcom-
ing territory became trickier. Today one can visual-
ize a failure or, worse, a disaster had that crucial
education at Fort Mandan not occurred. Indian instruction during the enforced layover at the Knife
River villages was used by the captains to the advantage of the expedition and, later, the nation.

That winter educational bivouac made much of
the difference between the journey of the Corps of
Discovery and those of many later expeditions,
where the intent was too often solely commercial or

imperial, with operations conducted by ill-prepared soldiers or greedy entrepreneurs woefully short on comprehension of and sympathy for native ways of living. Considered as a military probe, the entrance of the Corps into the northwest quadrangle of the United States was the beginning of the numerous campaigns that would eventually bring down George Armstrong Custer and his cavalry in 1876 before finally terminating armed Indian resistance at Wounded Knee in South Dakota in 1890, eighty-four years after the two Blackfeet fell to Field and Lewis.

There is no irony, only logic, that I have written these words with my favorite implement, a cedar pencil made by the Blackfeet of Montana, and the logic is this: after Meriwether Lewis, William Clark, Benjamin Rush, and Thomas Jefferson, far too few people of humane intelligence continued the American opening of the West. Jefferson's grand hope, expressed in his instructions to Lewis, looks today sadly empty: "Considering the interest which every nation has in extending & strengthening the authority & justice among the people around them, it will be useful to acquire what knolege you can . . . as it may better enable those who may endeavor to civilize and instruct them, to adopt their measures to the existing notions & practices of those on whom they are to operate." What Jefferson and the Corps began promisingly soon collapsed almost utterly—an indictment of a nation that so believes in "progress" and claims to value and to be inspired by the humane wisdom and efforts of those who go before.

Common among the aboriginal peoples of America is something called a vision quest, typically a ritual trek into a natural remoteness where isolation and deprivation lead the sojourner into a new and keen awareness of existence, even of the cosmos itself, which brings about harmony and gives purpose to one's days. To me it seems that Lewis and Clark, on behalf of America, set off up the great Missouri on a kind of national, if unrecognized, vision quest that succeeding generations have the chance to continue as we search for identity, purpose, harmony, and the fair sharing of an abundant country. How far we have yet to go and how much we have failed Lewis and Clark I see in this thing in my hand, this product of the Blackfeet, today a nation of pencil makers.

CHAPTER 5

*Perfect
Harmony*

When you white people met our Mandan people we gave to the whites the name Mací, meaning nice people, or pretty people. We called them by this name because they had white faces and fine clothes. We said also, "We will call these people our friends."

WOUNDED FACE

WITH THEIR NEIGHBORS the Hidatsas, the
Mandans lived in five large permanent villages of earth
lodges—home to forty-five hundred people, a population greater than that of St. Louis or Washington,
D.C., at the time.

They were prosperous farmers and the middlemen for a complex upper Missouri trading system. Each fall, delegations of Crows, Assiniboins, Cheyennes,
Crees, and sometimes even their enemies the Lakotas arrived to swap buffalo
hides, horses, and firearms for the Mandans' corn.

Over the previous seventy years, Europeans had visited, too: representatives
of France, Spain, and England—even a Welshman pursuing a persistent rumor
that they were somehow descended from a long-lost Welsh Prince.

When Lewis and Clark arrived, the Mandans welcomed the Americans with
open arms, seemed to agree with the captains' call for a peace with their enemies,
the Arikaras, and were particularly happy that the expedition, with its big boat
of merchandise, would be building a fort nearby and staying for the winter.

*Our wish is to be at peace with all. . . . If we eat, you shall eat; if we
starve, you must starve also.*

SHEHEKE, BIG WHITE

Fort Mandan, 1609 miles above the entrance of the Missouri.
Dear Mother, . . .
   The near approach of winter, the low state of the water, and the

known scarcity of timber which exists on the Missouri for many hundreds of miles . . . determined my friend and companion Capt. Clark and myself to fortify ourselves and remain for the winter in the neighbour-hood of the Mandans . . . who are the most friendly and well disposed savages that we have yet met with. . . .

. . . Give yourself no uneasiness with rispect to my fate, for I assure you that I feel myself perfectly as safe as I should do in Albemarle; and the only difference between 3 or 4 thousand miles and 130, is that I can not have the pleasure of seeing you as often as I did while at Washington.

MERIWETHER LEWIS

Winter came early that year on the northern Plains. By November 13 ice was running in the river. The water in some cottonwoods expanded as it froze, shattering the trees with a sound like cannon fire. The northern lights filled the night skies. Snow began to fall. The wind never seemed to stop. The men hurried to complete their fort.

The temperature kept dropping—it was "colder," wrote Sergeant John Ordway, "than I ever knew it to be in the States."

Among the cold facts Lewis recorded in his weather diary for January 1805 were a reading of 12 degrees below zero at sunrise on January 18 and an estimate the next day that the ice on the Missouri was now three feet thick.

December 6th, 1804. In the night the river froze over, and in the morning was covered with solid ice an inch and a half thick.

PATRICK GASS

December 8th. The Thermometer Stood at 12 degrees below zero, which is [44] degrees below the freesing point. . . . Several men returned a little frost bit, one of the men with his feet badly frost bit. My Servents feet also frosted & his P——s a little.

WILLIAM CLARK

December 10th. The weather Gits colder verry fast, So that the Sentinel had to be relieved every hour.

JOHN ORDWAY

December 11th. 21 degrees below zero . . . and getting colder. The Sun Shows and reflects two imigies, the ice floating in the atmospear being So thick that the appearance is like a fog Despurceing.

WILLIAM CLARK

December 12th. Clear and cold. The frost was white in the Guard chimney where their was a fire kept all last night. It is Several degrees colder this morning than it has been before, so that we did nothing but git wood for our fires. Our Rooms are verry close and warm, So we can keep ourselves warm and comfortable, but the Sentinel who Stood out in the open weather had to be relieved every hour all day.

JOHN ORDWAY

December 17th. A very cold morning . . . 45 degrees below zero.

WILLIAM CLARK

December 18th. Verry cold last night, So that the Sentinel had to be relieved everry half hour.

JOHN ORDWAY

On Christmas Eve, the temperature climbed above zero—and almost above freezing. Fort Mandan was deemed officially complete, and the captains handed out dried apples, pepper, and extra flour for the next day's meal and celebration. Just before Christmas dawn, the captains were awakened by the men, all of them, Clark noted, "merrily disposed."

December 25th, 1804. We ushred [in] the morning with a discharge of the Swivvel [gun], and one round of Small arms of all the party. Then another from the Swivel. Then Capt. Clark presented a glass of brandy to each man of the party. We hoisted the american flag, and each man had another Glass of brandy. The men prepared one of the rooms and commenced dancing. At 10 o'c[lock] we had another Glass of brandy, at one a gun was fired as a Signal for diner. Half past two another gun was fired to assemble at the dance, and So we kept it up in a jov[ia]l manner untill eight o'c[lock] at night, all without the company of the female Seck [sex].

JOSEPH WHITEHOUSE

The expedition endured the harsh Plains winter in Fort Mandan, completed by Christmas Eve of 1804. "Our Rooms are verry close and warm, So we can keep ourselves warm and comfortable," wrote John Ordway, "but the Sentinel who Stood out in the open weather had to be relieved every hour all day." The McLean County Historical Society of North Dakota built this replica near the original site.

The Mandans were asked not to visit the fort on Christmas because, the captains explained, it was a "great medicine" day for the expedition. But on New Year's, the men celebrated with their Indian hosts.

January 1st, 1805. We . . . went up to the 1st village of Mandans to dance as it had been their request. carried with us a fiddle & a Tambereen & a

The Bison Dance of the Mandan Indians, by Karl Bodmer. In early January 1805, the Mandans invited the expedition to take part in their sacred ritual, meant both to call the buffalo herds to the vicinity of the villages and to pass along the skills, or "medicine," of older men to younger hunters. A French fur trader living among the Indians that winter recorded that the Mandans attributed the quick arrival of buffalo to the explorers' participation in the ceremony.

Sounden horn. as we arived at the entrence of the vil[lage] we fired one round. then the music played. loaded again. then marched to the center of the village [and] fired again. then commenced dancing. a frenchman danced on his head and all danced round him for a Short time, then went in to a lodge & danced a while, which pleased them verry much. they then brought vectules from different lodges . . . & Some buffalow Robes which they made us a present off. So we danced in different lodges untill late in the afternoon. then a part of the men returned to the fort. the remainder Stayed all night in the village.

JOHN ORDWAY

Before the week was out, the Mandans held a special ceremony of their own—a buffalo-calling ritual, meant to lure buffalo herds to the vicinity and, through the intercession of women, transfer special powers to the young hunters.

A Buffalow Dance (or Medeson) for 3 nights passed in the 1st Village, a curious Custom. [T]he old men arrange themselves in a circle & after

Smoke[ing] a pipe which is handed them by a young man, Dress[ed] up for the purpose, the young men who have their wives back of the Circle go [each] to one of the old men with a whining tone and request the old man to take his wive (who presents [herself] necked except a robe) and (Sleep with her). [T]he Girl then takes the Old Man (who verry often can scarcely walk) and leades him to a convenient place for the business, after which they return to the lodge. . . .

If the old man (or a white man) returns to the lodge without gratifying the Man & his wife, he offers her again and again; it is often the Case that after the 2d time without Kissing the Husband throws a new robe over the old man &c. and begs him not to dispise him & his wife. We Sent a man to this Medisan Dance last night, they gave him 4 Girls.

All this is to cause the buffalow to Come near So that they may Kill them.

WILLIAM CLARK

Two days later, a herd of buffalo showed up.

Inside Fort Mandan, where the men had been consuming the equivalent of one buffalo a day from an earlier hunt, food supplies were running low. They had been supplementing their diet with corn bartered from the Mandans in exchange for metalwork that Privates John Shields and Alexander Willard performed on a portable forge. But the men preferred meat.

The temperature had plummeted to below zero again. Despite the cold, the hunt was joined.

Captain Lewis and eleven more of us went out . . . and saw the prairie covered with buffaloe and the Indians on horseback killing them. They killed 30 or 40, and we killed eleven of them. They shoot them with bows and arrows, and have their horses trained that they will advance very near and suddenly wheel and fly off in case the wounded buffaloe attempt an attack.

PATRICK GASS

January 9th, 1805. Blustry and exceeding cold. A nomber of the Savages out hunting the Buffalo [again] & came in towards evening with their horses loaded with meat and told us that two of their young men was froze to death in the prarie.

JOHN ORDWAY

January 10th. 40 degrees below zero [this morning]. The Indians . . . turned out to hunt for a man & a boy who had not returned from the hunt of yesterday, and borrowd a Slay to bring them in, expecting to find them frozed to death. About 10 oclock the boy, about 13 years of age, Came to the fort with his feet frosed . . . had layen out last night without fire, with only a Buffalow Robe to Cover him. . . . We had his feet put in Cold water and they are Comeing too. . . .

Soon after the arrival of the Boy, a man Came in who had also Stayed out without fire, and verry thinly Clothed. This man was not the least injured. . . . Customs & the habits of those people has [inured] them to bare more Cold than I thought possible for a man to indure.

WILLIAM CLARK

January 14th. . . . killed one buffaloe, a wolf & 2 porkapines, & I got my feet So froze that I could not walk to the fort.

JOSEPH WHITEHOUSE

An Indian hunter climbs a snowy bank in this photograph by Richard Throssel. While many of the Corps of Discovery suffered from frostbite during the winter, Clark marveled that the Mandans and Hidatsas seemed much better at bearing the frigid temperatures, including one hunter who returned uninjured after spending a night on the Plains, without a fire or heavy clothing, when the temperature dropped to 40 degrees below zero.

Lewis's medical skills were continually pressed into service. The Indian boy who had been caught out all night in the cold had to have his toes amputated, though the expedition had no anesthesia and no surgical saw. One Mandan child had an abscess lanced, and another was given a dose of Rush's Thunderbolts for a fever. Men suffered ax wounds when cutting wood, and had their blood drawn for other ailments. When Sergeant Nathaniel Pryor dislocated his shoulder, four attempts were required to put it back in place (it would pop out two more times during the expedition). By late January many of the men showed early signs of venereal disease, which Lewis treated with a salve of mercury.

And on the bitterly cold evening of February 11, Lewis made his most unusual house call. A baby was being born; the young mother was having trouble with the delivery.

Her name was Sacagawea—Bird Woman—a Shoshone girl who had been

The Trapper's Bride, by Alfred Jacob Miller, 1837. Like many European fur traders, Toussaint Charbonneau had taken an Indian wife—two wives, in his case, both young Shoshones—when Lewis and Clark met him. One of them was Sacagawea, whom Charbonneau had purchased from the Hidatsas after they captured her during a raid at the Three Forks of the Missouri.

captured several years earlier by the Hidatsas and then sold to Toussaint Charbonneau, a French Canadian fur trader living among them. Learning that the Shoshones lived near the Missouri's source, and thinking they might need a good interpreter when they reached it, the captains had hired her and Charbonneau in November.

But now she was in labor with her first child. It was "tedious," Lewis noted, "and the pain, violent." Someone suggested that the rings of a rattlesnake, crushed into powder and administered with water, sometimes helped ease and speed delivery. Lewis got some from his collection of animal skins and plants. Sacagawea was given the rattlesnake potion.

Whether this medicine was truly the cause or not I shall not undertake to determine, but . . . she had not taken it more than ten minutes before she

brought forth. Perhaps this remedy may be worthy of future experiments,
but I must confess I want faith as to it's efficacy.

MERIWETHER LEWIS

It was a boy, whom Charbonneau named Jean-Baptiste—now the youngest member of the Corps of Discovery.

They showed me their passports and letters of recommendation from the
French, Spanish and British ministers at the city of Washington, which
say the object of their voyage is purely scientific and literary, and no
ways concerning trade. . . . They told me that it was not the policy of the
United States to restrain commerce and fetter it . . . that we and all
persons who should come on their territories for trade will never be
molested by an American officer. . . . In short, during the time I was
there, a very Grand Plan was schemed, but its taking place is more than
I can tell, although the Captains say they are well assured it will.

FRANÇOIS-ANTOINE LAROCQUE

Captain Lewis could not make himself agreeable to us. He could speak
fluently and learnedly on all subjects, but his inveterate disposition
against the British stained, at least in our eyes, all his eloquence. Captain
Clark was equally well-informed, but his conversation was always
pleasant, for he seemed to dislike giving offense unnecessarily.

CHARLES MCKENZIE,
North West Fur Company

During the long winter, Lewis and Clark found themselves entangled in diplomatic conflicts.

British and French Canadian traders from the Hudson's Bay and the North West companies, headquartered in Canada, were informed they could continue doing business with the Mandans and Hidatsas as long as they did not try to undermine the new American sovereignty. But Lewis suspected them of telling their long-standing Indian clients to distrust any promises of better trade goods from United States companies.

Far to the south, Spanish authorities feared that the expedition—led by a man they referred to in secret communications as "Captain Merry"—had less to do with discovery and more to do with preparing the United States to conquer Texas, New Mexico, and perhaps Mexico itself.

Nothing would be more useful than the apprehension of Merry, and even though I realize it is not an easy undertaking, chance might proportion things in such a way that it might be successful.

NEMESIO SALCEDO,
*Commandant-General
Interior Provinces, New Spain*

Unbeknownst to the captains, New Spain had already sent one detachment of soldiers and Comanche Indians to intercept the expedition. It had failed—reaching the Platte River a month after Lewis and Clark had already passed—but the viceroys in Mexico City were planning another attempt to catch the explorers on their return trip.

In the East, President Jefferson had been elected to another term, but that winter, in his second inaugural address, he was still defending the Louisiana Purchase.

Black Moccasin, a Hidatsa chief who befriended Lewis and Clark during the winter of 1804. As an old man, when he sat for this portrait by George Catlin in 1833, he inquired about the captains and asked the painter to pass on his regards to Clark, whom he called Red Hair.

I know that the acquisition of Louisiana has been disapproved by some, from a candid apprehension that the enlargement of our territory would endanger its union. But who can limit the extent to which the federative principle may operate effectively? The larger our association, the less will it be shaken by local passions; and in any view, is it not better that the opposite bank of the Mississippi should be settled by our brethren and children, than by strangers from another family? With which shall we be most likely to live in harmony and friendly intercourse?

THOMAS JEFFERSON

A successful exploration, he hoped, might do more than mere words to quiet his critics.

Meanwhile, at the Mandan and Hidatsa villages, Indian politics and diplomacy were equally complicated.

When the Indians of the different villages heard of your coming . . . they all came in from hunting [and] expected great presents. They

The interior of a Mandan earth lodge, as painted by Karl Bodmer. Sergeant Patrick Gass, a carpenter by trade, devoted a journal entry to describing how the Indians built such dwellings, often large enough to house an extended family and all their belongings. During the harsh winters, he added, even the prized horses "are brought into the lodges, with the natives themselves, and fed upon cottonwood branches; and in this way are kept in tolerable case."

were disappointed and some dissatisfied. As to myself, I am not so much, but my village are.

BLACK CAT

Many chiefs could not understand why these white men—unlike the fur traders they were used to—had so many manufactured goods they were unwilling to sell or trade. Trying to corner the market on the limited supply that *was* available, the Mandans spread a rumor that the Americans would kill any Hidatsa who came to the white man's fort.

And the captains' talks of an American-inspired peace among the Plains Indians kept running into the hard realities of long-standing rivalries and tribal customs. Raiding and warfare were not just for wealth, self-protection, and revenge; they were part of the ritual by which young men gained standing among their own people. Without wars, one puzzled warrior asked Lewis after hearing the captain speak, "what would we do for chiefs?"

Despite Lewis and Clark's urgings, the most formidable Hidatsa leader, called Le Borgne, or One Eye, went ahead with plans to send raiding parties against the Shoshones in the spring, just as the Hidatsas had always done. The Americans didn't worry him, he said; if necessary, his own warriors could handle the soldiers like "so many wolves" on the prairie. "There are only two sensible men among them," he scoffed, "the worker of iron and the mender of guns."

Only one member of the expedition truly impressed him, according to the captains' account:

The chief observed that some foolish young men of his nation had told him there was a person among us who was quite black, and he wished to know if it could be true. We assured him it was . . . and sent for York. Le Borgne was very much surprised at his appearance, examined him closely, and spit on his finger and rubbed the skin in order to wash off the paint; nor was it until [York] uncovered his head and showed his short hair that Le Borgne could be persuaded that he was not a painted white man.

Mato-Tope, or Four Bears, was an important Mandan chief when Karl Bodmer visited the villages and painted this portrait in 1834. His bravery is displayed in his attire: six colored sticks in his hair, representing gunshot wounds; a split turkey feather for an arrow injury; a wooden knife for the real one he wrestled from a Cheyenne in combat; and a handprint on his chest, showing that he had captured prisoners in battle. Three years later, however, Four Bears died at the hands of a hidden enemy: smallpox swept through the Mandan villages and killed 90 percent of the tribe.

But the biggest trouble came from the Lakotas. In mid-February they stole some horses from an expedition hunting party, then bragged about it to the Arikaras, whom they also berated for having befriended the Americans. A French fur trader sent the captains news of the Lakotas' intentions.

They Say if they can catch any more of us they will kill us for they think that we are bad medicine. . . . Mr. [Tabeau said] to keep a good lookout for he heared the Souix Say that they Should Shurely come to war in the Spring against us and the Mandanes.

JOHN ORDWAY

But Lewis and Clark were already planning to be much farther west by that time. They asked their Indian friends what lay ahead, and the chiefs drew lines on the dirt floors of their lodges, with mounds of earth to show the terrain. Clark transferred the information onto a map he was preparing for Jefferson.

There was a tremendous waterfall farther upriver, one chief told them, and then they would have to pass through a great range of "shining mountains." The captains calculated that portaging their canoes around the falls would take only half a day. And the mountains they imagined were like the ones they knew in Virginia—a single ridge, no more than three hundred miles from the ocean: two or three days at most to cross.

"Big Medicine." Along the Missouri River, most of the Indian tribes had encountered whites before, but Clark's slave, York, was the first black man they had ever seen, and he thoroughly fascinated them. Some attributed special power, or "medicine," to his dark skin. This painting by Charles M. Russell (above) portrays the moment when a Hidatsa chief, Le Borgne, spit on his finger and rubbed it against York's bare skin to make sure he wasn't a painted white man.

Karl Bodmer painted these two portraits (left) of Pehriska-Ruhpa, or Two Ravens, a prominent Hidatsa warrior.

A present for Mr. Jefferson. From Fort Mandan, Lewis and Clark dispatched the keelboat back downriver in the spring of 1805, along with boxes and trunks filled with items they had collected during the expedition's first year. Besides maps, plant specimens, animal hides, and even a live prairie dog, they sent the President a trove of Indian materials, including this buffalo robe. On it, a Mandan had drawn a picture of a battle pitting the Mandans and Hidatsas against the Lakotas and Arikaras. Jefferson is said to have displayed the robe in his entryway at Monticello; it is now at Harvard's Peabody Museum.

They could make it to the Pacific and back to the Mandan villages, they were confident, before the next winter.

Invoice of articles from Fort Mandan to the President
First box, skins of the male and female antelope, with their
skeletons; . . . horns and ears of the black tail, or mule deer; . . . skeletons
of the small, or burrowing wolf of the prairies, the skin having been lost
by accident.
Second box, four buffalo robes and an ear of Mandan corn.
Third box, skins of the male and female antelope, with their skeletons.
Fourth box, specimens of earths, salts and minerals; specimens of
plants; . . . one tin box containing insects.
In a large trunk: one buffalo robe painted by a Mandan man
representing a battle which was fought eight years [ago], by
the Sioux and [Arikaras] against the Mandans and
[Hidatsas].
One cage, containing four living magpies.
One cage, containing a
living burrowing
squirrel of the prairies.
One cage, containing one
living hen of the prairies.
One large pair of elk's horns,
connected by the frontal bone.

By the end of March, the ice was no longer on the river. Lewis and Clark sent a small detachment back to St. Louis with the big keelboat, loaded with materials for Jefferson: maps, lengthy reports about the populations and customs of Indian tribes in the Louisiana Territory and the prospects for trade, and box after box of specimens they had collected from this newest region of the United States.

There were sixty-seven samples of soil and minerals; sixty plants, including one that supposedly cured bites from rattlesnakes and rabid animals; embalmed insects; coyote bones and antelope skins; ears of Arikara and Mandan corn and roped coils of Indian tobacco; bows and arrows and painted buffalo robes; and wooden cages containing a sharp-tailed grouse, four magpies, and the prairie dog they had flooded out of its home—all alive.

With the shipment went a letter from Lewis, whose description of the Corps of Discovery demonstrated that they were no longer the undisciplined collection of frontiersmen who had left St. Louis a year earlier. The trip up-river—and the long Plains winter—had forged them into something else.

At this moment, every individual of the party are in good health and excellent sperits; zealously attached to the enterprise, and anxious to proceed; not a whisper of discontent or murmur is to be heard among them; but all in unison act with the most perfect harmoney. With such men I have every thing to hope, and but little to fear.

MERIWETHER LEWIS

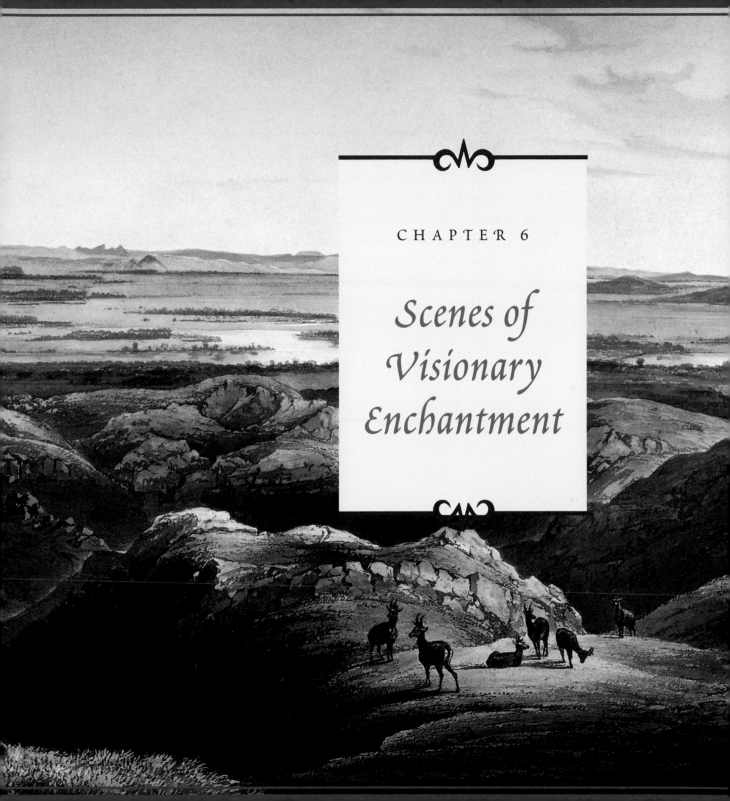

CHAPTER 6

*Scenes of
Visionary
Enchantment*

April 7th, 1805. Our vessels consisted of six small canoes, and two large perogues. This little fleet, altho' not quite so rispectable as those of Columbus or Capt. Cook, were still viewed by us with as much pleasure as those deservedly famed adventurers ever beheld theirs. . . .

We were now about to penetrate a country at least two thousand miles in width, on which the foot of civilized man had never trodden; the good or evil it had in store for us was for experiment yet to determine . . . [yet] entertaining as I do, the most confident hope of succeeding in a voyage which had formed a da[r]ling project of mine for the last ten years, I could but esteem this moment of my departure as among the most happy of my life.

MERIWETHER LEWIS

ON APRIL 7, 1805, the Corps of Discovery headed west once more.

They pushed into what is now Montana, farther west than any white man had gone before on the river. Fierce headwinds slowed their progress, sometimes stopping them for entire days. Sand blew in their faces and scratched their eyes; it was "so penetrating," Lewis wrote, "we are compelled to eat, drink and breathe it." The days began to grow warm, though nights were still frosty. There were occasional snows, and one morning was so cold, John Ordway reported, that "our moccasins froze near the fire."

But the abundance of wildlife astounded them all.

The buffaloe, Elk and Antelope are so gentle that we pass near them, while feeding, without appearing to excite any alarm among them; and when we attract their attention, they frequently approach us more nearly to discover what we are, and in some instances pursue us a considerable distance apparently with that view. I believe that two good hunters could conveniently supply a regiment with provisions.

MERIWETHER LEWIS

Saw large gangs of buffaloe Swimming the River just before our cannoes & we would not Shoot them as we had meat enofe on board.

JOHN ORDWAY

The first bighorn sheep they had ever seen appeared on the riverbank. Geese, swans, and cranes flew overhead. Bald eagles nested in the cottonwood trees; when one was shot, John Ordway took its quill feathers and used them when writing in his journal. Beaver were so numerous that the smacking of their tails on the water kept Clark awake at night. Lewis's Newfoundland dog caught one beaver in the river, then an antelope as it swam past. The men briefly made pets of buffalo calves and a litter of wolf pups.

Roasted beaver tails were considered a special treat by the hungry men, but buffalo meat soon became a staple of their diet. Each man consumed nine pounds of it a day.

The Game is gitting so pleanty and tame in this country that Some of the party clubbed them out of their way.

JOHN ORDWAY

We saw also many tracks of [a] bear of enormous size. . . . We have not as yet seen one of these anamals, tho' their tracks are so abundant and recent. The men as well as ourselves are anxious to meet with some of these bear. The Indians give a very formidable account of the strength and ferocity of this anamal, which they never dare to attack but in parties of six, eight or ten persons; and are even then frequently defeated with the loss of one or more of their party.

MERIWETHER LEWIS

A bighorn sheep, drawn by Clark on May 25, 1805, the day the expedition saw their first one, and Karl Bodmer's sketch of the head of a female bighorn (top). The sheep were agile and fast, according to Joseph Whitehouse, "running along in flocks where the bluffs were to appearence nearly perpenticular," and the head and horns of one that George Drouillard shot weighed 27 pounds. Clark noted that Indians made water cups and spoons from the horns, which "might probably answer as maney valuable purpoces to civilized man," such as elegant hair combs.

The Mandans and Hidatsas had warned the explorers they would encounter a new animal that was *not* so friendly—a bear so big, so ferocious, and so hard to kill that they needed to be particularly careful around it.

On April 29 Lewis and another hunter killed their first one: it was a grizzly. "The Indians may well fear this anamal, equipped as they generally are with their bows and arrows," Lewis bragged in his journal that evening, "but in the hands of skillful riflemen they are by no means as formidable or dangerous as they have been represented."

On May 5 they met another one, "a monster," Lewis called it, weighing an estimated six hundred pounds. Ten shots—five of them through the lungs—were required to kill it. There were more to come.

May 14th. About 4 oClock the men in the canoes Saw a large . . . bear on the hills. . . . 6 men went out to kill it. They fired at it and wounded it.

JOHN ORDWAY

[But the bear] took after them and chased 2 men in to a cannoe. They Shoved off in the River and fired at him. Some of the men on Shore wounded him worse.

JOSEPH WHITEHOUSE

He pursued two of them . . . so close that they were obliged to throw aside their guns and pouches and throw themselves into the river, altho' the bank was nearly twenty feet perpendicular; so enraged was this anamal that he plunged into the river only a few feet behind [them].

MERIWETHER LEWIS

One of the men on Shore Shot the bear in the head, which killed him dead after having nine balls Shot in him. We got him to Shore and butchered him. His feet was nine Inches across the ball. . . . His nales was Seven Inches long.

JOSEPH WHITEHOUSE

Not all the animals were so tame or easy to kill. Grizzly bears—new to science when Lewis described his first one on April 29, 1805—became such a persistent threat that the captains finally ordered the men to travel at least in pairs for their own safety. This painting by John Clymer depicts the moment when a wounded grizzly chased two of the explorers back into their canoes and, later, another man off the river bank, before the ninth bullet finally brought it down.

Over the next two months, grizzlies would chase the explorers across prairies, up trees, through willow thickets, and back into the river again and

Bird Woman

Novels have described her guiding the Corps of Discovery through the West. Paintings have shown her pointing the way to the Pacific. Movies have depicted a steamy romance with William Clark, and even a fistfight between the captains for her affections. Over time, oral traditions of different Indian tribes have come to claim her as their own. Her death—and even her name—are topics of dispute. And there are more statues of her than of any other woman in American history.

No other member of the Corps of Discovery has inspired more mythology than Sacagawea, the young Indian woman who joined the expedition at the Mandan villages. Lewis's and Clark's journals—which provide virtually the entire written record about her—are indispensable in trying to separate myth from fact.

Translated, her name means "Bird Woman," and in their attempts to spell the Indian words, Lewis and Clark used variations of "Sah-ca-gah-we-ah" and "Sah-kah-gar-we-a." (In 1814, when a version of the journals appeared, an editor changed the spelling to Sacajawea,

Although no painting or sketch was ever made of her during her lifetime, there are now more statues of Sacagawea than of any other woman in American history. This statue of the young Shoshone mother and her baby boy, Jean-Baptiste, stands on the grounds of North Dakota's state capitol in Bismarck.

which was the preferred spelling until recently, when most historians and official publications reverted back to Sacagawea.)

She was not their guide and did not point the way. Most of the route the expedition followed was across territory as alien to her as it was to the men from Virginia. In two areas—near her home country and on a stretch close to what is now Bozeman Pass on the return trip—she recognized familiar landmarks and pointed them out to the explorers. But for the thousands of other miles, Sacagawea more likely followed than led.

Saying this does not diminish her vital role in the expedition. From the start, Lewis considered her "our only dependence for a friendly negociation with the Snake [Shoshone] Indians on whom we depend for horses to assist us in our portage from the Missouri to the columbia river." The captains needed her services as an interpreter—and as a friendly introduction to her people.

But even far from the home of her own people, when she was neither guiding nor interpreting, Sacagawea proved valuable. On the Missouri, Lewis noted her "fortitude and resolution" in rescuing the medicines and other essential supplies that nearly washed away in a boat accident. On the Columbia, where one tribe at first viewed the expedition suspiciously, Clark commented: "[A]s Soon as they Saw the Squar wife of the interpreter they pointed to her and . . . they immediately all came out and appeared to assume new life, the sight of This Indian woman . . . confirmed those people of our friendly intentions, as no woman ever accompanies a war party of Indians in this quarter." She was a living, breathing flag of peace.

Some of her contributions were less dramatic. On different occasions, she supplied the captains with wild artichokes, currants, prairie turnips, and wild licorice she had foraged for their meals—and a fennel root that relieved stomachaches. When Lewis and Clark wanted an otter-skin robe to bring back to Jefferson from the Pacific, the local Indians refused to trade for anything but blue beads. The expedition's supply was nearly depleted. Sacagawea gave up a blue-beaded belt from around her waist so the exchange could be made.

If all these accomplishments do not quite match the romanticized, glorified, and overembroidered roles of the mythic Sacagawea, they are nevertheless acts worthy of a legend.

The captains named a river in her honor. And when the crucial decision was to be made about choosing winter quarters on the Pacific, Sacagawea's opinion was solicited along with everyone else's. But as Clark wrote to Charbonneau at the journey's end, "Your woman who accompanied you that long dangerous and fatigueing rout to the Pacific Ocian and back diserved a greater reward for her attention and services on that rout than we had in our power to give her."

If we remember—rather than glamorize—the Bird Woman and her genuine achievements, perhaps she will finally receive that "greater reward."

again. Lewis's dog would bark throughout many nights, warning of bears near the camp. The captains would order that the men sleep with their guns nearby, and that no one venture away from the group alone.

And the swagger evident in Lewis's earlier accounts of the grizzly bear quickly disappeared from his writings. "I would rather fight two Indians than one bear," he admitted to his journal, adding, "I find that the curiossity of our party is pretty well satisfyed with rispect to this anamal."

The woman that is with us is a squaw of the Snake [Shoshone] nation of Indians, and wife to our interpreter. We expect she will be of service to us, when passing through that nation.

PATRICK GASS

With part of the original crew sent back with the keelboat, there were just thirty-three members of the party now, including its three newest members:

The name of each member of the Corps of Discovery, including Lewis's Newfoundland dog, was eventually given by the captains to at least one landmark in the new territory. Lewis's journal of May 20, 1805, describes a "handsome river," which the captains named Sacagawea, or Bird Woman's, River. A map drawn by Clark shows York's Dry River, a tributary of the Yellowstone now known as Custer Creek.

much the same in appearance as that we saw when
we were, or broken, and that about five miles above the mouth of
shell river a handsome river of about fifty yards in
width discharged itself into the shell river on the
Stard. or upper side; this stream we called Sah-câ-gee (Sah ca gah we a)
Me-âh or bird woman's River, after our interpreter
the Snake woman. Shields also found a bould spring
or fountain issuing from the foot of the Lard. hills
about 4 miles up the Missouri; a fountain in this
plain country is a great novelty; I have not seen
a bold fountain of pure water except one since I left the
Mandans; there are a number of small ones but all without

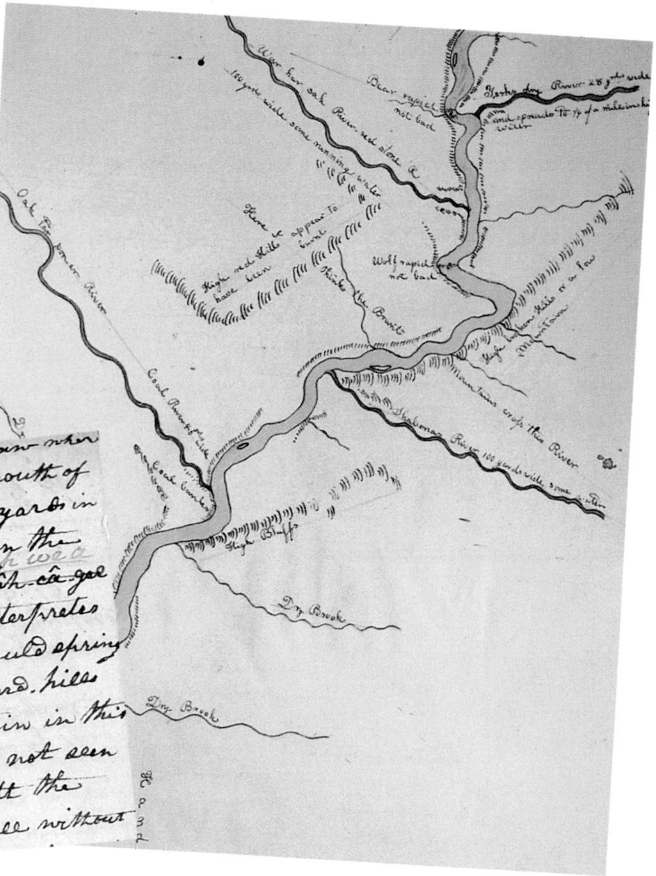

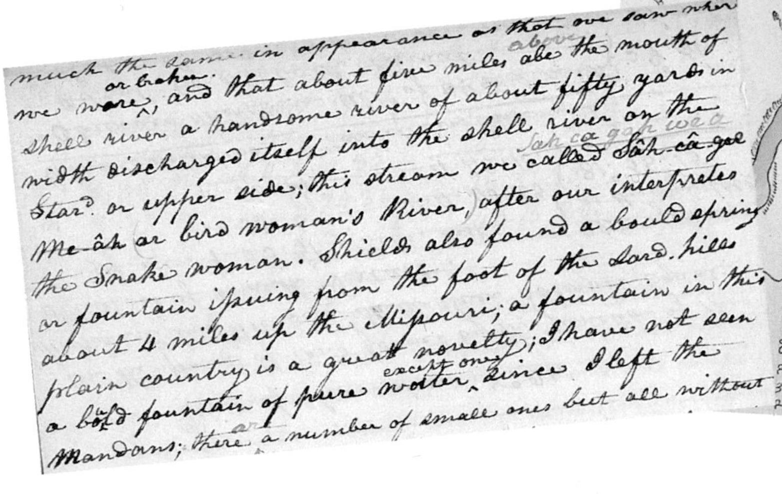

Charbonneau, Sacagawea, and their newborn son, Jean-Baptiste, whom Clark nicknamed "Little Pomp." Every day, he was carried on his mother's back as the expedition pressed forward.

Sacagawea dug for artichokes and prairie turnips, and picked currants and wild licorice for the captains' dinners. And she quickly won their confidence.

During one blustery day, Charbonneau lost control of the pirogue he was steering. Lewis and Clark watched helplessly from the shore as it turned in the current and began taking in water. It contained their books, scientific equipment, medicines, and many of the expedition's trade goods—"almost every article indispensably necessary to further the views, or ensure the success of the enterprize," according to Lewis. He briefly considered diving into the river to attempt a rescue before realizing "the madness" of it.

Fortunately, the combined efforts of Pierre Cruzatte and Sacagawea saved the day.

Charbono, still crying to his god for mercy, had not yet recollected the rudder, nor could the repeated orders of the bowsman, Cruzat, bring him

On May 26, Lewis climbed out of the river valley and for the first time saw what he thought were the Rocky Mountains in the distance, probably the Bears Paw Mountains shown here in Karl Bodmer's painting. Lewis's "secret pleasure" at gazing on the mountains was tempered by the prospect of "the sufferings and hardships of myself and party in thim," he wrote, "but as I have always held it a crime to anticipate evils I will believe it a good comfortable road untill I am compelled to believe differently."

to his recollection untill he threatened to shoot him instantly if he did not
take hold of the rudder and do his duty. . . .

 The Indian woman, to whom I ascribe equal fortitude and resolution
with any person on board at the time of the accident, caught and
preserved most of the light articles, which were washed overboard.

MERIWETHER LEWIS

Charbonneau, Lewis would write, was "perhaps the most timid waterman in the world" and "a man of no peculiar merit." The only thing he did well, the captain believed, was cook. His specialty was called *boudin blanc*—a "white pudding" of chopped buffalo meat and kidneys, stuffed into an intestine, which Lewis said, "we all esteem as one of the greatest delacies of the forrest."

About 6 feet of the lower extremity of the large gut of the Buffaloe is the
first mo[r]sel that the cook makes love to. This he holds fast at one end
with the right hand, while with the forefinger and thumb of the left, he
gently compresses it, and discharges what he says is not good to eat. . . .
Fillets are next saught; these are [kneaded] up very fine with a good
portion of kidney suet; to this composition is then added a just proportion
of pepper and salt and a small quantity of flour. . . .

 It is then baptised in the missouri with two dips and a flirt, and bobbed
into a kettle; from whence after it be well boiled it is taken and fryed with
bears oil untill it becomes brown, when it is ready to esswage the pangs of a
keen appetite [which] travelers in the wilderness are seldom at a loss for.

MERIWETHER LEWIS

May 20th. The large creek which we passed . . . we Call Blowing fly Creek,
from the emence quantities of those insects which geather on our meat in
Such nombers that we are obledged to brush them off what we eate.

JOHN ORDWAY

About five miles above the mouth of [the Musselshell] river, a handsome
river of about fifty yards in width discharged itself. . . . This stream we
called Sah-ca-gah-we-a or bird woman's River, after our interpreter
the Snake [Shoshone] woman.

MERIWETHER LEWIS

With each mile they traveled now, they were mapping new territory. The captains struggled to think of names for every landmark they encountered: Bratton's, Wiser's, Windsor's, and Thompson's creeks, Shields' River, and York's Dry Fork—and so on, until the name of every member of the Corps of Discovery was affixed to the land.

A dead tree caught fire near one campsite, and its sparks damaged a tent—Burnt Lodge Creek.

The water in one river reminded Lewis of the color of tea with milk in it, so he named it Milk River. The creek they called Teapot had almost no water in it, while the stream bed of Big Dry Creek, Lewis marveled when they named it, "is as wide as the Missouri . . . or half a mile wide, and not containing a single drop of water." There was Butter Island and No Preserves Island, marking places where the expedition ran out of both—and Onion Island, where they came across a field of wild onions. One creek Clark called "Roloje, a name given me last night in my sleep."

May 29 was an especially eventful day.

In the darkness before dawn, a buffalo bull emerged from the river and charged into camp, nearly trampling some of the sleeping men before Lewis's dog, Seaman, chased it away—Bull Creek.

Later in the day, they came upon the rotting remains of a hundred buffalo on the riverbank, which probably washed up there after drowning in the high waters of the spring thaw. Wolves were feeding on the putrid carcasses. The captains named a nearby stream Slaughter River.

And they passed another tributary whose waters seemed much clearer than others they had observed. Clark considered it an especially pretty stream and named it the Judith River, in honor of a young girl back in Virginia he hoped would one day be his wife.

May 30th. Many circumstances indicate our near approach to a country whos climate differs considerably from that in which we have been for many months. The air of the open country is asstonishingly dry as well as pure. I found by several experiments that a table spoon of water exposed to the air in a saucer would evaporate in 36 hours. . . . My inkstand so frequently becoming dry put me on this experiment. I also observed the well seasoned case of my sextant shrunk considerably and the joints opened.

MERIWETHER LEWIS

I remarked, as a singular circumstance, that there is no dew in this Country, and very little rain. Can it be owing to the want of timber?

PATRICK GASS

This country may with propriety be called the Deserts of North america for I do not conceive any part of it can ever be Sitled [settled], as it is deficient of . . . water except in this River, & [deficient] of timber, & too Steep to be tilled.

JOHN ORDWAY

Distances were deceiving. The captains dispatched a man to reconnoiter a hill they estimated was fifteen miles away. He showed up at nightfall saying he had turned back after walking ten miles without even getting halfway there.

Suddenly it was the scenery, not the wildlife, that fascinated them. They had entered a new section of the river, now called the White Cliffs of the Missouri. The Indians had not told them about it, and they were unprepared for its wild beauty.

May 31st. The hills and river Clifts which we passed today exhibit a most romantic appearance. . . . The bluffs of the river rise to the hight of from 2 to 300 feet and in most places nearly perpendicular; they are formed of remarkable white sandstone. . . .

The water in the course of time in decending from those hills and plains on either side of the river has trickled down the soft sand clifts and woarn it into a thousand grotesque figures, which with the help of a little immagination . . . are made to represent eligant ranges of lofty freestone buildings, having their parapets well stocked with statuary. . . .

[C]ollumns of various sculpture both grooved and plain, are also seen supporting long galleries in front of those buildings; in other places on a much nearer approach and with the help of less immagination we see the remains or ruins of eligant buildings; some collumns standing and almost entire with their pedestals and capitals. . . . [N]itches and alcoves of various forms and sizes are seen at different hights as we pass. . . . [T]he tops of the collumns did not the less remind us of some of those large stone buildings in the U. States.

MERIWETHER LEWIS

In maney places . . . we observe on either Side of the river extraodanary walls of a black Semented Stone which appear to be regularly placed one Stone on the other. . . . [T]hose walls Commence at the waters edge & in Some places meet at right angles.

WILLIAM CLARK

We passed some very curious cliffs and rocky peaks, in a long range. Some of them 200 feet high and not more than eight feet thick. They seem as if built by the hand of man, and are so numerous that they appear like the ruins of an antient city.

PATRICK GASS

[H]ere it is . . . that nature presents to the view of the traveler vast ranges of walls of tolerable workmanship, so perfect indeed are those walls that I should have thought that nature had attempted here to rival

"A most romantic appearance." The White Cliffs of the Missouri, seen here as painted by Karl Bodmer, astounded the explorers, who compared the white sandstone formations and darker outcroppings to elegant buildings, grotesque statuary, and the ruins of an ancient civilization. It is one of the few long stretches of Lewis and Clark's route across the West that remains today virtually unchanged.

Scenes of Visionary Enchantment

the human art of masonry had I not recollected that she had first began
her work. . . . As we passed on it seemed as if those seens of visionary
inchantment would never have and [an] end.

MERIWETHER LEWIS

But if the views were enchanting, the going was torturous. The river was swifter here, and marked by shallow rapids. The men had to get out and pull their canoes, wading chest deep in cold water or walking on shore, where slick mud stripped off their mocassins.

After four days, Lewis noted, some of them could "scarcely walk or stand." The captains thought it best to stop for a while. Besides, an unexpected challenge faced them.

June 2nd. Camped at a fork of the river. We could not determine which
[one] was the Missourie.

JOSEPH WHITEHOUSE

To ascend [the wrong] stream . . . would not only loose us the whole of
this season, but would probably so dishearten the party that it might
defeat the expedition altogether.

MERIWETHER LEWIS

June 3rd. Our officers & all the men differ in their opinions [of] which
river to take. . . . The Capts. Gave each man a dram of ardent Spirits.

JOSEPH WHITEHOUSE

The Hidatsas had not mentioned such a fork in the river, and the explorers could not agree on which course to take. The northern fork was muddy, just as the river had been all the way from St. Louis, and most of the men believed it was therefore the true Missouri. Lewis and Clark thought otherwise—that the Missouri should be getting clearer, like a mountain river, if it was to lead them to the Northwest Passage.

Everyone realized the critical importance of making the correct choice. Rather than impose an arbitrary command on the tired and nervous men, the captains decided to reconnoiter the area, despite the delay it would cost. Lewis followed the muddy stream for forty miles, far enough to assure himself that it led not westward toward the Pacific but northward, toward the endless Canadian plains. (He named it the Marias, in honor of a cousin in Virginia.) Clark

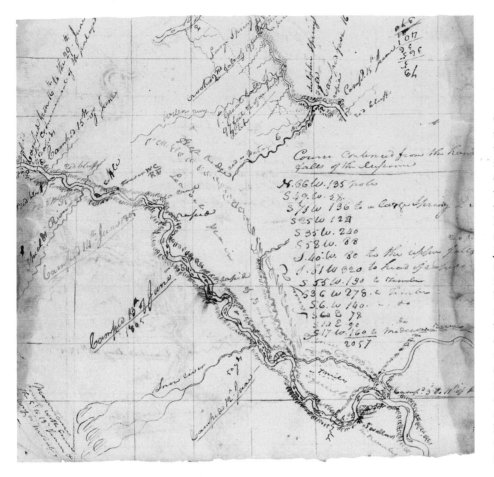

Clark's draft map, drawn as they traveled, clearly shows the fork in the river (bottom right) that perplexed the expedition for more than a week as they tried to discern which stream was the true Missouri. (He marked the spot where they camped from June 3 to June 11.) After scouting up the right-hand fork for 40 miles, Lewis became convinced it would not lead them to the great waterfall that the Indians had described, and he named it the Marias River, after a cousin of his in Virginia. The men still disagreed with the captains but "cheerfully" agreed to follow them up the left-hand fork, demonstrating the confidence they now had in their two leaders.

agreed with Lewis, but to a man the rest of the expedition remained convinced that the captains were wrong.

> *They said very cheerfully that they were ready to follow us any where we thought proper to direct, but that they still thought that the other was the [main] river and that they were affraid the South fork would soon termine-ate in the mountains and leave us at a great distance from the Columbia.*
>
> MERIWETHER LEWIS

On foot, Lewis and four men pushed ahead, along the other fork this time, hoping to encounter the mighty waterfall that the Indians had described to them in the winter.

On the morning of June 13, Lewis began hearing a constant roar in the distance, and then, on the horizon, he saw what looked like columns of smoke rising from the river channel. He hurried forward for seven miles.

The Great Falls of the
Missouri, photographed by
F. J. Haynes in 1880 before a
hydroelectric dam was built
behind it. Reaching the falls
confirmed to Lewis that the
expedition was on the route
the Hidatsas had sketched on
the dirt floor of their earth
lodge the previous winter, and
its beauty, he wrote, "formes
the grandest sight I ever
beheld." But there were four
more waterfalls just upstream,
and portaging around them all
would seriously delay the
expedition.

At last he reached the source of the noise and spray, and knew that he and
Clark had been right: there before him—three hundred yards wide, eighty feet
high—was the Great Falls of the Missouri.

*To gaze on this sublimely grand specticle . . . formes the grandest sight
I ever beheld. . . . Irregular and somewhat projecting rocks below receives
the water in it's passage down and brakes it into a perfect white foam,
which assumes a thousand forms in a moment, sometimes flying up in jets
of sparkling foam to the hight of fifteen or twenty feet and are scarcely
formed before large roling bodies of the same beaten and foaming water is
thrown over and conceals them. . . .*

*From the reflection of the sun on the sprey or mist which arrises from
these falls there is a beatifull rainbow produced, which adds not a little to
the beauty of this majestically grand senery.*

*After wrighting this imperfect discription, I again viewed the falls and
was so much disgusted with the imperfect idea which it conveyed of the scene*

that I determined to draw my pen across it and begin agin, but then reflected
that I could not perhaps succeed better than pening the first impressions of
the mind. I wished . . . that I might be enabled to give to the enlightened
world some just idea of this truly magnifficent and sublimely grand object
which has from the commencement of time been concealed from the view of
civilized man.

MERIWETHER LEWIS

Lewis sent a message back downriver telling Clark to bring up the rest of the expedition. Meanwhile, he scouted ahead and soon realized that their plans for a half-day portage had been wildly optimistic. Within ten miles, there were four more waterfalls.

They would have to portage around them all—eighteen and a half miles over rocky, broken ground under a broiling summer sun. They made crude carts from cottonwood trees, buried some of their heavier cargo in a cache, and began the excruciating work of moving everything overland.

The men has to haul with all their strength, [weight] & art; maney times
every man catching the grass & knobes & stones with their hands to give
them more force in drawing on the canoes & Loads.

WILLIAM CLARK

The buffaloe have troden up the prairie very much; [it] having now
become dry, the sharp points of earth [are] as hard as frozen ground [and
prickly pears] stand up in such abundance that there is no avoiding them.
This is particularly severe on the feet of the men, who have not only their
own weight to bear in treading on those hacklelike points, but have also
the addition of the burthen which they draw. . . .

At every halt, these poor fellows tumble down and are so much
fortiegued that many of them are asleep in an instant; . . . others faint
and unable to stand for a few minutes.

MERIWETHER LEWIS

Sergeant Pryor dislocated his shoulder again. Another man was bitten by a rattlesnake. After one hot day, Joseph Whitehouse drank too much water and became feverish. Lewis treated him by using a penknife to draw blood from his arm.

Sacagawea became seriously ill; "her case is somewhat dangerous," Clark confided to his journal. When bleeding her didn't help, the captains grew alarmed.

They were counting on her help in getting horses from her people when they reached the Missouri headwaters. Lewis gave her doses of opium and had her drink from a sulfur spring he had discovered. Slowly, she began to recover.

Violent storms punctuated the summer heat. In one, a flash flood nearly drowned Clark, Charbonneau, Sacagawea, and her baby in a gully. Another brought hail. It fell with such fury that it knocked the men to the ground, cut their exposed heads and skin, and so thoroughly frightened them all that the captains ordered an extra ration of grog and liquor to calm them that night.

> *The party . . . returned [to camp] in great confusion [on] the run, leaving their loads in the Plain. The hail & wind being so large and violent . . . and them naked, they were much brused, and some nearly killed. One knocked down three times, and others without hats or anything on their heads, bloody & complained very much. I refreshed them with a little grog.*
>
> William Clark

Along with the backbreaking work, there were more close calls with dangerous grizzly bears. But the greatest banes of their existence were more mundane: gnats, prickly pear cactuses, and the constant swarms of mosquitoes, "our great trio of pests," Lewis wrote, "equal to any three curses that ever poor Egypt labored under." (The journal writers struggled mightily to adequately describe

During the exhausting portage of the Great Falls, the men wore through a pair of moccasins every two days, developed infections on their blistered hands, suffered from heat stroke, hailstorms, prickly pear cactus, and plagues of mosquitoes. Robert Orduño's modern mural of the ordeal hangs at the Great Falls, Montana, airport.

just how bad the mosquitoes had become. As the days went by, they were called "troublesome," then "very troublesome," then "extremely troublesome," and finally "immensely numerous and troublesome.")

July 3rd, 1805. The men not other[wise] directed are dressing Skins to make themselves mockinsins, as they have about wore them all out in the plains. One pair of good mockinsons will not last more than about 2 days.

JOHN ORDWAY

By early July the torturous portage was nearly complete.

Lewis had brought along a light, collapsible iron frame that could be assembled, covered with skins, and turned into a large canoe capable of carrying nearly a ton of supplies. Having designed it himself and supervised its construction at Harpers Ferry in 1803, he had great hopes for its usefulness in conquering the Northwest Passage. He called it the *Experiment.* The men used elk and buffalo hides to cover the thirty-six-foot frame and caulked the seams with a mixture of buffalo tallow, beeswax, and pounded charcoal (since no tar or pine pitch was available).

When they set it on the river upstream from the falls, Lewis proudly reported, "she lay like a perfect cork in the water." But the seams soon began to leak, and a "mortified" Lewis "relinquished all further hope of my favorite boat." The *Experiment* was taken apart and buried. Building two new dugout canoes out of cottonwoods to replace it required a delay of five more days.

*July 4th. A beautiful, clear, pleasant warm morning. . . . It being the
4th of Independence, we drank the last of our ardent Spirits. . . . The
fiddle [was] put in order, and the party amused themselves dancing all
the evening until about 10 oClock in a jovi[a]l manner.*

JOHN ORDWAY

With the portage behind them, the Corps of Discovery celebrated their
second Fourth of July of the journey with a meal of beans, suet dumplings, and
heaping portions of buffalo meat, a "very comfortable dinner," Lewis wrote.
"We had no just cause to covet the sumptuous feasts of our countrymen on this
day." Their supply of whiskey was running low, but the captains let the men
finish it off as "they continued their mirth with songs and festive jokes and were
extremely merry until late at night."

The captains, however, had other things on their minds. In their winter
plans, they had estimated a half-day portage of the falls. Instead, it had taken
nearly a month. The delay at the river fork had cost them another ten
days.

They were way behind schedule. And off in the distance, they could now
see the mountains that awaited them.

*The Mountains to the N.W. and West of us are still entirely covered
[with snow], are white and glitter with the reflection of the sun. I do
not believe that the clouds that pervale at this season of the year reach
the summits of those lofty mountains; and if they do the probability is
that they deposit snow only, for there has been no p[er]ceptable
diminution of the snow which they contain since we first saw them. I
have thought it probable that these mountains might have derived their
appellation of* Shineing Mountains *from their glittering appearance
when the sun shines in certain directions on the snow which covers
them.*

WILLIAM CLARK

While the men danced, sang, and emptied the whiskey barrel, Lewis and
Clark privately abandoned their original plan to send a few men back from the
waterfalls with more information and a progress report for Jefferson. The mot-
ley collection of Americans that the captains had molded into a Corps of Discovery would need every bit of their collective strength and emerging unity of
purpose to face the challenges still ahead.

We have conceived our party sufficiently small and therefore have concluded not to dispatch a canoe with a part of our men to St. Louis as we had intended early in the spring. We fear also that such a measure might possibly discourage those who would in such case remain, and might possibly hazzard the fate of the expedition. We have never once hinted to any one of the party that we had such a scheme in contemplation, and all appear perfectly to have made up their minds to succeed in the expedition or purish in the attempt.

MERIWETHER LEWIS

CHAPTER 7

The
Most Distant
Fountain of
the Mighty
Missouri

We all believe that we are now about to enter on the most perilous and difficult part of our voyage, yet I see no one repining; all appear ready to meet those difficulties which await us with resolution and becoming fortitude.

MERIWETHER LEWIS

On JULY 15, 1805, the Corps of Discovery pushed its canoes onto the waters of the Missouri once more. Maddeningly, however, instead of taking them straight west toward the mountains and the Pacific, the river now led them south.

Clark, York, and two other men set off overland ahead of the main party, hoping to find the Shoshones and their all-important horses. Lewis took charge of the canoes.

North of what is now Helena, Montana, the canoes entered a constricted canyon with "the most remarkable cliffs that we have yet seen," according to Lewis—solid rock rising perpendicularly from the river's edge more than a thousand feet above them. "From the singular appearance of this place," he wrote, "I called it the Gates of the Rocky Mountains."

But farther on, the Missouri again entered a broad plain. Clark had come across signs of Indians, including a campfire that was still burning, but had not seen any. Sacagawea provided the only solace. Up to this point, the route the expedition had taken was as unknown to her as to the other explorers. Now she was returning to familiar territory.

July 22nd. The Indian woman recognizes the country and assures us that this is the river on which her relations live, and that the three forks are at no great distance. This peice of information has cheered the sperits of the party, who now begin to console themselves with the anticipation of shortly seeing the head of the missouri, yet unknown to the civilized world.

Meriwether Lewis

On July 19, the Missouri took them through a narrow gorge of nearly six miles. "The river appears to have forced it's way through this immence body of solid rock," Lewis wrote, adding that "every object here wears a dark and gloomy aspect." He gave it the name it still holds: the Gates of the Rocky Mountains.

Near the end of July, almost twenty-five hundred miles from St. Louis, they came to the Three Forks, where three smaller rivers join to form the Missouri. Lewis considered it "an essential point in the geography of this western part of the continent" and took celestial readings to mark its latitude and longitude.

The captains named the tributaries the Gallatin, after the Secretary of the Treasury, Albert Gallatin, who had helped arrange the financing of the Louisiana Purchase; the Madison, after Secretary of State James Madison, who had helped win its approval; and the Jefferson, "in honor," Lewis wrote, "of that illustrious personage Thomas Jefferson, the author of our enterprize."

The Jefferson pointed west, and they followed it. Lewis recorded the agonizingly slow progress against its swift, shallow current and the deteriorating health and spirits of the men:

July 31st. Nothing killed today and our fresh meat is out. When we have plenty of fresh meat, I find it impossible to make the men take any care of it, or use it with the least frugallity, tho' I expect that necessity will shortly teach them this art. . . . We have a lame crew just now, two with tumers or bad boils on various parts of them, one with a bad stone bruise, one with his arm accedently dislocated but fortunately well replaced, and a fifth has streigned his back by sliping and falling backwards on the . . . canoe.

August 2nd. The tops of these mountains [are] yet partially covered with snow, while we in the valley [are] suffocated nearly with the intense heat of the midday sun. The nights are so cold that two blankets are not more than sufficient covering. . . . Capt. Clark discovered a tumor rising on the inner side of his ankle this evening, which was painfull to him.

August 3rd. The currant more rapid & much more shallow than usual. In many places they were obliged to double man the canoes and drag them over the stone and gravel.

LEWIS & CLARK

August 4th. Charbono complains much of his leg, and is the cause of
considerable detention to us. . . . Capt. Clark's ancle became so painfull
to him that he was unable to walk.

August 5th. Drewyer [Drouillard] missed his step and had a very dangerous
fall. He sprained one of his fingers and hirt his leg very much. . . . The
men were so much fortiegued today that they wished much that navigation
was at an end, that they might go by land.

MERIWETHER LEWIS

Nothing seemed to be going right. Tow ropes snapped, and canoes capsized
in the swift water. Trying to prevent his dugout from being swamped, Joseph
Whitehouse was caught between the rocky stream bed and the boat, before it
finally floated over him. "Had the water been two inches shallower," Lewis
wrote, "it must inevitably have crushed him to death."

Clark's feet had become infected from prickly pear punctures, and he was
treating his fever with doses of Rush's Thunderbolts. By August 1, his thirty-
fifth birthday, a huge boil was festering on his ankle and he was virtually unable to walk. As a small consolation, Lewis named a small stream they passed
Birth Creek in honor of his friend.

The Jefferson itself forked into smaller rivers, causing yet another delay
when the main party missed a message left by the scouts (a beaver had chewed
down a pole to which the note was attached) and made a false start up the
wrong fork. Young George Shannon went hunting and got separated from the
expedition again for several worrisome days.

And still no sign of the Shoshones and their horses. "If we do not find
them," Lewis confided to his journal, "I fear the successful issue of our voyage
will be very doubtful."

Once more, the only bits of encouraging news came from Sacagawea. Earlier, at the Three Forks, she had shown the men the spot where the Hidatsas
had captured her five years earlier. Now she pointed out another landmark that
proved the explorers were at least on the right path. It was Beaverhead Rock,
north of present-day Dillon, Montana.

August 8th. The Indian woman recognized the point of a high
plain . . . which she informed us was not very distant from the summer
retreat of her nation on a river beyond the mountains which runs to the
west. This hill she says her nation calls the beaver's head from a conceived

re[se]mblance of it's figure to the head of that animal. She assures us that we shall either find her people on this river or on the river immediately west of it's source; which from it's present size cannot be very distant.

As it is now all important with us to meet with those people as soon as possible, I determined to proceed [ahead] tomorrow with a small party to the source of . . . this river and pass the mountains to the Columbia; and down that river until I f[i]nd the Indians. In short, it is my resolusion to find them, or some others who have horses, if it should cause me a trip of one month.

MERIWETHER LEWIS

Beaverhead Rock. This outcropping was a familiar sight to Sacagawea, who told the captains they were at last nearing the land of her people. The next day Lewis took three men to make one final push to find the Shoshones and their horses. This time Clark, suffering from a swollen and infected foot, stayed behind with the canoes. "I Should have taken this trip had I have been able to march," he wrote, "from the rageing fury of a tumer on my anckle musle."

On August 9, with George Drouillard, John Shields, and Hugh McNeal, Lewis left the main party and canoes under Clark's command on the Beaverhead River and pushed ahead in search of the Shoshones. Two days later, as they followed a small creek leading toward the mountains, the advance party saw an Indian on horseback in the distance—the first Indian they had seen since leaving the Mandan villages four months earlier.

Lewis was overjoyed at the sight, and laid down his gun to signal that his intentions were friendly. The lone horseman seemed suspicious as the four explorers walked forward. Lewis got within two hundred yards of the Indian and shouted out "tab-ba-bone, tab-ba-bone," which Sacagawea had told him was the word her people would use for "white man."

The Shoshone edged away.

The Indian halted again and turned his horse about as if to wait for me, and I believe he would have remained untill I came up whith him had it not been for Shields, who still pressed forward. When I arrived within about 150 paces I again repeated the word "tab-ba-bone" and held up the trinkits in my hands and striped up my shirt sleve to give him an opportunity of seeing the colour of my skin, and advanced leasurely towards him.

The Scout, by Edward S. Curtis. The mounted Shoshone whom Lewis cautiously yet excitedly approached on August 11 was the first Indian the expedition had seen in four months. "I . . . had no doubt of obtaining a friendly introduction to his nation provided I could get near enough to him to convince him of our being whitemen," Lewis wrote, but every method he tried at signaling peaceful intentions failed. Adding to the disappointment, after the Indian rode away, a heavy rain drenched the explorers and made following the horse's trail more difficult.

Shields, who was some distance from his captain, did not see Lewis signaling him to hold back. Perhaps the Indian feared a trap, as both Lewis and Shields approached from different directions. Or perhaps it was the fact that since the Shoshones had never before encountered whites, there was no special word to describe them, a nuance lost when Lewis had been questioning Sacagawea in anticipation of this moment. In Shoshone, "tab-ba-bone" means "stranger."

Whatever the cause, the result, Lewis wrote, was the same. When the captain was within a hundred yards of the Shoshone,

he soddenly turned his horse about, gave him the whip, leaped the creek, and disappeared in the willow brush in an instant, and with him vanished all my hopes of obtaining horses for the preasent. I now felt quite as much mortification and disappointment as I had pleasure and expectation at the first sight of this indian.

On August 12, 1805, the same day Lewis reached the Continental Divide, Lewis and Clark's shipment from Fort Mandan arrived in Washington, D.C. In the entryway of his home in Monticello, shown here, Jefferson proudly displayed the elk antlers his Corps of Discovery had sent him, and after planting the Indian corn outside, he diligently recorded its progress in his garden book.

The next day was August 12. That day, the shipment the captains had sent from Fort Mandan finally reached the East, having traveled down the Missouri and Mississippi, through the port of New Orleans, and by ship around Florida and up the Atlantic coast.

President Jefferson would plant the Indian corn in his Monticello garden, hang the elk antlers on the wall of his home, and send the two surviving animals, a magpie and the prairie dog, to the nation's preeminent natural science museum of the time: Independence Hall in Philadelphia, where thirty years earlier Jefferson and others had created the nation that now stretched to the Rocky Mountains.

As he sifted through the specimens, read Lewis's confident letter about their proposed schedule, and spread Clark's map out on the floor to follow their anticipated route, Jefferson must have imagined them already through the Northwest Passage and at the western ocean.

But in fact, they were nowhere near the sea. Instead, the Corps of Discovery was about to learn the difference between imaginary mountains on a map and the real thing.

———

August 12th. This morning I sent Drewyer [Drouillard] out as soon as it was light, to try and discover what rout the Indian had taken. He followed the track of the horse we had pursued yesterday to the mountain where it had ascended, and returned to me in about an hour and a half. . . .

We fell in with a large and plain Indian road. . . . I therefore did not dispair of shortly finding a passage over the mountains and of taisting the waters of the great Columbia this evening.

MERIWETHER LEWIS

The well-worn Indian trail led west, up a gentle rise toward a ridge line. A small creek ran beside it. Hugh McNeal straddled the stream with his feet and "thanked his god," Lewis wrote, that he had "lived to bestride the heretofore deemed endless Missouri." They hurried forward, climbing the slope toward the source of the creek.

Lewis's spirits were exuberant on the afternoon of April 12, as he was about to become the first United States citizen to reach the Missouri's head-waters. He had no idea that mountains like these might still block the expedition's path to the Pacific.

Lewis's First View of the Rockies, by Olaf Seltzer. This painting depicts the moment on May 26, 1805, when Lewis first saw the mountains on the far western horizon. Three arduous months later, standing at Lemhi Pass, he would have to report "immence ranges of high mountains still to the West of us with their tops partially covered with snow." In those mountains, the myth of a Northwest Passage finally died.

Further [up was] the most distant fountain of the waters of the Mighty Missouri, in surch of which we have spent so many toilsome days and wristless nights. Thus far I had accomplished one of those great objects on which my mind has been unalterably fixed for many years. Judge then of the pleasure I felt in allaying my thirst from this pure and ice-cold water.

MERIWETHER LEWIS

Lewis paused at the small spring a few minutes to rest himself and the others. Refreshed and eager with excitement, he pressed on. The ridge line was only a few hundred yards ahead.

He was approaching the farthest boundary of the Louisiana Territory, the Continental Divide—the spine of the Rocky Mountains beyond which the rivers flow west. No American citizen had ever been there before. This, he believed, was the Northwest Passage: the goal of explorers for more than three centuries, the great prize that Thomas Jefferson had sent him to find and claim for the United States.

With each stride, Lewis was nearing what he expected to be the crowning moment of the expedition and his life. From the vantage point just ahead, all of science and geography had prepared him to see the watershed of the Columbia and beyond it, perhaps, a great plain that led down to the Pacific.

Instead, there were just more mountains—"immence ranges of high mountains still to the West of us," he wrote, "with their tops partially covered with snow."

At that moment, in the daunting vista spread out at the feet of Meriwether Lewis, the dream of an easy water route across the continent—a dream stretching back to Christopher Columbus—was shattered.

But Lewis had no time now to contemplate his disappointment. He had more pressing business pushing him onward. He desperately needed to find horses for the expedition to cross the Divide; and he needed to find a river they could navigate to the western sea.

The success—perhaps the very survival—of all of them depended on it.

FRIENDS

STEPHEN E. AMBROSE

ON JUNE 19, 1803, Captain Meriwether Lewis wrote William Clark a letter that contained what Lewis and Clark scholar Donald Jackson described as "one of the most famous invitations to greatness the nation's archives can provide." The letter launched one of the great friendships of all time and started the friends on one of the great adventures, and one of the great explorations, of all time.

Lewis and Clark have become so entwined by history that for many Americans the name is Lewisandclark, but in 1803 they had spent very little time together. Although Clark was born in Virginia four years earlier than Lewis, he had moved to Kentucky as a small boy. They had served together in the army, for six months, with Clark as Lewis's commanding officer. No anecdotes survive, or any correspondence between them in the next decade except for a business letter from Lewis to Clark, asking him to make inquiries about land in Ohio.

But in those six months together they had taken each other's measure and they had become friends. Their trust in each other was complete, even before they took the first step west together. How this friendship came about cannot be known in any de-tail, but that it existed long before they became Lewisandclark cannot be doubted, as is clear from their exchange of letters. After describing the scope of the enterprise, Lewis wrote, "Thus my friend, you have a summary view of the plan, the means and the objects of this expedition. If therefore there is anything under those circumstances which would induce you to participate with me in it's fatigues, it's dangers and it's honors, believe me there is no man on earth with whom I should feel equal pleasure in sharing them as with yourself."

Lewis then made an extraordinary offer: Clark would have a captain's commission and be co-commander. Lewis did not have to do it; he could have proposed a lieutenant's commission. Divided command almost never works and is the bane of all military men, to whom the sanctity of the chain of command is basic and the idea of two disagreeing commanders in a critical situation is anathema. But Lewis did it anyway. It felt right to him. It was based on what he knew about Clark, and what he felt for him.

Lewis wanted Clark along, even if not as an official member of the party. He closed his letter by

Marks of friendship. Clark named the Lewis River (now the Salmon and the Snake) in his friend's honor, and Lewis returned the favor by naming the next major stream Clark's River (now the Bitterroot and Clark's Fork).

saying that if personal or business or any other affairs prevented Clark from accepting, Lewis hoped that he could "accompany me as a friend part of the way up the Missouri. I should be extremely happy in your company."

In reply, Clark said he was free and would "chearfully join" Lewis. He concluded, "This is an undertaking fraited with many difeculties, but My friend I do assure you that no man lives with whome I would perfur to undertake Such a Trip &c. as yourself." And in a follow-up letter he concluded, "My friend, I join you with hand & Heart."

On October 15, 1803, the keelboat brought Lewis to Clarksville. He tied her up and set off to meet his partner, who was living with his older brother, General George Rogers Clark. They met on General Clark's porch. As they stuck out their hands to each other, both men had smiles on their faces which were as broad as the Ohio River, as big as their ambitions and dreams, as deep as their friendship. That evening, over dinner, there were the two would-be heroes with the authentic older hero, all three great talkers, full of ideas and images and memories and practical matters and grand philosophy, of Indians and bears and mountains never before seen. Excitement and joy ran through their questions and answers, words coming out in a tumble.

They proceeded down the Ohio, then up the Mississippi to Wood River, across from St. Louis. Lewis taught Clark astronomy and the use of the sextant for making celestial observations, skills he had learned from Mr. Jefferson, among others; Clark taught Lewis the craft of the waterman on western rivers, skills he had learned in the army. They made the winter camp at Wood River. One or the other of them was in St. Louis nearly always, purchasing items necessary for the trip—an exceedingly complex and difficult task.

Thus they were separated when Lewis received Clark's commission from the War Department. It was a lieutenant's commission, not a captain's, as Lewis had promised. Lewis was mortified and apparently helpless. He felt not the slightest temptation to take advantage of the situation. It never occurred to him that here was an opportunity for him to assume sole command. Instead, he immediately wrote Clark, giving him the bad news but adding, "I think it will be best to let none of our party or any other persons know any thing about the grade."

For the next seven years, only the Secretary of War, Jefferson, and Meriwether Lewis and William Clark knew that as far as the army was concerned, Captain Lewis was in command of the Corps of Discovery, with Lieutenant Clark as his second-in-command.* For the men of the expedition, it was Captain Clark and Captain Lewis, co-commanders. That was what counted.

That, and their friendship. The situation was fraught with dangerous possibilities. They had ahead of them four thousand miles of wilderness, peopled by Indians who had to be regarded as potentially hostile until proven otherwise, Indians who were thought to regard all strangers as prey. They had mountains to cross, rapids to run, falls to portage. If at any time they disagreed over one of the daily, often life-threatening decisions they would have to make, Lewis could have pulled rank on Clark. But he was confident that would never happen. So was Clark.

A small incident a week before they began the ascent of the Missouri illustrates their relationship. Lewis, in St. Louis, sent a note to Clark asking Clark to send to him "the specimines of salt which you will find in my writing desk, on the shelves where our

* And then only Nicholas Biddle knew; he found out while interviewing Clark in the process of preparing his paraphrased edition of the journals.

books are, or in the drawer of the Instrument case." The invitation to rummage through Lewis's writing desk spoke to the trust between the two men.

On the expedition, they disagreed on the necessity for salt, and over dog meat—Lewis wanted salt and rather liked dog; Clark was indifferent about salt and could not reconcile himself to eating dog. They did not disagree on decisions. The best-known and most difficult came at the junction of the Missouri and the Marias. Which was the true Missouri? The men, many of them experienced watermen, to a man thought it was the Marias. The captains conferred, and then announced that the others were wrong. In a splendid tribute to their leadership qualities, the men said to the captains "very cheerfully that they were ready to folow us any wher we thought proper to direct but that they still thought that the other was the river."

Lewis and Clark had it right. As they made their way up the Missouri to the Three Forks, they frequently separated, with one of them hiking overland, looking for the Shoshones. Previously they had been together when they discovered new rivers; Clark or Lewis would suggest a name and they would agree on it. When the two separated, the man who first saw the river or stream would name it, confident that the other would agree. Clark named a river after Lewis; Lewis named a river after Clark.

The captains were ready to die for each other. Although they were not together when the single Indian fight of the expedition occurred, they were in a number of situations in which they were right on the edge of violence, most of all with the Sioux both going and coming. They stood together, prepared to fight if necessary, hoping they would not have to, thinking as one.

They worried about and ministered to each other. In August 1805 Lewis helped Clark pull thorns from his feet and bathed Clark's feet in warm water. Clark had been hiking in search of the Shoshones; the prickly pears had rendered his feet a raw, bloody mass of torn flesh. "I opened the bruses & blisters of my feet which caused them to be painfull," Clark wrote, in his own get-to-the-point fashion.

The captains talked. They agreed that another overland expedition was necessary. Clark wanted to lead it; he wanted another chance at finding Indians, never mind the prickly pears. Lewis wrote, "altho' Capt. C. was much fatiegued his feet yet blistered and soar he insisted on pursuing his rout in the morning nor weould he consent willingly to my releiving him. Finding him anxious I readily consented to remain with the canoes."

In September 1805, when Lewis had severe gastrointestinal distress, it was Clark's turn to be the nurse. His intentions were good, his treatment a near disaster. He wrote that Lewis was so sick he was "scercely able to ride on a jentle horse." He gave Lewis Rush's Pills, an emetic of legendary strength, better known as "Rush's Thunderbolts." That was probably the worst thing he could have done. The next day, Lewis was suffering worse than before. Clark was nothing if not persistent: he gave Lewis some salts and "Tarter emetic," another laxative. The following day, he tried "Salts Pils Galip [jalap, another purgative] Tarter emetic &c," again with unhappy results.

Clark wasn't doing so well himself. Like Lewis and the men (who were also sick), he was on a diet of boiled roots and dried salmon at the time. On October 5 Clark reported, "Capt Lewis & my Self eate a Supper of roots boiled, which filled us So full of wind, that we were Scercely able to Breathe all night felt the effects of it." Two days later, he opened his journal entry, "I continu verry unwell but obliged to attend every thing," because Lewis was so sick he couldn't even supervise the men's work.

Fortunately, they were young and in great shape. They recovered.

On the return journey, they parted on July 4, Clark heading south to explore the Yellowstone, Lewis north to make further discoveries. Each had nearly a thousand miles to go through country neither had seen. As they said good-bye, they promised to meet in six weeks at the mouth of the Yellowstone.

Lewis got shot in the buttocks in a hunting accident; when he arrived for the reunion he was lying on his belly in the canoe. Informed of his friend's condition, Clark dashed to the canoe. He was much alarmed to see Lewis in this state, but Lewis raised his head to assure him that the wound was slight and would be healed in three or four weeks. "This information relieved me very much," Clark wrote.

Clark washed Lewis's wound and packed it with lint, a process he repeated twice a day for the next three weeks. Then he was able to write, "I am happy to have it in my power to Say that my worthy friend Capt Lewis is recovering fast, he walked a little to day for the first time."

When they got back to St. Louis, Lewis immediately wrote Jefferson to set him straight on this business of Clark's commission. "With rispect to the exertions and services rendereed by that esteemable man Capt. William Clark in the course of our voyage I cannot say too much; if sir any credit be due for the success of the arduous enterprise in which we have been mutually engaged, he is equally with myself entitled to your consideration and that of our common country." Over the next year, Lewis worked on the President and the Congress to make certain that Clark was treated equally with himself when it came to handing out rewards and honors. And it was Lewis who first referred to the voyage as the "Lewis and Clark Expedition."

Clark married shortly after the expedition and

brought his bride to St. Louis, where Lewis was governor of Upper Louisiana and Clark was superintendent of Indian Affairs. Lewis gave Mrs. Clark as her wedding present a complete set of Shakespeare. For some months the three of them lived in the same house; when Lewis got a place of his own, he continued to share his office with Clark. When Clark's firstborn son came along, Clark named him Meriwether Lewis Clark.

Lewis's financial and mental decline in 1808 and 1809 distressed his friend greatly. He loaned Lewis money, kept him out of scenes at taverns and balls, and generally looked after him as best he could. Among other problems, Lewis had been stuck with chits he had written on the War Department in good faith. He headed for Washington to set things right. The day after Lewis's departure, Clark wrote his brother Jonathan: "Govr. L I may Say is ruined by Some of his Bills being protested for a Considerable Sum. . . . I have not Spent Such a day as yesterday for maney years. His Crediters all flocking in . . . distressed him much, which he expressed to me in Such terms as to Cause a Cempothy [sympathy] which is not yet off—I do not believe there was ever an honester man in Louisiana nor one who had pureor motives than Govr. Lewis. [I]f his mind had been at ease, I Should have parted Cherefully.

"I think all will be right and he will return with flying Colours to this Country—prey do not mention this about the Govr. excup Some unfavourable or wrong Statement is made."

The two men never saw each other again. But on the last day of his life, before his sad and lonely death on the Natchez Trace, Lewis said to his servant that Clark had heard of his difficulties and was coming on. He would put things straight. He always had. Perhaps, just before he died, Lewis found one brief moment of comfort thinking of his friend.

In a famous interview in November 1972 with Italian reporter Oriana Fallaci, Henry Kissinger described himself as the cowboy who rode into town alone to restore law and order. He said that the American people loved that image (he didn't add that the Germans did too; it was in Germany that he was captured by the image as a boy). That lone cowboy, the quintessential rugged individualist—like his predecessor the mountain man—holds the imagination as a symbol of the West. It got started with Owen Wister's novel *The Virginian* (1902). Wister was a Harvard friend of Theodore Roosevelt's and took Teddy as something of a model for the hero of the tale. He dedicated his novel to TR. In fact, Roosevelt had been more a tourist and investor in the West than a resident, but he had spent weeks and more on solitary hunts in North Dakota.

The movies greatly reinforced the Wister image. It lent itself perfectly to the scenery, the plots, the drama of the West. From Tom Mix through John Wayne to Kevin Costner, the lone cowboy has provided the most enduring of all Hollywood's themes. Not even World War II can top the Westerns.

But as they say out west, the high-risk-taking loner often ended up at the end of a rope, while the committee men watched from their horses. It was teamwork that made the West, something scarcely recognized in our western lore. Herein lies yet another price paid for Lewis's failure to get the journals published. Had the Lewis and Clark story been better known, the teamwork it exemplified would have provided a richer western experience for storytellers and moviemakers, one less encouraging to freemen and militia and more supportive of team players.

What Lewis and Clark and the men of the Corps of Discovery had demonstrated is that there is nothing that people cannot do if they get themselves together and act as a team. Here you have thirty-two men who had become so close, so bonded, that when they heard a cough at night they knew instantly who had a cold. They could see a man's shape in the dark and know who it was. They knew who liked salt on his meat and who didn't. They knew who was the best shot, the fastest runner, the one who could get a fire going the quickest on a rainy day. Around the campfire, they got to know about each other's parents and loved ones, and each other's hopes and dreams. They had come to love each other to the point where they would have sold their lives gladly to save a comrade. They had developed a bond, become a band of brothers, and together they were able to accomplish feats that just astonish us today.

It was the captains who welded the Corps of Discovery into a team. Indeed, a family. This was their greatest accomplishment. They made their divided command work as efficiently and effectively as a Roman legion or any other elite outfit in history, not one of which had risked a divided command.

Consider the situation in August 1805, when the Corps of Discovery was making its way up the Jefferson River. The men were footsore, exhausted, standing chest-deep in cold mountain water most of the day, hauling the canoes forward. They had reached the breaking point. As Clark described it, "men complain verry much of the emence labour they are obliged to undergo &c wish much to leave the river. I passify them." Lewis gives us a bit more detail: he wrote, "Men geting weak soar and much fortiegued; they complianed of the fortiegue to which the navigation subjected them and wished to go by land. Capt. C. engouraged them and passifyed them."

One would love to know more about how Clark did it, but it is certain that Lewis approved. In a situation fraught with difficulties, when there were a

[Handwritten excerpt 1:] ...cumstance which I did not learn untill we were about to set out and it was then too late to take a Vocabulary). The river here called Clark's river is that which we have heretofore called the Flat-head river, I have this named it in honour of my worthy friend and fellow traveller Capt. Clark. for this stream we know no indian name and...

[Handwritten excerpt 2:] ...they would be supplied &c. or — I am happy to have it in my power to Say·· my worthy friend Capt Lewis is recovering fast, he walked a little to day for the first time. I have discontinued the tent in the hole the bale came out — I have before mentioned that the beans are Mahubter...

Neither captain was particularly emotionally demonstrative when writing in his journal, but these two excerpts are evidence of their remarkable bond. On May 6, 1806, Lewis refers to "my worthy friend and fellow traveller Capt. Clark." On August 22, 1806, Clark, who had been worriedly tending his comrade's bullet wound, reported, "I am happy to have it in my power to Say that my worthy friend Capt. Lewis is recovering fast."

dozen times a day when the captains might have disagreed with each other—which branch to take, whom to send out as hunters, whom to send out as scouts for the Shoshones, how hard to push the men, where to camp, and so many more—they instinctively agreed. When they were apart, as on this occasion, so confident were they that they would respond alike to whatever the challenge there might be, they assumed the other would do what they would do. This was due to their high level of professional competence—and to their friendship.

Friendship is different from all other human relationships. Unlike acquaintanceship, it is based on love. Unlike that between lovers and married couples, it is free of jealousy. Unlike that between children and parents, it knows neither criticism nor resentment. Friendship has no status in law. Business partnerships are based on a contract. So is marriage. Parents are bound by the law, as are children. But friendship is freely entered into, freely given, freely exercised.

Friends never cheat each other, or take advantage. Friends glory in each other's successes and are downcast by the failures. Friends minister to each other. Friends give to each other, worry about each other, stand always ready to help. Friends will go hungry for each other, freeze for each other, die for each other. It is rarely achieved, but at its height, friendship is an ecstasy. For Lewis and Clark, it was an ecstasy, and the critical factor in their great success.

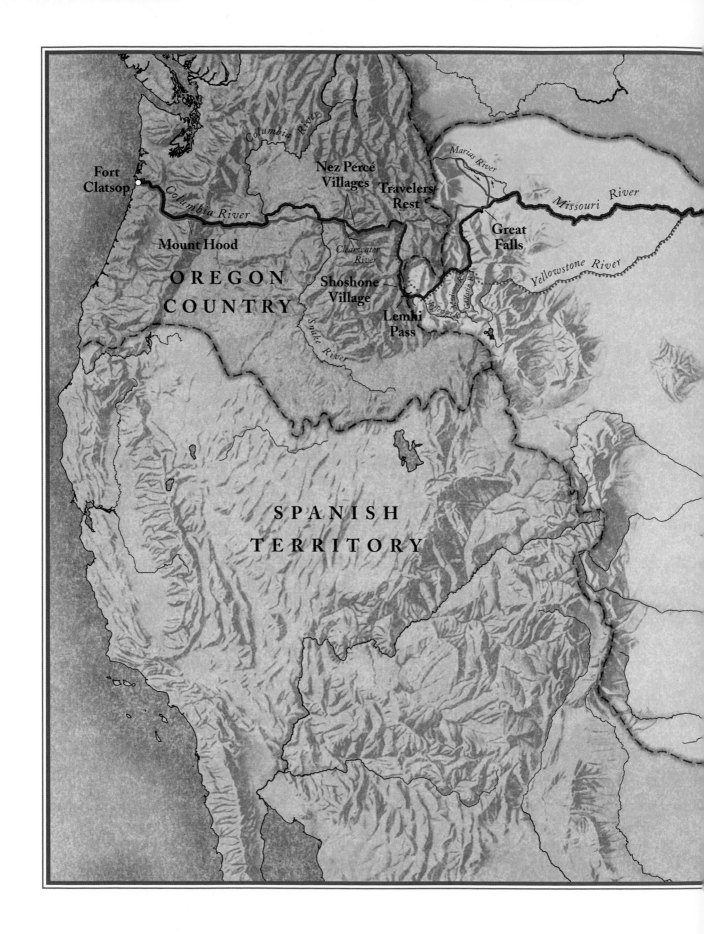

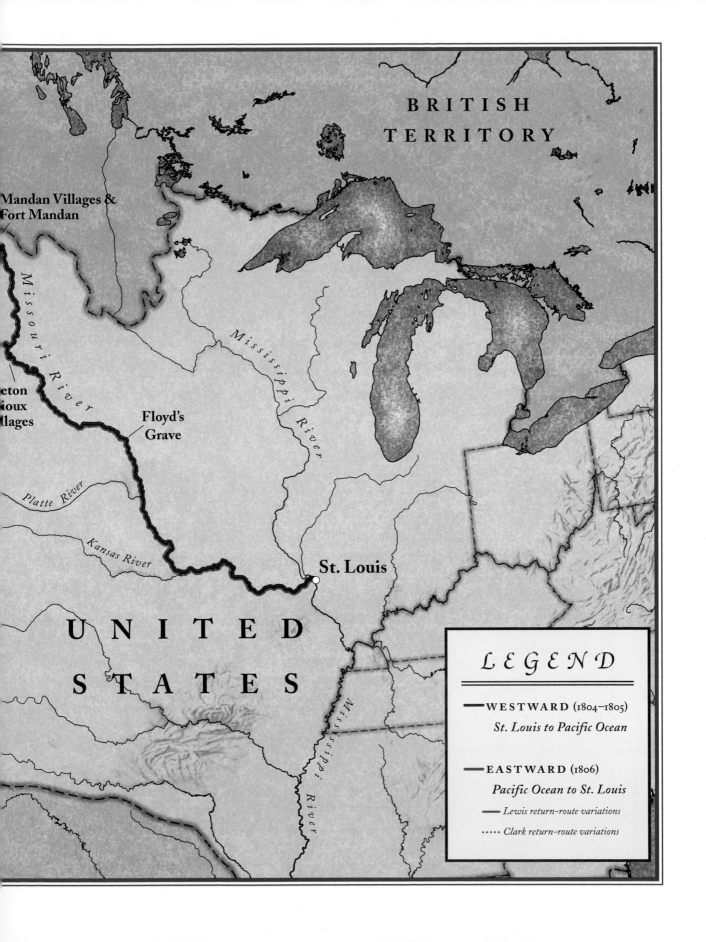

BRITISH
TERRITORY

Mandan Villages &
Fort Mandan

Missouri River

eton
ioux
llages

Floyd's
Grave

Mississippi River

Platte River

Kansas River

St. Louis

UNITED

STATES

Mississippi River

LEGEND

WESTWARD (1804–1805)
St. Louis to Pacific Ocean

EASTWARD (1806)
Pacific Ocean to St. Louis

— *Lewis return-route variations*

····· *Clark return-route variations*

CHAPTER 8

Hungry Creek

A great many snows past, when I was a child, our people were in continual fear. . . . During our excursions for buffalo, we were frequently attacked by [our enemies], and many of our bravest warriors fell victims to the thunder and lightning they wielded. . . . The lips of our women [were] white with dread, there [were] no smiles on the lips of our children. . . . [Our chief said], "Let us fly to the mountains. Let us seek their deepest recesses where, unknown to our destroyers, we may hunt deer and the bighorn, and bring gladness back to the hearts of our wives and our children."

FARO

THE LEMHI SHOSHONES HAD once lived on the rich buffalo plains of what is now Montana. They had brave warriors and were skilled horsemen. But in recent years, they had been driven into the mountains by their enemies far to the north and east—the Blackfeet, Atsinas, and Hidatsas—who had acquired muskets from Canadian fur traders.

In August 1805, desperately hungry from having lived for a year on roots, berries, and occasional fish and small game, they were preparing to make a brief venture back onto the plains to hunt buffalo. It was always risky. That very spring, the Atsinas had attacked them, killed or captured twenty men, stolen many horses, and destroyed all their tepees except one.

On the morning of August 13, three of their women, out gathering food a few miles from their village, looked up to see strangers approaching. It was Lewis and his three companions.

One of the Shoshones fled, but the two others, a young girl and an old woman, were too startled to run away. As he advanced toward them, Lewis laid down his gun, but the Indians seemed frozen to the ground with fear, he wrote, "holding down their heads as if reconciled to die, which they expected no doubt would be their fate."

Lewis gave them beads, moccasin awls, and some pewter mirrors, and he painted their faces with vermilion, "which with this nation is emblematic of peace."

Just then, sixty mounted warriors galloped up, expecting to meet an enemy war party. Instead, Lewis stepped forward with gifts and an American flag, while the Shoshone women explained that the newcomers were friendly.

These were the first white people the Shoshones had ever seen.

They were unlike any people we had hitherto seen, fairer than ourselves, and clothed with skins unknown to us. . . . They gave us things like solid water, which were sometimes brilliant as the sun, and which sometimes showed us our own faces. . . . We thought them the children of the Great Spirit. . . . [And] we soon discovered that they were in possession of the identical thunder and lightning that had proved in the hands of our [enemies] so fatal to our happiness.

FARO

The village chief, Cameahwait (the One Who Never Walks), installed the strangers in the village's only skin tepee and provided them with food—

Of all the Indians Lewis and Clark met, the Lemhi Shoshones led the most precarious lives. Without guns to protect themselves, they were constantly raided by enemy tribes such as the Hidatsas, who had kidnapped Sacagawea. "They live in a wretched stait of poverty," according to Lewis, but they were "generous with the little they possess, extreemly honest, and by no means beggarly." William Henry Jackson took this photograph in 1870.

including a piece of salmon, which convinced Lewis that he was now on the Pacific side of the continent. They were also offered a small, boiled root that Lewis found "naucious to my pallate." It was later given the scientific name *Lewisia rediviva*, in honor of the captain, but it is better known as bitterroot.

Impressed by the large herd of Shoshone horses—seven hundred mounts that Lewis said were as good as any in Virginia—the captain had Drouillard use sign language to explain that he needed horses and that more white men were on their way. Many of Cameahwait's people suspected it was a trap, that the strangers were in league with the Shoshones' well-armed enemies.

Cameahwait, with his ferce eyes and lank jaws grown meager for the want of food . . . [said,] "If we had guns, we could live in the country of the buffaloe and eat as our enimies do, and not be compelled to hide ourselves in these mountains and live on roots and berries as the bear do."

I told [him] . . . that after our finally returning to our homes towards the rising sun, whitemen would come to them with a number of guns and every other article necessary to their defence and comfort.

MERIWETHER LEWIS

Reluctantly, Cameahwait agreed to accompany the strangers back across the Continental Divide to the Beaverhead to join Clark and the others—

Captain Lewis, with Drewyer and Shields, Meeting the Shoshoni Indians, August 13, 1805, by Charles M. Russell. Lewis left his gun on the ground and advanced with an American flag. The Shoshones "embraced me very affectionately in their way," he wrote, by putting one arm over his shoulder and touching their left cheek to his. "Bothe parties now advanced and we wer all carresed and besmeared with their grease and paint," he added, "till I was heartily tired of the national hug."

Though desperately poor, the Shoshones had large herds of horses, many of which Lewis believed would "make a figure on the South side of James River or the land of fine horses." The success of the Corps of Discovery now rested on whether the Indians would be willing to trade with the expedition.

although as Lewis and Cameahwait and a group of warriors left the village two days later, some of the women sang mournful chants for the men they feared they might never see again.

But when the horse caravan reached the point on the other side of the Divide where Lewis had promised they would meet more white men, no one was there. Some of the warriors accused Cameahwait of leading them into an ambush.

Lewis had to think fast. He gave Cameahwait his hat and his gun and put on a Shoshone cape, symbolizing that if it *was* a trap, Lewis would be the first to die. The Indians warily agreed to wait a little longer. That night, Lewis wrote, he was more nervous than the Shoshones.

I slept but little. . . . My mind [was] dwelling on the state of the expedition, which I have ever held in equal estimation with my own existence, and the fait of which appeared at this moment to depend in great measure upon the caprice of a few savages who are ever as fickle as the wind.

MERIWETHER LEWIS

LEWIS & CLARK

The next day Clark arrived with the rest of the expedition and the boats. Sacagawea was walking out in the lead when they saw the Shoshones. She "danced for the joyful sight," Clark wrote, and sucked her fingers as a signal that they were her own people. "Those Indians," he added of the reunion, "sung all the way to their camp."

Now it was time to begin the important negotiations for horses to portage the Continental Divide. Then occurred one of the greatest coincidences in American history.

The moccasins of the whole party were taken off, and after much ceremony the smoking began. . . . Glad of an opportunity of being able to converse more intelligibly, Sacagawea was sent for; she came . . . sat down, and was beginning to interpret, when, in the person of Cameahwait, she recognized her brother. She instantly jumped up, and ran and embraced him, throwing over him her blanket, and weeping profusely.

WILLIAM CLARK

Sacagawea was the chief's sister. With her acting as the interpreter, Cameahwait agreed to sell the Corps of Discovery all the horses they needed. A relieved Lewis and Clark named the spot Camp Fortunate.

———

The following day, August 18, was Lewis's thirty-first birthday. When he opened his journal that night, he wrote that the day had gone well. Eager for any manufactured goods they could get, the Shoshones were trading horses at bargain prices. Lewis himself had purchased three good ones for an old uniform coat, a pair of leggings, a few handkerchiefs, and three knives, worth less than twenty dollars back in the states. The Indians had also given him three "ear bobs" as ornaments and a long cape made of white weasel tails and otter skins.

Then his thoughts turned inward:

This day I completed my thirty first year, and conceived that I had in all human probability now existed about half the period which I am to remain in this . . . world. I reflected that I had as yet done but little, very little, indeed, to further the hapiness of the human race, or to advance the information of the succeeding generation. I viewed with regret the many hours I have spent in indolence, and now soarly feel the want of that information which those hours would have given me, had they been judiciously expended. But since they are past and cannot be recalled, I

and cannot be recalled, I dash from me the gloomy thought and resolved in future, to redouble my exertions and at least indeavour to promote those two primary objects of human existence, by giving them the aid of that portion of talents which nature and fortune have bestoed on me; or in future, to live for mankind, as I have heretofore lived for myself. ———

A portion of Lewis's intriguing journal entry for August 18, 1805, his thirty-first birthday, and what should have been a moment of triumph. He had successfully traced the Missouri to its headwaters, and the Shoshones were willingly providing horses for the expedition to continue westward. Still, Lewis chastised himself for "the many hours I have spent in indolence" and urged himself "to live *for mankind,* as I have heretofore lived *for myself.*"

dash from me the gloomy thought, and resolved in future, to redouble my exertions and at least indeavour to promote those two primary objects of human existence, by giving them the aid of that portion of talents which nature and fortune have bestoed on me; or in future, to live for mankind, *as I have heretofore lived* for myself.

———

August 20th, 1805. They are the poorest and most miserable nation I ever beheld, having scarcely any thing to subsist on, except berries and a few fish. . . . They have a great many fine horses, and nothing more. . . . We had a long talk with them, and they gave us very unfavorable accounts with respect to the rivers.

PATRICK GASS

The explorers could not afford to tarry for long among the Shoshones. The captains had originally planned to be at the Pacific by this time. Instead, the expedition hadn't even crossed the mountains or found the river that would take them west.

They asked Cameahwait about the stream Lewis had seen near the Shoshone village and the river it flowed into. It was impassable, the chief told them, with no game for food or trees big enough with which to make canoes.

This information, if true, is alarming. I deturmined to go in advance and examine the Countrey, [and] See if those dificuelties presented themselves in the gloomey picture in which they painted them.

WILLIAM CLARK

Clark scouted ahead far enough to establish that the Shoshones were correct. He named the rugged river Lewis's River. Today it is the Salmon—sometimes called the River of No Return.

They would have to go on horseback.

An elderly Shoshone they called Old Toby told them of a route to the north, a rough trail through the mountains with little game but used each year by a tribe traveling from the Columbia to the buffalo plains. The captains decided it was their best chance to reach the Pacific.

Having buried some of their heavy baggage and stashed their canoes at Camp Fortunate, the expedition set off on twenty-nine horses and one mule. Rather than remain with her own people, Sacagawea moved on as part of the Corps of Discovery.

They crossed a steep mountain pass and descended into the valley of a beautiful river, the Bitterroot. It was September now. The days were pleasant, but on the high mountains immediately to the west, snow was already accumulating.

They came across a new tribe—the Salish—who also had never before encountered white men and who spoke what Clark called "a gugling kind of language, spoken much through the throat."

> September 4th. These natives are well dressed, decent looking Indians; light complectioned. . . . They have the most curious language of any we have seen before. They talk as though they lisped or have a bur on their tongue. . . . We suppose that they are the Welch Indians, if there is any such.
>
> JOHN ORDWAY

Perhaps, the explorers speculated at first, these were the fabled, fair-skinned Welsh Indians who for centuries had been rumored to be living somewhere in the West.

Communicating with them was difficult. Through a misinterpretation of sign language, the captains referred to the Salish as the "Flatheads," even though the tribe did not perform head-flattening rituals on their young.

Finally, a Shoshone boy was discovered living among them who could speak their language. Each time the Salish spoke, he would translate it into Shoshone for Sacagawea, who translated it into Hidatsa for Charbonneau. Charbonneau, in turn, passed it on in French to the expedition's François Labiche, who changed it into English for the captains. Their responses went back through the same cumbersome, six-language chain of translation.

Despite the obstacles, the captains were able to negotiate for fresher horses

Face-to-Face with Another Myth

The dream of a Northwest Passage had been shattered by the view of endless mountains from Lemhi Pass only a few weeks earlier. But when the Corps of Discovery met the Salish Indians, a different myth briefly flared to life.

It was nearly as old as the myth of an easy water route across the continent—and equally persistent, though more fantastic. It was said that in 1170 a Welsh prince named Madoc had discovered America, "a land unknowen . . . where he saw many strange things." Madoc had returned to Wales, the story went, recruited three thousand colonists, and taken them to the New World, landing by various accounts from Newfoundland to Florida to South America.

The "Madocians," as they were called, reportedly moved westward, assimilating with Indian people. Different versions of the tale held them responsible for the great Aztec, Mayan, and Inca cultures, and for the Mound Builders of the lower Mississippi. Even George Rogers Clark, William Clark's famous older brother, thought that the mound ruins near Kaskaskia, Illinois, were remnants of their fortifications. Always, the tribal members just over the next horizon were said to have light skin, blue eyes, blond or red hair, and a language similar to Welsh. Until they became better known, the Delawares, Tuscaroras, Shawnees, Pawnees, and Comanches—more than a dozen tribes in all—were cast in people's imaginations as the long-lost descendants of Prince Madoc.

By the late eighteenth century, speculation centered on a cluster of villages on the upper Missouri. A white American named William Bowles appeared in London, claiming to be an Indian and riveting audiences with tales of the Madocians. Excited Welshmen raised enough money to send John Evans to find them in 1795. They turned out to be the Mandans.

By the time Lewis and Clark departed St. Louis for the fabled Northwest Passage, the Welsh Indians were rumored to be living farther yet up the Missouri. Jefferson himself gave at least passing credence to the notion. Even in December 1804, while the explorers wintered with the Mandans, the latest tribe to explode the myth, a Kentucky newspaper published a fanciful report that some years earlier a Kentuckian had traveled the length of Missouri and discovered the Madocians, skin pure white, speaking proper Welsh, able to raise fifty thousand fighting men, and living in cities that spread along the river for fifty miles.

Then on September 4, 1805, in what is now Ross's Hole in western Montana, the Corps of Discovery encountered what Patrick Gass called "the whitest Indians I ever saw." Their language was different from any the explorers had ever encountered: a "brogue," Joseph Whitehouse called it; an "impediment" and a "burr on their tongue," wrote others.

For explorers already bracing themselves to cross trackless mountains where a Northwest Passage had been supposed to exist, the thought that at least *one* rumor might be true must have caused a flurry of excitement.

"Capt. Lewis took down the names of everry thing in their Language," Whitehouse wrote on September 6, "in order that it may be found out whether they are or whether they Sprang or origenated first from the welch or not." They weren't, and they hadn't. Within a few days, the expedition was struggling over the *real* mountains that had replaced the *mythic* Passage, and the notion of Welsh Indians had disappeared from the journals forever.

Lewis and Clark Meeting the Flatheads at Ross' Hole, by Charles M. Russell. The Salish spoke "the most curious language of any we have seen before," wrote John Ordway, and for a brief moment the expedition thought they might be the fabled "Madocians," long-lost descendants of a Welsh prince. Through a misinterpretation of sign language, the captains called the tribe Flatheads.

from the Salish (and determine that the Indians were not descended from a Welsh prince). The expedition moved on down the Bitterroot to a campsite south of what is now Missoula, Montana. They called the spot Travelers Rest. Here they paused to prepare the exhausted men to cross the snowy barrier still to the west of them.

> *September 10th. As our road [next] leads over a mountain to our left, our Captains conclude to Stay here this day to take observations, and for the hunters to kill meat to last us across the mountains and for our horses to rest, etc. . . . Though the day is warm, the Snow does not melt on the mountains a short distance from us. . . . The Snow makes them look like the middle of winter.*
>
> JOSEPH WHITEHOUSE

Old Toby now told them some startling news. From Travelers Rest, he said, the Missouri River and the Great Falls were only four days' travel due east.

By following the Missouri to its source, the Corps of Discovery had missed this shortcut. Instead of four days, it had taken them fifty-three.

Summer was already over. And still they had more mountains to cross—"the most terrible mountains," Sergeant Patrick Gass wrote, "that I ever beheld."

Following what is now Lolo Creek, the expedition began the ascent into the Bitterroot Mountains on September 11. Indians had told the captains that the

The Bitterroots. Crossing the mountain barrier became the expedition's severest test, an 11-day ordeal of cold, hunger, and treacherous travel. "I have been wet and as cold in every part as I ever was in my life, indeed I was at one time fearfull my feet would freeze in the thin mockersons which I wore," Clark wrote on September 16. "To describe the road of this day would be a repitition of yesterday excpt the Snow which made it much wors[e]."

crossing would take five days of hard travel, after which they would reach a broad plain on the Columbia River, which would take them to the Pacific. But Old Toby, the expedition's guide, lost the trail. Before they regained their bearings, they wandered for two days, up and down mountainsides, one man wrote, "as steep as the roof of a house."

Horses slipped and rolled down embankments. Some gave out from exhaustion. In one accident, Clark's field desk was crushed. It quickly became clear that five days would not be enough to surmount the seemingly endless jumble of peaks and valleys.

Food began running short. The men, who only recently had each been feasting on nine pounds of buffalo meat a day, started looking anywhere they could for something to eat.

September 14th. None of the hunters killed anything except 2 or 3 [grouse], on which, without a miracle it was impossible to feed 30 hungry men and upwards, besides some Indians. So Capt. Lewis gave out some portable soup, which he had along, to be used in cases of necessity. Some of the men did not relish this soup, and agreed to kill a colt; which they immediately did, and set about roasting it; and which appeared to me to be good eating.

PATRICK GASS

The Mountains which we passed to day much worst than yesterday, the last excessively bad. . . . Encamped opposit a Small Island at the mouth of a branch [of] the river. . . . We named [it] Colt killed Creek.

WILLIAM CLARK

The men ate a young horse to stave off hunger. Another night, camping without water, they melted snow and mixed it with the dried-soup concoction, packed in lead canisters, that Lewis had purchased in Philadelphia.

On the fifth day, Clark climbed to a vantage point. It was a discouraging sight. "From this mountain," he wrote, "I could observe high rugged mountains in every direction, as far as I could see."

The next day, things got even worse.

September 16th. When we awoke this morning to our great Surprize we were covred with Snow, which had fallen about 2 Inches the latter part of last night, & [it] continues a verry cold Snow Storm. Capt. Clark Shot at a deer but did not kill it. We mended up our mockasons. Some of the men without Socks, wrapped rags on their feet, and loaded up our horses and Set out without anything to eat, and proceeded on. Could hardly See the old trail for the Snow.

JOSEPH WHITEHOUSE

September 17th. The want of provisions, together with the dificu[lt]y of passing those emence mountains [has] dampened the Spirits of the party.

WILLIAM CLARK

September 18th. Some places [are] so steep and rocky that some of our horses fell backwards and rolled 20 or 30 feet among the rocks, but did not kill them. . . .

We came to the highest part of the mountain, we halted. . . . The Mountains continue as far as our eyes could extend. They extend much further than we expected.

JOHN ORDWAY

Through blinding snow they trudged up and down the rugged mountain-sides cluttered with fallen trees. Clark worried that his feet, ravaged earlier by cactus spikes and infection, would now freeze in his thin moccasins.

They killed a second colt and ate it; then a coyote, two grouse, and some crayfish they caught in a mountain stream. One meal consisted of the portable soup and some tallow candles. Another, John Ordway recorded, was "a handful or 2 of Indian peas and a little bears oil which we brought with us. We finished the last morcil of it and proceeded on, half Starved and very weak."

> *September 18th. Encamped on a bold running Creek . . . which I call Hungery Creek, as at that place we had nothing to eate.*
>
> WILLIAM CLARK

By September 19, Lewis noted that skin rashes, mild diarrhea, lack of energy, and other early signs of malnutrition had become "common" among the men. Clark and six others had been sent ahead in a desperate attempt to find food and a way out of the mountains. "I find myself growing weak for the want of food," Lewis admitted in his journal on September 21. "Most of the men complain of a similar deficiency, and have fallen off very much."

On the twenty-second, the ordeal of the Bitterroot crossing finally ended. Eleven grueling days after leaving Travelers Rest, the entire expedition staggered out of the mountains, almost more dead than alive.

Then, in their greatest hour of vulnerability and need, they encountered another Indian tribe.

———

> *Long ago when the world was young, Coyote learned that all the animals were being swallowed by a monster who dwelled on the Clearwater River. Coyote killed this monster and set free the animals inside. Then he cut the monster into pieces and threw them in all directions, as far as he could throw them. Where the pieces landed, Indian people sprang up—the Salish, the Cayuse, the Crow, the Blackfeet, the Bannocks, all of them.*
>
> *But there, on the best country of all, Coyote took the blood from the monster's heart, mixed it with water from the river, and sprinkled it on the land.*
>
> *"This," he said, "will be my greatest creation. People made from the blood of the heart will be brave and strong. You will be the Nimipu—the 'real people.'"*
>
> NEZ PERCÉ CREATION STORY

They called themselves the Nimipu—"the people"—but in sign language their name was indicated by a motion that Clark translated as "pierced nose"—the Nez Percé.

They lived along the Clearwater and Snake rivers, where they fished for salmon, harvested the rich bulbs of camas plants in the mountain meadows, and once a year—but in better weather—dispatched buffalo-hunting parties eastward over the same mountain trail the Corps of Discovery had just traveled and barely survived.

Lewis and Clark were the first white men ever to reach their homeland. In the absence of more prominent leaders, who were out on a war party, a chief named Twisted Hair and his band had to decide what to do with the weak but wealthy strangers suddenly in their midst. According to the tribe's oral tradition, some of the Nez Percé proposed killing the white men and confiscating their boxes of manufactured goods and weapons. The expedition's rifles and ammunition, in particular, would have instantly made the Nez Percé the region's richest and most powerful tribe.

But once again an Indian woman came to the Corps of Discovery's aid.

As a young girl, she had been captured by an enemy tribe on the Plains, who

Like the Shoshones and the Salish, the Nez Percé (seen here in a photograph from 1880) had never seen any white people before the Corps of Discovery emerged from the mountains, weak with hunger. At first, according to tribal history, the Nez Percé debated whether to kill or befriend the strangers.

in turn sold her to another tribe farther to the east. Eventually, she had been befriended by white people in Canada before escaping and making her way back to her own people. They called her Watkuweis—"Returned from a Far-away Country"—and for years she had told them stories about the fair-skinned people who lived toward the rising sun. She was aged and dying by the time the explorers arrived.

When she learned about possible plans to destroy the expedition, tribal tradition says, she intervened. "These are the people who helped me," she said. "Do them no hurt."

She told history about the whites and every Nez Percé listened . . . told how the white people were good to her, treated her with kindness. That is why the Nez Percés never made harm to the Lewis and Clark people. . . . We ought to have a monument to her in this far West. She saved much for the white race.

MANY WOUNDS

September 22nd. These Savages was verry glad to see us. The men, women & children ran meeting us & Seemed rejoiced to See us. We Camped near [the] village . . . [and] the natives gave us Such food as they had to eat, consisting of roots of different kinds which was Sweet and good. . . . They are much like potatoes when cooked. . . . The natives [also] gave us Some excelent fat Sammon to eat with the root or potatoe bread.

JOSEPH WHITEHOUSE

This branding iron, carrying the mark "U.S., Capt. M. Lewis," is one of the few authenticated original objects from the Lewis and Clark expedition. The men used it to mark their horses, before turning them loose with the Nez Percé herds to await the return journey. The brand was found in 1892 on an island in the Columbia River.

Twisted Hair, Clark noted, was "a cheerful man with apparent sincerity," who urged his people to provide the strangers with food. The half-starved explorers gorged themselves on salmon and camas roots. Soon, most of the men—three quarters of the expedition, by Clark's estimate—were violently ill with vomiting and diarrhea from the sudden change of diet.

Clark treated them all with doses of Rush's Thunderbolts, which only made matters worse. Out of their desperation to avoid the fish and roots, the men pleaded again for permission to butcher a horse. They enjoyed it, Joseph Whitehouse wrote, "as ever we did fat beef in the States."

Twisted Hair directed them to a grove of pon derosa pines along the Clearwater, and the men cut

The Clearwater River was the first stream whose current the expedition did not have to fight; it would speed Lewis and Clark away from the Bitterroot Mountains toward the Columbia River.

some down. But they were not yet strong enough to hollow out the thick tree trunks with their tools, Patrick Gass noted, so the chief showed them how the Nez Percé used fire to "save them from hard labor." Twisted Hair also agreed to accompany them part of the way downriver and promised that his people would look after the expedition's horse herd until their return the next spring. The men branded their horses with the words "U.S., Capt. M. Lewis," and finished work on the five small vessels that would take them the rest of the way west.

On October 7 the Corps of Discovery pushed their boats into the swift waters of the Clearwater. It had been nearly two months since they had last been on a river. Both Lewis and Clark, as well as most of the men, were still weak from the ordeal over the mountains and still suffering from dysentery.

But for the first time since leaving St. Louis, they now had the current at their back.

CHAPTER 9

O!
The Joy

October 8th. One of the canoes Struck a rock in the middle of the rapid and Swang round and Struck another rock and cracked hir So that it filled with water. The waves roared over the rocks and Some of the men could not Swim. Their they stayed in this doleful Situation untill we unloaded one of the other canoes and went and released them. 2 Indians went in a canoe to their assistance also.

JOHN ORDWAY

*T*HE CURRENT propelled them down the Clearwater, then the Snake River—"swifter," one man wrote, "than any horse could run." "We should make more portages," Clark added, "if the season was not so far advanced, and time so precious with us." But constant spills in rocky rapids kept their progress to twenty or thirty miles a day.

October 14th. Our stern canoe . . . turned broad Side [in a rapid]. The Canoe filled and Sunk. A number of articles floated out . . . the greater part of which were caught by 2 of the [other] Canoes. . . . Our loss of provisions is verry Considerable. All our roots was in the Canoe that Sunk. . . . Our loose powder was also in the Canoe. . . .

We found some Split timber, the parts of a house which the Indians had verry securely covered with Stone. . . . We have made it a point at all times not to take any thing belonging to the Indians, even their wood. But at this time we are Compelled to violate that rule and take a part of the split timber we find here . . . for firewood, as no other is to be found in any direction.

WILLIAM CLARK

They were in the semidesert of the Columbian Plain now, where less than ten inches of rain falls per year. Game was scarce. So was firewood. "The country is barren and broken," John Ordway noted. "No timber. We can scarcely get wood enough to cook a little victuals."

They bought provisions from the Indians they encountered. But at an unguarded site, for the first time on their long journey, they simply took some-

A Wishram fisherman lowers his dip net into the Columbia for salmon. With the dried fish the Wishrams operated what Clark called a "great mart of trade."

thing that belonged to the natives: a pile of house timbers for a warming fire after another river accident.

On October 16 they reached the great river of the Northwest—the Columbia.

This river is remarkably clear and crouded with salmon in maney places. . . . Salmon may be seen at the depth of 15 or 20 feet. . . . The number . . . is incrediable to say.

WILLIAM CLARK

Huge crowds of Yakima and Wanapam Indians turned out on the riverbanks to see the strangers. A group of two hundred men strode into the expedition camp, beating on drums and singing a chant of greeting. A few days later, the Walla Wallas also welcomed the explorers.

Not all of the river tribes were happy to encounter the expedition. At one Umatilla village, after watching Clark shoot down a crane, the people rushed to their mat houses as the captain and a few men approached. Clark entered one lodge uninvited.

Found 32 persons . . . in the greatest agutation, Some crying and ringing their hands, others hanging their heads. . . . They said we came from the clouds and were not men. . . . [But] as Soon as they Saw the Squar wife of the interpreter they pointed to her and . . . imediately all came out and appeared to assume new life. The sight of This Indian woman . . . confirmed those people of our friendly intentions, as no woman ever accompanies a war party of Indians in this quarter.

WILLIAM CLARK

Clark jotted down the differences between the Columbia River tribes and the Indians they had met so far. These lived in large mat houses, wore fewer clothes, and owned as many canoes as horses. And everywhere he looked, they depended on the great numbers of salmon for everything—for food, for trade, even dried salmon for fuel. At one place, Clark estimated he saw ten thousand pounds of salmon drying along the riverbank.

But despite the astounding abundance of fish, the Americans were wary of eating it.

They wanted meat.

The fish being out of season and dying in great numbers in the river, we did not think proper to use them. . . . We purchased forty dogs for which we gave articles of little value.

WILLIAM CLARK

For the remainder of their time on the Columbia—one of the world's richest fisheries—whenever other meat was unavailable the expedition subsisted on dogs. The sometimes bemused Indians sold them at least 250.

Lewis would later comment that the diet kept the men at their healthiest since leaving the buffalo country, and that he personally preferred dog meat to lean venison or elk. It was one of the few points of disagreement between the two captains. "As for my own part," Clark noted in his journal, "I have not become reconsiled to the taste of this animal."

Mount Hood had been seen and named by a British seafaring explorer in 1792, and it was marked on a map of the Pacific Coast that Lewis and Clark brought along. After crossing thousands of miles of previously uncharted territory, the sight of the snowcapped peak was proof that they were at last nearing their goal.

A Comfortable Supper

We roasted and eat a hearty supper of our venison, not having taisted a morsel before during the day; I now laid myself down on some willow boughs to a comfortable nights rest, and felt indeed as if I was fully repaid for the toil and pain of the day, so much will a good shelter, a dry bed, and comfortable supper revive the sperits of the w[e]aryed, wet and hungry traveler.

MERIWETHER LEWIS

The Corps of Discovery literally ate its way across the continent. They began their journey on a rather bland three-day rotation of salt pork and flour, salt pork and Indian meal, and corn and "voyagers grease" (lard, deer tallow, and bear fat). But by the end of the expedition— out of both curiosity and necessity—they had tasted nearly everything the new territory had to offer.

They had prairie turnips and jackrabbit; goose eggs and grouse; grapes, plums, and raspberries in season; Missouri River catfish, Rocky Mountain cutthroat trout, and sturgeon from the Columbia.

The Arikaras gave them beans and dried squash. The Mandans offered hominy and bushels of corn. Though near famine themselves, the Shoshones shared small cakes made with serviceberries and chokecherries. The Nez Percé supplied salmon and the rich root of the camas. The Clatsops sold them wappato. Sacagawea provided currants, fennel roots, wild licorice, and onions she had foraged along the trail.

Meat, however, was the staple of their diet. Elk, deer, antelope, bighorn sheep, bears, coyotes, and raccoons—all were roasted over expedition campfires. So were dogs and horses. Buffalo provided the most meat, up to nine pounds of it a day per man when it was easily available, but the captains also made at least one small meal out of a roasted prairie dog.

Lewis was the gourmand of the group, and he wrote the most vividly about the expedition's culinary adventures. (He had, after all, spent several years dining each night in the White House with Thomas Jefferson, a connoisseur who spent three thousand dollars a year on wine—five hundred dollars more than the original appropriation for Lewis and Clark's entire expedition.) Lewis listed beaver tail as among everyone's favorites and, after a lengthy description of its

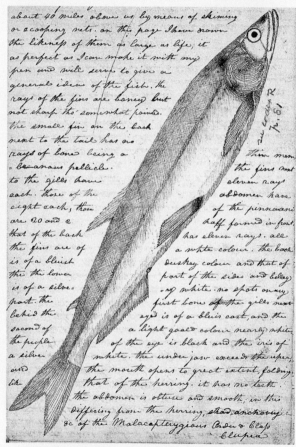

The small eulachon, or candlefish, drawn by Lewis "as large as life" in his journal on February 24, 1806. (Clark did the same thing the next day.) "I find them best when cooked in Indian stile," Lewis wrote, "which is by roasting a number of them together on a wooden spit without any previous preparation whatever. They are so fat they require no additional sauce, and I think them superior to any fish I ever tasted."

preparation, counted Charbonneau's *boudin blanc* (a stuffed buffalo intestine) as "one of the greatest delacies of the forrest." The bitterroot, however, was "naucious to my pallate," and after one helping among the Shoshones he refused to eat any more of it. (Nonetheless, the plant's scientific name, *Lewisia rediviva*, still honors the man who couldn't stomach it.)

If Clark ever took a turn as camp cook, no record exists of the event. But Lewis described in elaborate detail the suet dumplings he made from boiled buffalo meat "by way of a treat" for the exhausted men during the portage of Great Falls.

As the resident food critic at Fort Clatsop, Lewis explained that whale blubber looked like pork and "resembled the beaver or the dog in flavour," which he described as "pallitible and tender." Writing like a well-traveled restaurant reviewer, he declared the tiny candlefish "superior to any fish I ever tasted, even more delicate and lussious than the white fish of the [Great] Lakes, which have heretofore formed my standart of excellence among the fishes." Then he drew a candlefish, full scale, on a page of his journal.

And on January 1, 1806, he compared their meager New Year's dinner of spoiled meat and pounded roots to the meal he anticipated having on January 1, 1807. The future meal would be eaten with "zest" and "in the bosom of our friends," he wrote, surely thinking of elaborate dinners and fine wines in the White House once more with Jefferson. "At present," he concluded, homesickness dripping from every word, "we were content with eating our boiled Elk and wappe-toe, and solacing our thirst with our only beverage *pure water*." A weary traveler, he could at least be thankful that night for a good shelter and a dry bed.

October 18th. Saw a mountain bearing S.W., conocal form, Covered with Snow.

WILLIAM CLARK

Thirteen years earlier, in 1792, the American sea captain Robert Gray, in command of the ship *Columbia,* had sailed into the mouth of the great river and given it his vessel's name. That same year, a British explorer had gone a hundred miles up the river—far enough to see the snowcapped, volcanic peaks of the Cascade Mountains and name the biggest one Mount Hood before turning back.

Seeing the mountain on October 18 confirmed to the Corps of Discovery that they were slowly emerging out of unknown territory and back onto the maps of previous explorers.

Farther downriver, the broad Columbia began a fifty-five-mile stretch of cascades and rapids. Some required painstaking portages, accomplished with the help of the tribes who lived and fished there. But as often as possible, in their rush to the sea the expedition shot through in their canoes.

At the Columbia Gorge, where the river cuts through the Cascade Mountains, the climate changed dramatically. Suddenly the explorers observed misty forests and magnificent waterfalls like Multnomah Falls, photographed by C. E. Watkins in 1868.

I deturmined to pass through this place, notwithstanding the horrid appearance of this agitated gut swelling, boiling & whorling in every direction, which from the top of the rock did not appear as bad as when I was in it. However, we passed Safe, to the astonishment of all the Ind[ian]s . . . who viewed us from the top of the rock.

WILLIAM CLARK

They passed between the mountain ranges of the Columbia Gorge and entered an entirely different world, totally unlike the desert environment only a few miles upstream.

Here, moist Pacific winds dump more than five feet of rainfall per year. Magnificent trees, larger than any of them had ever seen in their lives, rose in dense forests on both sides. Huge flocks of waterfowl—ducks, geese, cormorants, gulls—were everywhere. "I could not sleep for the noise kept [up] by the swans [and] ducks," Clark wrote one morning. "They were immensely numerous and their cries horrid."

The Indians were different, too. Some flattened their children's heads between boards as a mark of beauty and distinction. Others wore clothes made from cedar bark. They lived in houses made of wooden planks, "the first wooden houses in which Indians have lived since we left those in the vicinity of Illinois," Clark noted. They harvested plants called wappato from the rich soil, had no horses at all, and navigated the river in elaborately carved canoes so superior to the expedition's dugouts that the captains bought one.

By late October the expedition was seeing daily signs that they were drawing nearer to the coast, where American and European ships had been trading for sea otter pelts for more than a decade. Some Indians wore blue jackets and hats obtained from sailors. Brass teakettles hung over cook fires.

November 3rd. Towards evening we met Several Indians in a canoe who were going up the River. They Signed to us that in two Sleeps we Should See the Ocean vessels and white people.

JOSEPH WHITEHOUSE

Interior of a Ceremonial Lodge, Columbia River, by Paul Kane. Having encountered Indians who lived in buffalo-hide tepees, in rounded earth lodges, and in shelters made of grass and sticks, the expedition now saw plank houses. Clark called them "the first wooden houses in which Indians have lived since we left those in the vicinity of Illinois."

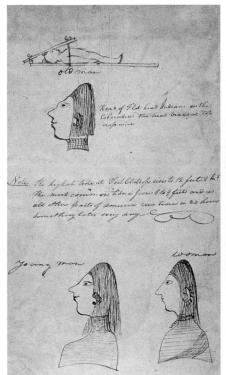

"They have all flat heads in this quarter both men and women," Clark observed along the lower Columbia. Then he drew these pictures in his journal (far left) and described in detail the way mothers pressed the heads of their babies between two boards to achieve the desired look. "This amongst those people," Clark added, "is considered as a great mark of buty." The Canadian artist Paul Kane, who visited the region in the 1840s, painted this portrait of a mother cradling her baby (left) in a similar device.

I saw the name of J. Bowmon marked or picked on a young squars left arm. They ask high prices for what they sell and say that the white people below give great prices for everything.

WILLIAM CLARK

The persons who usually visit the entrance of this river for the purpose of traffic or hunting, I believe, are either English or American. The Indians inform us they speak the same language with ourselves and give us proofs of their varacity by repeating many words of English, as musquit, powder, shot, knife, file, damned rascal, sun of a bitch, etc.

MERIWETHER LEWIS

After passing through the Columbia River Gorge, seen here in a photograph by Harold Lampert, the men began noticing evidence of tidal movement in the river's current and knew they were finally approaching the Pacific.

The river widened still further, and the men detected signs of tidal movement. The weather got continually damper.

On the morning of November 7, the expedition pushed off into a mist so dense they couldn't see across the river. An Indian (dressed in a sailor's coat)

situated ½ a mile in the river 5
& 20 Diameter. Some high
to the S.W. on the top of one
Ocian in view! O! the joy.
8th November 1805
to a point on the Star. Side a high
Country Several low
in the Bay or deep bend opposit

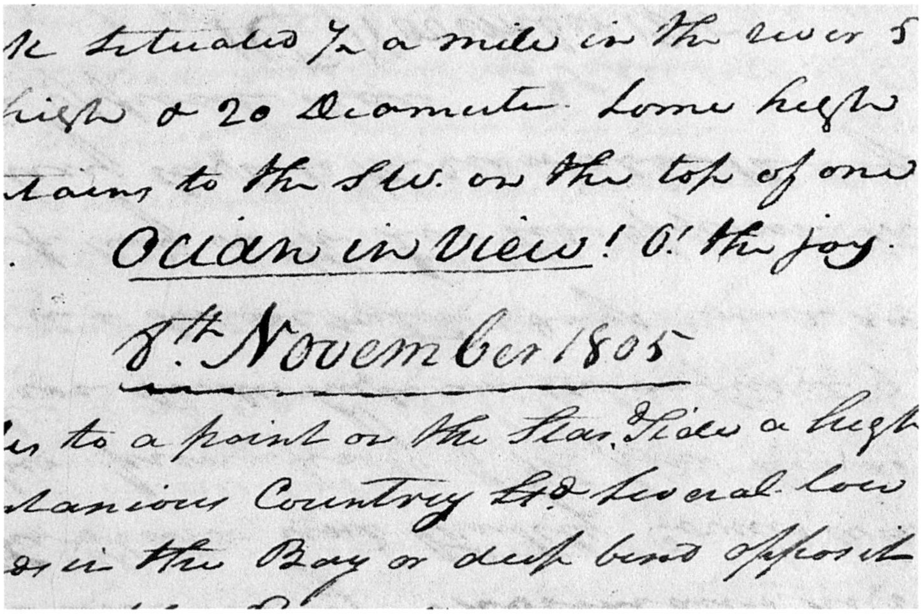

Probably William Clark's most famous journal entry, written after nineteen months of sometimes exhausting and perilous travel across the continent. On November 7, 1805, near the mouth of the Columbia, he looked up from his canoe and wrote: "*Ocian in view!* O! the joy."

was hired to pilot them through the thick fog and find the main channel. In the afternoon, a light rain fell, but the fog finally lifted. Off toward the west, the Corps of Discovery could see nothing but horizon and water.

"Ocian in view!" Clark excitedly scribbled in his field book. "O! the joy."

Since leaving St. Louis a year and a half earlier, the Corps of Discovery had considered this their principal objective—reaching the continent's farthest shore—and they all paddled furiously toward it. By day's end, though they had covered thirty-four miles, they were still on the Columbia and were forced to make camp on a small, rocky spot along the river.

A hard rain was now falling. A campfire would be difficult to start. There was no chance to hunt for food. The men's buckskin clothes were tattered and rotten from the constant dampness. But as Clark sat down that evening to record the day's events in his journals, the Corps of Discovery seems to have had something other than the miserable conditions around them in mind.

> *Great joy in camp. We are in* View *of the* Ocian, *this great Pacific Octean which we [have] been So long anxious to See, and the roreing or noise made by the waves brakeing on the rockey Shores . . . may be heard disti[n]ctly.*
>
> WILLIAM CLARK

The elation did not last long. It wasn't the ocean they were seeing and hearing, but the eastern end of Gray's Bay. They soon learned they were still more than

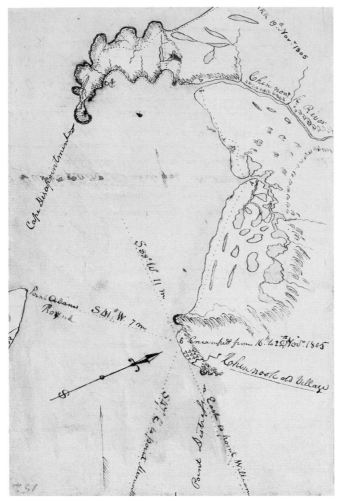

Clark's map of the mouth of the Columbia River. Cape Disappointment had been named by an earlier, seafaring explorer who could not navigate *into* the river, but it captures the same emotion of the Corps of Discovery when turbulent waves prevented them from getting *out* of the river. (Joseph Whitehouse was under the impression that the captains were the first to use that name.) Cold, wet, and hungry, they camped for more than a week at a spot Clark designates as Point Distress.

twenty miles from the coast, where they hoped to find a ship, and perhaps even a small trading post for fresh supplies. The tides, the waves, and the weather, however, made the final miles excruciatingly slow.

A huge storm was howling in from the Pacific, bringing eleven straight days of ceaseless rain, high winds, and flood tides that created rolling breakers far into the Columbia's estuary. On November 8 three of the men and Sacagawea became violently seasick as the canoes bobbed and rolled in the swells. They made a mere eight miles before setting up another cold, rainy camp on a sliver of shore. A rising tide in the middle of the night forced them awake and they rushed to save their luggage from ruin.

The next day, gigantic logs—some nearly two hundred feet long and seven feet in diameter—littered the churning water, threatening to crush the canoes. "At this dismal point we must spend another night," Clark complained, "as the wind and waves are too high to proceed." The estuary water was too salty to drink (although a few of the men had done so, paying a price for it with stomach ailments); the rain provided their only fresh water.

November 12th. It would be distressing to a feeling person to see our situation at this time, all wet and cold with our bedding etc. also wet, in a cove scercely large enough to contain us, our Baggage in a small holler about ½ a mile from us, and the canoes at the mercy of the waves & drift wood. . . . Our Situation is dangerous.

WILLIAM CLARK

For nearly three weeks, pinned down by storms and high waves among the rocks and driftwood, they huddled near the river's mouth, a few miles from the ocean they had crossed a continent to behold. It was "the most disagreeable time I have experienced," Clark wrote, "confined on a temp[estuous]

Coast, wet, where I can neither get out to hunt, return to a better Situation, or proceed on."

Scouting expeditions searched for food—and for any signs of a trading vessel from whom they could buy supplies with the voucher of credit Jefferson had given them. The members of those parties—about half of the total contingent—were the only ones who actually made it to the headlands overlooking the Pacific surf.

Our officers named this Cape, Cape disappointment, on account of not finding Vessells there.

JOSEPH WHITEHOUSE

The emence Seas and waves . . . roars like an emence fall at a distance, and this roaring has continued ever Since our arrival. . . . We [have] arrived in Sight of the Great Western (for I cannot say Pacific) Ocian, as I have not Seen one pacific day Since my arrival in its vicinity. . . . Its waters are foaming and [perpetually] breake with emence waves on the Sands and rockey coasts, tempestous and horiable.

WILLIAM CLARK

November 16th. We are now of [the] opinion that we cannot go any further with our Canoes, & think that we are at an end of our Voyage to the Pacific Ocean, and as soon as discoveries necessary are made, that we

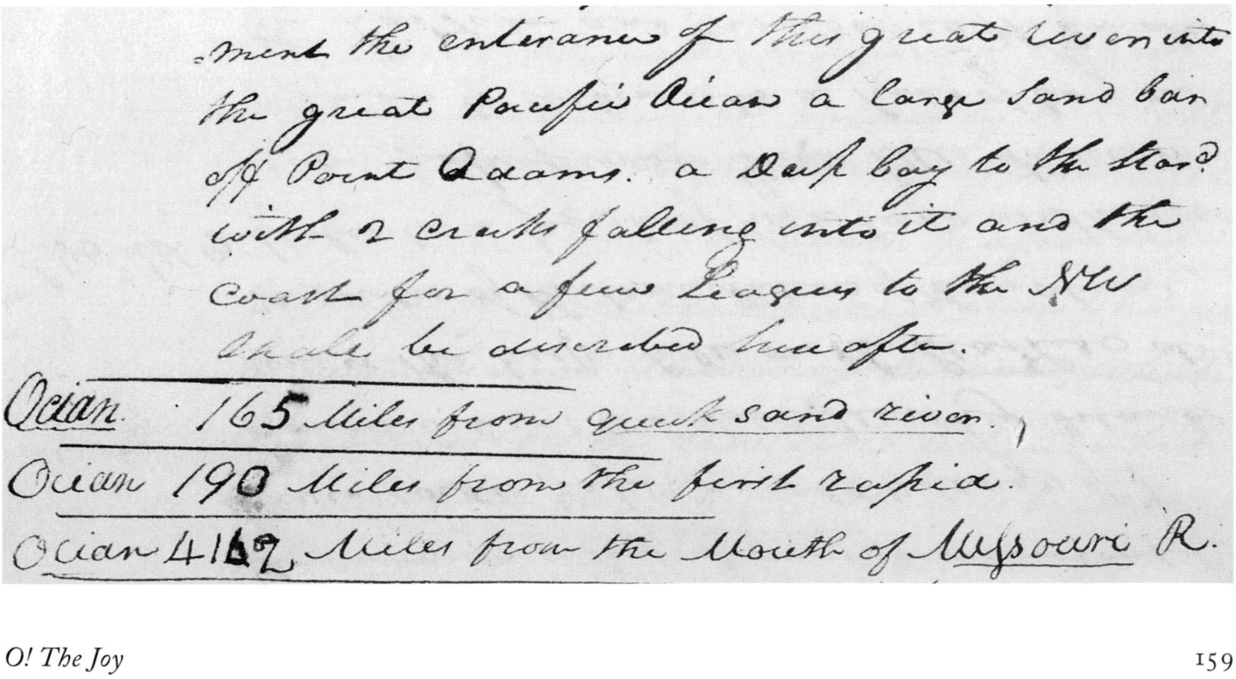

At the bottom of William Clark's notes for November 16, 1805, he calculated how far the expedition had come to reach the ocean. The "Quick Sand" River (Sandy River, east of today's Portland, Oregon) was 165 miles away, and the first rapids of the Columbia were 190 miles upriver. But the distance to the expedition's starting point at the mouth of the Missouri, Clark estimated, was a staggering 4,162 miles. That final estimate—compiled by dead reckoning during the long journey—was within 40 miles of the actual distance.

The farthest reach. Clark wondered how the Pacific got its name, "as I have not Seen one pacific day Since my arrival in its vicinity." But in making it to the ocean, they had fulfilled one of Jefferson's primary missions. The next task was finding a suitable place to spend the winter and preparing to bring word of their great achievement and discoveries back home.

shall return a short distance up the River & provide our Selves with Winter Quarters.

JOSEPH WHITEHOUSE

On November 24 the captains called everyone together. They had come 4,162 miles since leaving the Mississippi, Clark estimated. But now a decision was needed: where to spend the winter. Lewis and Clark explained the options.

Staying near the ocean meant they might yet meet a ship, get provisions, and perhaps send a man or two back to Washington by sea with word of their achievement. And being near ocean water, they could also make salt, which they would need for the return trip.

They could remain on the north side of the Columbia's mouth, though the local Chinook Indians charged what Clark considered extravagant prices for everything and there did not appear to be an abundance of game.

They could move to the south side (in what is now Oregon). Some Clatsops, who had crossed over from there, promised plenty of elk for food and clothing.

Or they could head back upriver—perhaps halfway back toward the Nez Percé—where they could count on drier weather.

Once again the captains broke with protocol in reaching an important decision. As military commanders—especially as commanders now operating in territory beyond the borders of the United States—Lewis and Clark could simply have imposed their own choice.

Instead, the Corps of Discovery would face this issue the same way it had already dealt with the grueling portage of the Great Falls, the deflating disappointment of Lemhi Pass, the biting cold and near starvation of the Bitterroot Mountains, and the rain-soaked gales of the lower Columbia. They would face it together, as a collection of diverse individuals who had molded themselves into a cohesive unit that was stronger than the sum of its particular parts. *E pluribus unum.*

One by one, the name of each member of the Corps of Discovery was called out. And each one's preference was recorded.

Clark's slave, York, was allowed to vote—nearly sixty years before slaves in the rest of America would be emancipated and enfranchised.

Sacagawea, the Indian woman, voted too—more than a century before either women or Indians were granted the full rights of citizenship.

In the end, a majority decided to cross to the south side of the Columbia. There, together, they would spend the winter with all of North America between themselves and their countrymen.

*Capt. Lewis Branded a tree with his name, Date, etc. . . . The party all
Cut the first letters of their names on different trees. . . . I marked my
name, the Day & year on an alder tree. . . . William Clark. By Land
from the U. States in 1804 & 1805.*

WILLIAM CLARK

CHAPTER 10

*Wet and
Disagreeable*

December 25th, 1805. Rainy & wet. Disagreeable weather. We all moved in to our new Fort, which our officers name Fort Clatsop after the name of the Clatsop nation of Indians who live nearest to us. The party saluted our officers by each man firing a gun at their quarters at day break this morning. They divided out the last of their tobacco among the men that used [it] and the rest they gave each a Silk hankerchief as a Christmast gift, to keep us in remembrence of it as we have no ardent Spirits. But all are in good health which we esteem more than all the ardent Spirits in the world. We have nothing to eat but poor Elk meat and no Salt to Season that with, but Still keep in good Spirits as we expect this to be the last winter that we will have to pass in this way.

JOHN ORDWAY

*I*N A SPRUCE FOREST near a small river several miles from the coast, south of what is now Astoria, Oregon, the Corps of Discovery built their winter quarters. They named it Fort Clatsop, in honor of the nearby Indian tribe.

Work was far enough along by the end of December that they could move in and celebrate Christmas. The captains distributed silk handkerchiefs and the last of the company's tobacco. Sacagawea presented Clark with two dozen white weasel tails.

The weather was rainy. The food was bad—so spoiled, Clark wrote, "that we eat it through mere necessity"—with no grog or whiskey to wash away the taste. The fleas infesting the fort, Clark added a few days later, "torment us in such a manner as to deprive us of half the nights Sleep."

In ways that no other Americans at that time could fully comprehend, the Corps of Discovery understood through hard experience just how broad the continent really was and how difficult it could be to cross. And now, having spent the year 1805 constantly on the move, making discovery after discovery, all they could do was seek shelter from the unending rains in their smoke- and flea-filled rooms, where they contemplated the yawning distance between themselves and everything they'd left behind. For the first time, the Corps of Discovery seems to have been afflicted with homesickness.

January 1st, 1806. Our repast of this day, tho' better than that of Christmass, consisted principally in the anticipation of the 1st day of January 1807, when in the bosom of our friends we hope to participate

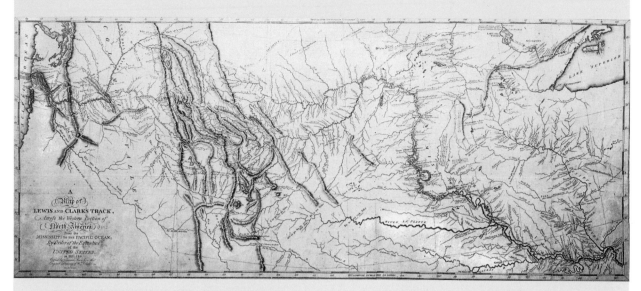

Filling in the great blank. William Clark's final map of the West (more than four feet wide in the original) was remarkable in its detail, noting places like Floyd's grave, Fort Mandan, and Fort Clatsop, and the names and estimated populations of Indian tribes. Most of all, where rumor and hope had once placed a single line of small mountains and the dream of a Northwest Passage, Clark showed for the first time a more daunting—and accurate—prospect.

Mapping the Unknown

As he stooped over a makeshift drafting table each day at Fort Clatsop, William Clark was creating a revolutionary document: his map of the West. With each line that he drew, a realistic view of the geography of North America slowly emerged from the fog of rumor, guesswork, conjecture, and wishful thinking that had been accumulating for centuries.

Two years earlier, in January 1804, Clark had surveyed maps that distilled the most up-to-date thinking about what the Corps of Discovery would encounter on its journey. A single, narrow ridge of mountains was shown, not all that distant from the Pacific. Major rivers headed in different directions from essentially the same height of land. Much of the West was simply a blank.

Using that information, Clark had estimated the distances that awaited the expedition. From St. Louis to the Mandan villages—a section already traveled and described by fur traders—Clark's estimate of 1,500 miles had been only 100 miles shy of the actual distance the explorers traveled in 1804. But from the Mandans to the Pacific, the early maps had led Clark to estimate 1,350 miles. Instead, in 1805 the Corps of Discovery had covered nearly twice that distance (2,550 miles) to reach the ocean.

At Fort Clatsop, Clark began correcting the record and filling in the blanks. Though not formally trained in cartography, he had a natural genius for it and turned out to be superb at mapmaking. Each day of the journey west, he had taken compass readings at every bend of the river or twist of the trail and used dead reckoning to note the mileage from point to point. These daily "courses and distances" were transferred to different sheets of paper (in one instance, Clark used the back of a blank certificate meant for Indian chiefs) and then transferred again onto larger strip maps that marked distinct sections of the journey.

As he compiled a master map of the West, Clark also added information about areas he had not personally seen. Fur traders along the Missouri River and at the Mandan villages were pumped for details about the big river's tributaries. And everywhere he met Indian peoples, Clark asked them for descriptions of the surrounding terrain. Some chiefs drew crude maps on hides, explaining distances not in miles but in "sleeps" (days of travel). Some sketched lines in the ashes of smoldering campfires. Others piled small heaps of dirt or sand on the earth floors of their homes to designate mountains and etched small furrows to denote the course of rivers.

With all that information—and hard-won personal experience—at his command, Clark's view from Fort Clatsop was much clearer than it had been two years earlier. The map he now drew depicted the Rockies more accurately: not as a single ridge but as a broad swath of unruly mountains not only wider but higher than those of the East and entirely distinct from two more ranges, the Cascades and the Coastals. The lengthy course of the Missouri (and many of its tributaries) finally bore some semblance to fact, and the gap between its headwaters and a navigable stream to the Columbia clearly ruled out any notion of a half-day portage.

"Lewis and Clark would return to civilization with a new image of the West," according to geographer and historian John Logan Allen. "In their new image there would be many dreams of the fertility and beauty and vastness of the West. But the dream was no longer the Passage to India."

Clark, characteristically, was more matter-of-fact about it all when he finished his work on February 14, 1806. "I compleated a *map* of the Countrey through which we have been passing from the Mississippi at the Mouth of the Missouri to this place," he wrote. "We now discover that we have found the most practicable and navigable passage across the Continent of North America." As his map so clearly demonstrated, "practicable" and "navigable" had been redefined.

in the mirth and hilarity of the day, and when with the zest given by the recollection of the present, we shall completely, both mentally and corporally, enjoy the repast which the hand of civilization has prepared for us.

MERIWETHER LEWIS

Men were put to work making candles, boiling ocean water for salt, preserving elk meat in a smokehouse, and sewing clothes from elk hides for the return trip home.

Clark labored over a new map that would replace eastern speculation with the hard facts of western geography.

Lewis wrote page after page of descriptions of animals and plants unknown to science—from the giant sitka spruce tree to the evergreen huckleberry; from ring-necked ducks and whistling swans to a small smelt—the candlefish—that the men roasted and ate whole.

In early January the boredom was broken when Indians reported that a whale had washed ashore several miles south of the salt-making camp. Clark and a few others decided to go see it and get some blubber to replenish the dwindling food supply. Sacagawea begged to go along.

With an entire continent between themselves and their homes, the explorers spent the soggy winter of 1805–1806 within the close confines of Fort Clatsop, named for the coastal Indian tribe that lived nearby. This reconstruction at Fort Clatsop National Memorial was built on the original site, using as a guide a floor plan Clark sketched on the cover of his elkskin journal.

January 6th. The Indian woman was very im[patient] to be permitted to go with me, and was therefore indulged. She observed that she had traveled a long way with us to see the great waters, and that now that [a] monstrous fish was also to be seen, she thought it very hard that she could not be permitted to see either.

WILLIAM CLARK

The two-day trip took Clark's party along the rocky coast to a spectacular site overlooking what is now Cannon Beach—"the grandest and most pleasing

prospects which my eyes ever surveyed," he said, "inoumerable rocks of emence Sise out at a great distance from the Shore and against which the Seas brak with great force gives this Coast a most romantic appearance."

But when they reached the whale, the Tillamook Indians had already stripped the carcass of any meat or blubber. All that was left was a skeleton, which Clark dutifully measured out at 105 feet long. Using his supply of trade goods, he bought three hundred pounds of blubber and a few gallons of whale oil from the Tillamooks. Then they all headed back to Fort Clatsop and its dreary routine.

January 17th. Continued stormey all last night, and this morning Wet & rainey.

JOSEPH WHITEHOUSE

January 18th. No . . . occurrence worthy of relation took place [today]. The men are still much engaged in dressing skins in order to cloath themselves and prepare for our homeward journey.

MERIWETHER LEWIS

January 19th. This morning we had moderate showers of rain.

JOSEPH WHITEHOUSE

The Captured Whale, by
Edward S. Curtis. Hoping to
augment the expedition's food
supply, Clark led a small group
down the coast to where the
Indians had reported a beached
whale (indicated by the
drawing on his map, right).
After buying 300 pounds of
blubber, Clark thanked
"providence for directing the
whale to us; and think him
much more kind to us than he
was to jonah, having sent this
Monster to be *Swallowed by us*
in Sted of *Swallowing of us* as
jonah's did."

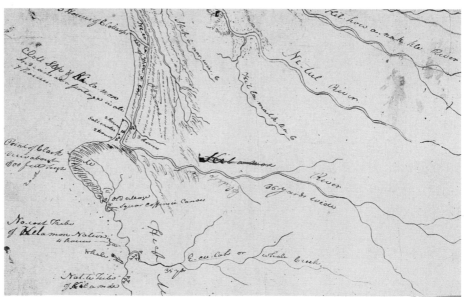

January 20th. Wet & rainey weather during the whole of this day. Nothing material occured worth mentioning.

JOSEPH WHITEHOUSE

February 22nd. Our sick consisting of Gibson, Bratton, Sergt. Ordway, Willard and McNeal are all on the recovery. We have not had as many sick at any one time since we left [the Mississippi]. The general complaint seams to be bad colds and fevers, something I beleive of the influenza.

MERIWETHER LEWIS

March 3rd. No movement of the party today worthy of notice. Every thing moves on in the old way, and we are counting the days which seperate us from the 1st of April and which bind us to Fort Clatsop.

MERIWETHER LEWIS

Lewis's weather table for January 1806 tells a dreary story. The sun was seldom seen for more than a few hours, and the phrases "rained incessantly all night" and "rained the greater part of night" describe the soggy winter.

Some of the men busied themselves sewing moccasins—exactly 338 pairs, according to Patrick Gass, who also kept a precise count of other items: 131 elk and 20 deer killed during the winter; only twelve days in which it didn't rain, and of those, a mere six with clear skies. On March 7, when their supply of tobacco ran out, Gass noted that twenty-six of the men were now without anything but the bark of crab trees to satisfy their chewing and smoking habits.

The Clatsops and Chinooks made regular visits, but they were not as welcome as the Mandans and Hidatsas had been at Fort Mandan. The captains considered their new neighbors somehow not quite so trustworthy and complained often about the sharp bargaining of these coastal Indians. At Fort Mandan, Indians often remained overnight, just as many of the explorers often stayed in the earth lodge villages. At Fort Clatsop, strict orders were issued restricting access to the fort and requiring all Indians to be outside the palisades by nightfall; and there is no record of any extended visit at Clatsop or Chinook villages.

March 15th. We were visited this afternoon by Delashelwilt, a Chinook Chief, his wife and six women of his nation, which the old ba[w]d had brought for market. This was the same party that had communicated the venerial to so many of our [men] in November last, and of which they have finally recovered. I therefore gave the men a particular charge with rispect to them, which they promised me to obey.

MERIWETHER LEWIS

On March 16 Lewis took stock of the remaining trade items, which the expedition would need on the return trip to barter for horses and food. The entire supply, he noted, could be held in two handkerchiefs.

At the same time, a Chinook chief and band of women had arrived at the fort, offering to exchange sexual favors for expedition goods. Back in November, the men had traded knives and tools with the same Indian women at such an alarming rate that the captains had taken the hardware away and handed out ribbons for the bartering. Now, even ribbons were in short supply. Lewis, believing that his mercury treatments had finally cured the men of the venereal disease they had contracted, made them promise—for both health and economic reasons—to resist this time.

Lewis and Clark occasionally complained about the Indians of the Pacific Northwest, seen here in photographs (right and opposite) by Edward S. Curtis. "They are great higlers in trade and if they conceive you anxious to purchase will be a whole day bargaining for a handfull of roots," Lewis wrote. He grudgingly gave up one of his lace-adorned uniform coats for an Indian boat he admired. Clark never mentioned the price of a hat he purchased, woven out of cedar bark and bear grass with such precision "that it Casts the rain most effectually."

*March 17th. Old Delashelwilt and his
women still remain. They have formed a
camp near the fort and seem to be determined
to lay close sege to us, but I beleive notwithstanding every effort of their wining graces,
the men have preserved their constancy to the
vow of celibacy which they made on this
occasion to Capt. C. and myself.*

MERIWETHER LEWIS

———

Back in the East, President Jefferson was wel-
coming a delegation of Missouri, Oto, Arikara,
and Yankton Sioux chiefs who had met Lewis
and Clark more than a year earlier. Jefferson
thanked them for their assistance to Lewis,
whom he called "our beloved man," promised
trade goods from American companies, and
told them his hope was "that we may all live together as one household."

The Indians responded with both kind
words about Lewis and concern for their own
future.

*We have seen the beloved man, we shook
hands with him and we heard the words you put in his mouth. We wish
him well. . . . We have him in our hearts, and when he will return we
believe that he will take care of us, prevent our wants and make us
happy.*

*[But when] you tell us that your children of this side of the
Mississippi hear your word, you are mistaken, since every day they raise
their tomahawks over our heads. . . . Tell your white children on our
lands to follow your orders and to do not as they please, for they do not
keep your word.*

The President wrote a brief note to Lewis's brother and mother telling
them he was confident that the expedition was going well. But to someone else,
Jefferson confided, "We have no certain information of Captain Lewis since he
left Fort Mandan."

And in Santa Fé, the Spanish governor of New Mexico was organizing another attempt to intercept the American expedition. This one would include five hundred troops, one hundred Indian allies, and a packtrain of more than two thousand animals—the largest Spanish military party the Great Plains had ever seen, set to depart Santa Fé as soon as winter was over.

————

The Indians told the captains that ships often arrived on the coast to trade, and Jefferson had instructed Lewis to send back a few men and a copy of the journals by sea if possible. But while the expedition was at Fort Clatsop, no vessels appeared. After a long winter of boredom, homesickness, and rain, the entire Corps of Discovery set off for home the same way they had come.

March 20th. Altho' we have not fared sumptuously this winter and spring at Fort Clatsop, we have lived quite as comfortably as we had any reason to expect we should; and have accomplished every object which induced our remaining at this place except that of meeting with the traders who visit the entrance of this river. . . . Many of our men are still complaining of being unwell; Willard and Bratton remain weak, principally I beleive for the want of proper food. I expect when we get

under way we shall be much more healthy. It has always had that effect
on us heretofore.

MERIWETHER LEWIS

All winter, Lewis and Clark had hoped a trading vessel would show up, so they could replenish their supplies and, even more important, send back a copy of their journals, as insurance that word of their accomplishments and discoveries would reach Jefferson, even if they themselves did not. But during their five long months on the coast, no ship was sighted.

By late March they could wait no longer.

The captains wrote notes summarizing the expedition's achievements, sketched a rough map of the connection between the Missouri and Columbia, and listed the names of every member of the Corps of Discovery. They tacked one such note to the wall of Fort Clatsop and gave others to the Indians, with instructions to present it to the captain of any ship that arrived later in the spring.

The object of this list is, that through the medium of some civilized
person who may see the same, it may be made known to the informed
world, that the party consisting of the persons whose names are hereunto
annexed, and who were sent out by the government of the U'States in
May 1804 to explore the interior of the Continent of North America, did
penetrate the same by way of the Missouri and Columbia Rivers, to the
discharge of the latter into the Pacific Ocean, where they arrived on the
14th of November 1805, and from whence they departed the 23rd day of
March 1806 on their return to the United States by the same rout they
had come out.

MERIWETHER LEWIS AND WILLIAM CLARK

It was time to go home.

FINDING SACAGAWEA

ERICA FUNKHOUSER

Three Forks of the Missouri River, July 28th, 1805. Our present camp is precisely on the spot that the Snake [Shoshone] Indians were encamped at the time the Minnetares of the Knife R. first came in sight of them five years since. . . . O[u]r Indian woman was one of the female prisoners taken at that time; tho' I cannot discover that she shews any immotion of sorrow in recollecting this event, or of joy in being again restored to her native country; if she has enough to eat and a few trinkets to wear I beleive she would be perfectly content anywhere.

MERIWETHER LEWIS

Enough to eat and a few trinkets to wear . . . This is all there is to go on. Sacagawea kept no journal. She wrote no letters. No oral tradition preserved her story in her own words. If I wanted to learn something about the young Shoshone woman who traveled with the Lewis and Clark expedition, I had to begin here, with the captains' journals, in which Sacagawea is mentioned about three dozen times. With a few exceptions, the captains do not record Sacagawea's appearance, her language, or her mannerisms; they do not describe her temperament or her strengths and weaknesses or venture to guess what she is feeling.

Perfectly content anywhere . . . Sacagawea, her husband, and their baby slept in the same tent as Lewis and Clark for much of the voyage, yet the captains do not comment on this domestic arrangement. And what about the baby? Jean-Baptiste was two months old when the expedition began; Sacagawea carried him all the way across the country and back again. When she rode through rough rapids in a dugout canoe, she rode *with her baby;* when food was scarce, both she *and the baby* went hungry. Yet the journals of Lewis and Clark tell us almost nothing about Sacagawea's unique burden.

It is precisely this absence of information, the historian's nemesis, that drew me, as a poet, closer to the subject.* All the tantalizing gaps, like missing

* See the complete "Birdwoman," in *Sure Shot and Other Poems* (Houghton Mifflin, 1992), by Erica Funkhouser; poem passages excerpted with permission.

Nez Perce Babe, by Edward S. Curtis

Hidatsa Mother, by Edward S. Curtis

pieces from a prized mosaic, shimmered and murmured, coaxing me closer. If I paid close enough attention to the little we know of Sacagawea, would it be possible to discover, in my own imagination, a credible voice for this historical mystery? It could not be the factual voice—that was irrevocably lost—but it could be a voice with a truth of its own.

Let's return to the above journal excerpt. The kidnapping to which Lewis refers took place when Sacagawea was a girl of about twelve. We know that she had been foraging with others from her tribe when they were surprised by a Hidatsa raiding party. Sacagawea's mother was killed, and Sacagawea was taken by a Hidatsa brave, who brought her home to his village, a ride of several days. Possibly through a gambling match, Sacagawea became

the property of Toussaint Charbonneau, a forty-five-year-old French Canadian fur trader, who took her as one of his common-law wives. When Lewis and Clark met her during the winter of 1805, Sacagawea was a young woman of about seventeen and about to give birth to her first child.

Five months later, after five years among the Hidatsas and three months traveling with Lewis and Clark, Sacagawea found herself once again at the precise location where she had been kidnapped. I don't doubt that, as Lewis writes, she showed no "immotion" but that doesn't mean she felt none! What *had* she been feeling as she walked west with the Corps of Discovery? Where did she place herself in her own story, I wondered. As victim? As heroine? How did she speak to herself about all that was happening? What confluence of past and present experiences and emotions informed her vision as she and her child walked west toward the rivers where her own childhood had been stolen from her?

It was this interior life I was after, and the only way to get at it was through the rich imagery of the journals. Whatever the captains had seen, Sacagawea had probably seen; but what she made of those sights would have been an altogether different story. The task turned me, in essence, into a traveler. Starting from the observations of Lewis and Clark, I journeyed backward, as if through a telescope, into the imagined eye of a different beholder, Sacagawea, who was on a voyage unlike that of any other member of the expedition. She was not, like Lewis and Clark, charged with scientific purpose; she was not one of the Americans who now owned this new land; she was not, in the classic sense of the American pioneer, claiming alien territory; she was, at least in the first few months of the journey, walking home. As the newcomers Lewis and Clark walked west toward a dream, Sacagawea was making a return voyage to a land brimming with memories of childhood.

Mother and Child (Apsaroke Crow), by Edward S. Curtis

On the Missouri Between the Milk River and the River That Scolds All Others, May 1805

If the single quill of cloud in the sky
decided to come back to earth
it would find no place to land.
On both sides of the river
buffalo, antelope, and elk crowd together,
watching us work our way upstream.
The water is black with beaver.
We feast on the tail and the liver
until I forget I have ever been hungry.

What stands out, above all, in the captains' journals is Sacagawea's steadfastness and courage and, increasingly, her confidence and independence. From the captains' records, it's clear she viewed herself neither as a victim nor as a heroine. Only a month after she joined the expedition, in May 1805, Lewis took the time to record in his journal Sacagawea's "fortitude and resolution": the white pirogue had capsized, and the quick-thinking Sacagawea had caught most of the articles that had washed overboard, including the tin box that contained the captains' journals. What does this tell us about her? That, despite the baby on her back, she was attentive to and involved in every aspect of the expedition. She was keenly aware of both its higher purposes and the day-today dynamics of a large group traveling together—the persistent need for food, shelter, dry clothing, and reliable equipment. I envisioned that by May, Sacagawea had begun to see herself as a vital member of this community on the move, even to the point of having preferences among her traveling companions.

> I can already smell the pleasure
> on Clark's fingers as he spreads the dry pages,
> dips his pen in the shiny black ink,
> barely dry himself before he takes up the story
> of this evening's misfortunate squall.
>
> After supper, Cruzat, my favorite Frenchman,
> will play songs on his fiddle.
> In front of the fire, all of the men
> will dance in each other's arms
> like trees grown a long time together.
>
> On and off the river, we move as one people.
> When one of us falters, the others take on
>   more.
> When one of us swells with laziness or pride,
> the rest bare their teeth like coyotes.

By June, when Sacagawea became ill with fever, her importance to the expedition was well established. Clark noted in his journal that "our Indian woman [is] sick & low spirited"; he has been treating her with bark and laudanum. Lewis is concerned as well, writing that Sacagawea is "extremely ill and much reduced by her indisposition," adding that she is their "only dependence for a friendly negociation with the Snake Indians."

About a month later, the Corps of Discovery reached Three Forks, the spot from which the young Sacagawea had been kidnapped. Despite Lewis's description of her lack of "immotion of sorrow in recollecting this event," I couldn't help seeing this moment as a turning point for Sacagawea. The landscape itself must have resonated with meaning; it had been here, on these very shoals, that Sacagawea had seen her mother killed and where she herself had been kidnapped.

Then she had been a girl of about twelve, with no experience of any way of life other than that of the Shoshone. Now, five years later, she found herself beside the same stream. As she stood in this place which was for her both a personal and a tribal landmark, how could she help but ask herself what of that twelve-year-old Shoshone girl still remained? And what did not? Questions about her own identity must have converged with questions about her tribe. Were any of her family members still alive? Were there any Lemhi Shoshones left, and if so, would they recognize her? Would they welcome her return? Sacagawea knew Lewis and Clark were relying on her to secure horses from the Shoshones, but what if the Shoshones didn't comply? Would she be forced to take sides? How could this momentous return to her homeland have failed to stir up every fragment of Sacagawea's consciousness?

Already in her brief life, she had "belonged" to the Shoshones, the Hidatsas, a French Canadian fur trader, and, in a different sense, to Lewis and Clark. Was Sacagawea a lost Shoshone or a misplaced adopted Hidatsa or the slave-wife of a French Canadian with a half-breed son or the traveling companion of two white American captains? To whom would she "belong" from this point on? When I imagined her answering these questions, I couldn't help seeing her step into the river from which she had been stolen, reentering as fully as possible that previous experience in order to comprehend where it had taken her and where she must now go.

Now, as I bathe in the water of my childhood,
I rise like a stream in spring,
impatient for new destinations.
I scrape the white clay from the bank,
traverse fallen branches.
I am looking for the rivers
that do everything they can
to reach the Big Lake That Stinks.
Rivers where the sun lies down every night,
the lucky ones that carry the sun
back to the place from which it is possible
to rise up again in the morning.

By the time the baby and I are dry
I know what I will say to the captains.
I will tell them I have traveled far
in my thoughts, found room in my parfleche
for much I was never asked to carry.

Once, it was true, the only land
I could see myself entering was my old home
surrounded by mountains.
Now, without straining my eyes,
I see Sacagawea following many strange rivers
into the new world that has never heard of her
or any of the men in her party.

Within weeks, Sacagawea was reunited with the Shoshones. Lewis described the reunion as "really affecting," and in his edition of the journals, Nicholas Biddle wrote that Sacagawea began "to dance and show every mark of the most extravagant joy" when she first laid eyes on her people. Her reunion with her cousin, who had also been taken during the Hidatsa raid, was "ardent." When the captains and the Shoshone leaders sat down to confer, Sacagawea was sent for to begin interpreting. Just as the conference began, she recognized that Chief Cameahwait was her brother, and, we're told, "she jumped up, ran & embraced him, & threw her blanket over him and cried profusely."

Sacagawea must have been anticipating this reunion for weeks, even years, and now here she was, at last, reunited with her own family. Whatever she might have feared, the Shoshones had welcomed her back warmly; they wanted her to stay with them rather than continue on with Lewis and Clark. While she obviously reveled in their company, Sacagawea nevertheless decided not to remain with the Shoshones. Instead, she insisted on traveling west with the expedition, knowing full well the hardships she and her child would inevitably face.

Why did she decide to keep going? I imagine that at this point in the expedition, Sacagawea must have realized that she was not simply on a journey back to her homeland. She was on a different, larger journey now—Lewis and Clark's journey. She had got caught up in the spirit of discovery, and she wanted to see the expedition through to its end; she didn't want to stop here. There's stubbornness in this, but there's also loyalty.

Between April and August, it seems, Sacagawea had developed a relationship with her fellow travelers, and now she wanted to stay with them until their journey had been completed. I sense that her weeks among the Shoshones had demonstrated to Sacagawea that, for the moment at least, she belonged to a new and different tribe, the Corps of Discovery. Despite the early onset of winter and the captains' concerns about Jean-Baptiste crossing the mountains, Sacagawea insisted on continuing west with the expedition.

Clark looks up from his packing.
For the first time since we started walking
he and Charbonneau agree on one matter—
Sacagawea and her baby will be safer
if they stay here with the Shoshone.
Running Deer has made a place for us in her hut.

I hold a council with Baptiste,
the one who will starve if I am stupid.
Speak up now, *demi-lune*, I warn him,
if you fear your mother lacks the strength
to carry her halfblood over the Bitterroots.
He crawls into my lap and falls asleep.

"We figured as much," says Lewis,
a smile working its way over his face.
And then Clark hands me the reins
of a fine spotted pony.
What do you think of this, Baptiste?
From now on, your mother's good feet,
like your own, will journey
without touching the ground.

The trip through the Bitterroots, as anticipated, was arduous; nearly all the men were cold and sick and hungry. Hunger was nothing new to Sacagawea, and it's noteworthy that neither she nor the baby are mentioned in the journals during this time; apparently they suffered neither more nor less than the others. At last the expedition reached the mouth of the Columbia, where, on November 24, 1805, the famous vote was held in which Sacagawea and the black slave, York, were given equal say with the other members of the expedition about where to establish winter quarters.

Again, what the captains do not say in their journals becomes noteworthy: neither one makes a point about including Sacagawea and York in the vote, apparently taking for granted their right to participate equally in this first truly democratic moment in American history. I imagine that this experience served to confirm Sacagawea's sense of affinity with the Corps of Discovery. Lewis and Clark had given her more decision-making power than she had ever enjoyed among the Shoshones or the Hidatsas or, it's safe to assume, in her marriage to Charbonneau.

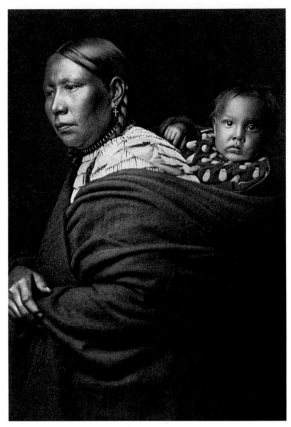

Sioux Woman with Papoose, by Edward S. Curtis

Camp was established at Fort Clatsop, where, on Christmas Day, Clark recorded in his journal a gift from Sacagawea of "two Dozen white weazils tails," a gift that figures like a brilliant dry white icon against the prevailing damp of the Northwest Coast winter. The gift appears to have been a surprise; if Lewis or anyone else received anything from Sacagawea, we're not told as much. Although Sacagawea had previously dug up roots and gathered wild plants for the men to eat, this is the first personal exchange of which the captains write. Did Sacagawea trap the weasels herself? Did she prepare the tails in secret? Did Clark give her something in return?

Although we can't definitively answer these

questions, asking them helps to prepare us for the Sacagawea that we next meet in Lewis's journal entry of January 6, 1806. Parties of salt-makers had been traveling back and forth between Fort Clatsop and the Pacific. When one group returned home with reports of a beached whale, Clark assembled a group of men to go down to the water to collect meat and blubber. Sacagawea wanted to go, too. In his journal Lewis noted, "The Indian woman was very impo[r]tunate to be permitted to go, and was therefore indulged; she observed that she had traveled a long way with us to see the great waters, and that now that monstrous fish was also to be seen, she thought it very hard she could not be permitted to see either (she had never yet been to the Ocean)."

What is the origin of this sudden boldness? Obviously Sacagawea must have been feeling more comfortable with the captains, at least with Clark. Perhaps she was motivated in part by boredom and restlessness, even jealousy. After all, between the fleas and spoiled food and the relentless rain, everyone had been going stir-crazy at Fort Clatsop; and for weeks the salt-makers had been returning to camp with talk of the ocean.

Now Sacagawea felt it was her turn to see the Pacific. Reaching this ocean had been, after all, the whole point of the expedition. I imagined that other desires were at work as well. The Pacific, about which the Shoshones had heard from other tribes, was part of her mythology. All the rivers in her homeland west of the Continental Divide found their way here eventually; why shouldn't she? And why shouldn't her little boy, now nearly a year old, complete his journey as well? She wanted to stand on the beach and touch the water herself, not just hear about it from the others.

The Sacagawea I saw arriving at the Pacific at last was no longer simply a young Shoshone; she was Lewis and Clark's *Indian woman,* away from her native tribe; she was also a frontier mother, but rather than being framed in the dark doorway of a sod house or a skin tepee, she was a woman without a house, without even a prairie.

More than any woman who came before or after her, Sacagawea seemed to me to belong to the whole unconquered landscape of the American West, and here she was at the far end of that land. I couldn't imagine that she would have reached the Pacific without wanting to enter it herself, with her son.

Like every member of the party, she must have had to abandon some piece of her tribal identity and some measure of her independence in order to join wholly in the spirit of the expedition. Still, the Sacagawea I saw arriving at the Pacific was one who felt she belonged not just to the Corps of Discovery but to the whole vast landscape she had traversed.

For once I was not hungry.
Not in a hurry to get anywhere.
The sun that had been hiding for so long
played among the pebbles.
I let Baptiste wade in the yellow foam.
Put his nose in the water
so he would never forget its stink.

Then I lay down in the sand beside the sea
    creature
and saw I could do so twenty more times
and still not reach the end of its tail.
I invited myself into its belly.
Ai! To stand inside another animal
when you are neither dead nor waiting to be
    born.

I took the hands of Baptiste and showed him a
    dance.
He moved with the sun on his shoulders.

I left him with Charbonneau,
who was making big talk
to the pretty Killamuck guide.

I said goodbye for a while
and walked to the edge of the water.
There was no thought of crossing or following,
none of the business surrounding rivers.
I knew I would stay with the others
until it was time to walk back.

For today I had less on my mind than the plovers
running back and forth with the waves.

Beyond them the green-black water
showed us nothing but the top of her head.

Think of her people, I said to myself,
their wisdom and stature.
Nearly every stream I ever crossed
is looking for this water,
and now I am entering it myself—
Sacagawea, Birdwoman, Boat Launcher,
one of the braided waves,
one of the silver ribbons
riding the crest of the waves.

CHAPTER 11

*See Our
Parents
Once More*

March 23rd, 1806. The rain Seased and it became fair about meridian, at which time we loaded our canoes, & at 1 P.M. left Fort Clatsop on our homeward bound journey.

JOHN ORDWAY

O N   M A R C H 23, 1806, after presenting Fort Clatsop to the neighboring Indians, the expedition slid its boats out onto the Columbia once again and pushed off for the United States.

So anxious were they to be on the move once more that they violated their rule guiding conduct with Indians a second time. On the way west, they had taken wood from an unoccupied Indian dwelling without paying for it. Now, needing an extra canoe, they simply stole one from the Clatsops as they left.

Going against the river's current proved maddeningly slow. The spring run of salmon had yet to start, and food was a problem. Tribes along the lower river charged high prices, crowded and jostled the men during portages, and sometimes pilfered things: a tomahawk, an ax—even Lewis's Newfoundland dog, recovered only after a two-mile chase and physical threats.

April 11th. Many of the natives crouded about the bank of the river where the men were engaged in taking up the canoes; one of them had the insolence to cast stones down . . . at the men. . . . These are the greatest thieves and scoundrels we have met with. . . . I hope that the friendly interposition of [their] chief may prevent our being compelled to use some violence with these people; our men seem well-disposed to kill a few of them.

MERIWETHER LEWIS

Lewis in particular seems to have become short-tempered. When his dog disappeared, he was prepared to burn down an Indian village if it wasn't

Without a supply of trade goods, the captains exchanged medical services with the Indians for food. Sore eyes were the most common complaint, Lewis wrote, and "my friend Capt. C. is their favorite phisician." One Indian gave him a "very eligant grey mare" for a vial of eyewater, while others provided dogs for the explorers to eat.

returned. He reprimanded Alexander Willard "more severely than had been usual with me," he admitted, for neglecting something at camp. And after an Indian took a piece of metal from a canoe pole, Lewis slapped him several times—"the first act of the kind," Patrick Gass confided in his journal, "that had happened during the expedition."

In his own journal, Lewis consoled himself that the rising river waters slowing their progress must mean that the snows were melting on the mountains, "that icy barier which seperates me from my friends and Country, from all which makes life esteemable." Then, as a personal reminder, he added, "Patience, patience."

Dismayed at what seemed a snail's pace on the river, they sold their canoes and bought horses with their remaining trade goods. The men were back on a diet of dogs again, and the captains had to figure out a way to pay for the meat. To their surprise, they learned that Clark had acquired a reputation as a healer among the Indians on the westward journey; now they made the most of it.

May 5th. Last fall . . . Capt. C. gave an indian man some . . . linniment to rub his knee and thye for a pain. . . . The fellow soon after recovered and has never ceased to extol the virtues of our medicines and the skill of my friend Capt. C. as a phisician. . . . In our present situation I think it pardonable to continue this deseption for they will not give us any provision without compensation. . . . We had several applications to assist their sick, which we refused unless they would let us have some dogs or horses to eat.

MERIWETHER LEWIS

May 6th. We received a second horse for medecine & proscription to a little girl with the rhumitism, whome I bathed in w[a]rm water and anointed her a little with balsom [resin]. . . . I was busily imployed for several hours this morning in administering eye water to a crowd of applicants. We once more obtained a plentiful meal, much to the comfort of all the party.

WILLIAM CLARK

*While at dinner, an indian fellow very impertinently threw a poor half
starved puppy nearly into my plait by way of derision for our eating
dogs, and laughed very heartily at his own impertinence. I was so
provoked at his insolence that I caught the puppy and threw it with great
violence at him and struck him in the breast and face, siezed my tomahawk and shewed him by signs if he repeated his insolence I would
tommahawk him. The fellow withdrew, apparently much mortifyed, and
I continued my repast* on dog *without further molestation.*

MERIWETHER LEWIS

Clark dispensed vials of eyewash and linament oil, lanced boils, and treated
Indians for wounds, colds, rheumatism, broken arms, and bad backs. Some
days, he had more than forty patients lined up to exchange food for medical
attention.

By early May they were back with Twisted Hair and the Nez Percé, and
eager to move farther east over the Bitterroots. But the mountains were still
covered with snow, and the Indians said it would be at least a month before the
trail was passable.

May 7th. This is unwelcom inteligence to men confined to a diet of horsebeef and roots, and who are as anxious as we are to return to the fat plains of the Missouri and thence to our native homes.

MERIWETHER LEWIS

Once again the Nez Percé befriended the explorers, who had been reduced to trading the brass buttons from their uniforms for roots and bread. A chief provided them with horses to eat—and refused any payment. There were dances and celebrations, and a tribal council meeting at which the Nez Percé promised always to stay at peace with the United States.

[The chief] said that the whitemen might be assured of their warmest attachment and that they would always give them every assistance in their power; that they were poor, but their hearts were good.

I think we can justly affirm, to the honor of this people, that they are the most hospitable, honest and sincere people that we have met with in our voyage.

MERIWETHER LEWIS

The captains made the most of their time with the Nez Percé, as they waited for the snows to recede on the nearby mountains. Lewis studied the Indians' method of gelding their horses and declared it "preferable to that practiced by ourselves." Clark drew up an inventory of "Indian Nations West of the Rocky Mountains," based on what the expedition had both seen and been told; he estimated their numbers at nearly a hundred thousand. And to get the men in shape for what they knew would be a difficult mountain crossing, Lewis and Clark turned to games, including one called "base," a precursor of baseball.

June 8th. Several foot races were run this evening between the indians and our men. . . . When the racing was over the men divided themselves into two parties and played prison base, by way of exercise which we wish the men to take previously to entering the mountains. In short, those who are not hunters have had so little to do that they are geting reather lazy and slouthfull. After dark, we had the violin played and danced for the amusement of ourselves and the indians.

MERIWETHER LEWIS

After five weeks of waiting, and despite the Nez Percé's warnings that it was still too early, they started out toward the Bitterroots. "Every body seems anxious to be in motion," Lewis noted, "convinced that we have not now any time to delay, if the calculation is to reach the United States this season. This I am detirmined to accomplish if within the compass of human power."

Even now I shudder with the expectation of great dificuelties in passing those Mountains, from the debth of snow and the want of grass sufficient [for] our horses.

WILLIAM CLARK

But at the higher elevations, they ran into snowbanks twelve feet deep. "Here was winter with all its rigors," Lewis marveled on June 17. "The air was

While the expedition waited more than a month for the snows to melt in the Bitterroots, the Nez Percé provided food and friendship—and played a game of "base" with the men. This picture was taken by Enoch Reeves in 1906, exactly one hundred years after Lewis called the Nez Percé "the most hospitable, honest and sincere people that we have met with in our voyage."

cold, my hands and feet were benumbed." After two torturous days, they had to turn back. To proceed on, Lewis admitted, would be "madness." This was the first time during the entire expedition that "we have ever been compelled to retreat or make a retrograde march," he added. "The party were a good deel dejected, tho' not as much so as I had apprehended they would have been."

They waited another week in the foothills, then tried again, this time with some Nez Percé guides.

June 27th. The day was pleasant throughout; but it appeared to me somewhat extraordinary, to be traveling over snow six or eight feet deep in the latter end of June. The most of us, however, had saved our socks, as we expected to find snow in these mountains.

PATRICK GASS

June 30th. Decended the mountain to Travellers rest, leaveing these tremendious mountains behind us, in passing of which we have experienced cold and hunger of which I shall ever remember. . . . Our food was horses, of which we [ate] three.

WILLIAM CLARK

By the end of June they were out of the mountains. The captains had decided they could now explore more of the Louisiana Territory, without seriously delaying their return, if they split into smaller groups at Travelers Rest.

Most of them would return to the Beaverhead River, where Clark would push on toward the Yellowstone while the others in his party retrieved the canoes and floated down to the Great Falls.

At the same time, Lewis would take a smaller party to check out the overland shortcut to the Great Falls which the Indians had described, then, with only three men, reconnoiter the upper reaches of the Marias River, which he believed would mark the new territory's northern border.

It would mean that the Corps of Discovery would be divided at some point into four groups separated by huge distances. But Lewis and Clark now had enough confidence in their men—and in their new understanding of the West's basic geography—to risk it.

Promising to reunite in a month where the Yellowstone meets the Missouri, they went their separate ways.

July 3rd. I took leave of my worthy friend and companion, Capt. Clark, and the party that accompanyed him. I could not avoid feeling much concern on this occasion although I hoped this seperation was only momentary.

MERIWETHER LEWIS

———

Clark's group reached the Beaverhead on July 8. Cached with the canoes was a supply of tobacco, and the men "became so impatient to be chewing it that they scarcely gave themselves time to take their saddles off their horses," he wrote, "before they were off to the deposit." Everything they had buried was safe, he added, although a little damp.

At the Three Forks, Sergeant Ordway and nine men paddled off down the Missouri toward Great Falls. "The Mosquetoes," he wrote, "are more troublesome than ever we have seen them before." Clark and twelve others—including York, Charbonneau, Sacagawea, and little Jean-Baptiste—headed overland, due east, traveling on horseback.

Sacagawea was familiar with this territory (her people had often frequented it when she was a young girl), and for the first and only time during the expedition, she served as an actual guide to the Corps of Discovery. She pointed them toward what today is Bozeman Pass, and Clark followed.

July 13th. The indian woman, who has been of great service to me as a pilot through this country, recommends a gap in the mountain more south, which I shall cross.

WILLIAM CLARK

On July 15 they reached the Yellowstone, and a few days later came across cottonwoods large enough to be hollowed into canoes. (While they stopped, unseen Indians made off with half of their horse herd. And when a smaller group was sent ahead on horseback with a message to the Mandans, their horses were also stolen by Indians no one ever saw.)

In two large dugouts lashed together for stability, Clark's group floated down the Yellowstone and out onto the Great Plains once more. He noted that grasshoppers had "destroyed every sprig of grass for miles" in one section, and later encountered a herd of buffalo so immense that the canoes had to wait an hour as the beasts swam across the river in front of them.

On July 25 Clark came across a remarkable sandstone formation, which he named "Pompy's Tower," after Sacagawea's son, now a year and a half old, whom he had grown fond of and had nicknamed "Little Pomp." A nearby creek was given the boy's real name, Baptiste.

East of what is now Billings, Montana, Clark came upon this "remarkable rock" standing by itself on the south bank of the Yellowstone. He climbed it, measured it, and then named it Pompy's Tower, in honor of Sacagawea's toddling son, the "little dancing boy" Clark had nicknamed Little Pomp. On a path leading to the top, where Indians had scratched the figures of animals in the soft rock, Clark etched his name and the date—where it can still be seen today.

And in the soft stone of the outcropping, near some Indian pictographs, Clark inscribed his name and the date—the only physical evidence the Corps of Discovery left on the landscape which survives to this day.

———

July 25th. I now begin to be apprehensive that I shall not reach the United States within this season, unless I make every exertion in my power, which I shall not omit when once I leave this place. . . . [Drouillard] found some wintering camps of the natives and a great number of a more recent date. . . . We consider ourselves extreemly fortunate in not having met with these people.

MERIWETHER LEWIS

That same day, Lewis and three men were nearly three hundred miles away, trying to mark the northernmost reach of the Marias River. Cloudy skies prevented him from taking precise celestial readings, so he named the spot Camp Disappointment and started back toward the Missouri and the remainder of the expedition.

It was Blackfeet territory. Their connection to British traders in Canada—and the guns and ammunition that went with it—made them the preeminent power of the northern Plains and Rockies, mortal enemies of the Shoshones, Flatheads, and Nez Percé. With so few men, Lewis was not anxious to meet the tribe. But on July 26 he looked through his telescope and saw eight warriors on a rise in the distance. *They* were watching the Americans.

This was a very unpleasant sight. However, I resolved to make the best of our situation and to approach them in a friendly manner.

MERIWETHER LEWIS

Warily, the two groups moved toward each other, neither one knowing how many others might be over the next hill. Suspicions seemed to ease when Lewis presented them with some handkerchiefs, flags, and peace medals. It was near evening, so they all shared dinner and camped together under three small cottonwoods.

While Clark explored the Yellowstone, Lewis was hundreds of miles away, in what is now northern Montana, searching for the northernmost extent of the Louisiana Territory. Instead, near the Two Medicine River, he came across some Blackfeet Indians. It was a "very unpleasant sight," Lewis wrote, because "I expected that we were to have some difficulty with them; that if they thought themselves sufficiently strong I was convinced they would attempt to rob us." Edward S. Curtis took this photograph of a young Piegan Blackfeet on the same river a hundred years later.

The Blackfeet, however, probably didn't appreciate Lewis's announced plans to open direct trade with their adversaries. In their eyes, it could only mean diminished economic power and better-armed enemies.

I told these people that I had come a great way from the East, up the large river which runs towards the rising sun, that I had been to the great waters where the sun sets and had seen a great many nations, all of whom I had invited to come and trade with me on the rivers on this side of the mountains. . . .
I fell into a profound sleep and did not wake untill the noise of the men and indians awoke me a little after light in the morning.

Karl Bodmer painted these Blackfeet portraits at Fort McKenzie on the upper Missouri in the 1830s, during an uneasy peace between the tribe and American fur companies. Iron Shirt (below) had just traded in a lace-trimmed British uniform, and Bull's Back Fat (right) was wearing a Jefferson peace medal.

Lewis was roused from his sleep by the sounds of a man shouting "Damn you, let go my gun." Joseph Field had caught the Indians trying to steal the explorers' rifles. Reuben Field, wrestling to recover his gun, had already stabbed one of the Blackfeet. George Drouillard was chasing after another one.

I then drew a pistol from my holster and terning myself about saw the indian making off with my gun. I ran at him with my pistol and bid him lay down my gun, which he was in the act of doing when the Fieldses returned and drew up their guns to shoot him, which I forb[ade] as he did not appear to be about to make any resistance or commit any offensive act. . . . He droped the gun and walked slowly off.

MERIWETHER LEWIS

Other Blackfeet were rounding up the horses. Lewis sprinted after two of them, threatened to shoot if they didn't stop, and raised his gun. One warrior jumped behind a rock. The other turned toward Lewis.

At the distance of 30 steps . . . I shot him through the belly. He fell to his knees and on his wright elbow, from which position he

LEWIS & CLARK

partly raised himself up and fired at me, and turning himself about
crawled in behind a rock. . . . He overshot me, [but] being bearheaded I
felt the wind of his bullet very distinctly.

MERIWETHER LEWIS

Two Blackfeet now lay dead. As the six others fled north to join their tribe, Lewis ordered his men to round up the horses, while he examined the corpses. On one, he left a grim token to commemorate the first act of bloodshed between representatives of the United States and western Indians.

While the men were preparing the horses I put four sheilds and two bows
and quivers of arrows . . . on the fire, with sundry other articles. . . .
I also retook the flagg but left the [peace] medal about the neck of the dead
man, that they might be informed who we were.

MERIWETHER LEWIS

Lewis and three men camped here with a small group of Blackfeet, who tried to steal the explorers' guns and horses. In the ensuing fight, two Indians were killed—the only act of bloodshed during the entire expedition. In later years, three former members of the Corps of Discovery would be killed by the tribe.

Convinced that a Blackfeet war party would soon be on their heels seeking revenge, they rode as hard and as fast as they could for the next twenty-four hours straight.

After 120 miles, they reached the Missouri.

Miraculously, at that very moment the combined expedition groups from the Beaverhead and the Great Falls rounded a bend in their canoes. Lewis's party jumped off their horses and into the dugouts. Back on the water, they raced toward the rendezvous with Clark, traveling seventy-three, then eighty-three, then eighty-eight miles a day.

On August 11 Lewis stopped to hunt for food. Nearby, a shot suddenly rang out. Lewis was hit.

I was in the act of firing on [an] Elk . . . when a ball struck my left thye, about an inch below my hip joint. Missing the bone it passed through the left thye and cut the thickness of the bullet across the hinder part of the right thye. The stroke was very severe. . . . In this situation, not knowing how many indians there might be concealed in the bushes, I thought best to make good my retreat to the perogue, calling out as I ran . . . that there were indians.

MERIWETHER LEWIS

As it turned out, the bullet hadn't come from an Indian. Lewis had been wounded by one of his own men—the one-eyed Pierre Cruzatte, who had mistaken the buckskin-clad captain for an elk in the underbrush.

The next day, August 12, downstream from the mouth of the Yellowstone, they arrived at Clark's camp. He was "alarmed" to discover his friend and co-commander injured with a "very bad flesh wound," and when he began dressing it, Lewis fainted for a while. But the bullet had not broken any bones, and both Lewis and Clark soon agreed that a full recovery was assured.

"And now (thanks to God), we are all together again," a relieved Patrick Gass wrote, as the reunited party pushed on to the Mandan villages. It took them only two days.

August 17th. Took our leave of Touisant Charbono, his Snake Indian wife and their child, who had accompanied us on our rout to the pacific ocean in the capacity of interpreter and interpretess. . . . Settled with Charbono for his services . . . in all amounting to 500 dollars and 33 and a third cents. . . . I offered to take his little son, a butifull promising child

The Sentinel, by Richard Throssel, 1905. As the expedition paddled past the villages of the Teton Sioux without stopping, Clark exchanged sharp words with Chief Black Buffalo, who had hailed them from a hilltop. They were "bad people," Clark shouted. In response, Black Buffalo struck the ground three times with his gun as a curse.

who is about 19 months old. . . . They observed that in one year the boy would be sufficiently old to leave his mother . . . if I would be so freindly as to raise the child in such a manner as I thought proper, to which I agreed.

WILLIAM CLARK

They all said good-bye to Charbonneau, Sacagawea, and little Baptiste. And after consulting the men, the captains permitted John Colter to join two American trappers who were on their way to the Yellowstone to hunt for beaver. He would be "lonely" in St. Louis, Colter said; he wanted to begin a new life in the West.

Fur Traders Descending the Missouri, by George Caleb Bingham. By the fall of 1806, other explorers and fur traders were heading up the Missouri and into the territory from which Lewis and Clark were returning. The expedition provided them with information, and in return received linen clothes, tobacco, sugar, chocolate, and the first whiskey they had tasted since July 4, 1805.

However, Sheheke, the Mandan chief, agreed to accompany the captains east to meet President Jefferson. He was in the canoes with them when they passed through the lands of the Teton Sioux—the Lakotas—who had tried to stop the Corps of Discovery from moving upriver two years earlier.

Black Buffalo, one of the chiefs they had met, hailed them from the riverbank, but the explorers refused to stop.

*I told this man to inform his nation that we had not forgot their treat-
ment to us as we passed up this river etc.; that they had treated all the
white people who had visited them very badly . . . [that] we viewed
them as bad people and no more traders would be Suffered to come
to them, and whenever the white people wished to visit the nations
above, they would Come Sufficiently Strong to whip any vilenous party
who dare to oppose them. . . . I also told them that I was informed that
a part of all their bands were gorn to war against the Mandans, & that*

they would be well whiped as the Mandans and [Hidatsa now] had
plenty of Guns, Powder and ball, and we had given them a Cannon to
defend themselves . . . and to keep away from the river or we Should
kill every one of them.

WILLIAM CLARK

From the top of a hill, the chief struck the ground three times with his gun. "This, I am informed," Clark noted, "is a great oath among the Indians."

Farther downriver they stopped briefly to pay their respects at the grave of Sergeant Floyd, miraculously the Corps of Discovery's only casualty.

At about the same time (and unbeknownst to the explorers), the massive Spanish military expedition, sent from Santa Fé in June to capture or destroy the Americans, reached the Pawnee villages on the Republican River, in what is now south-central Nebraska. The Missouri was only a few hundred miles away. With more than five hundred Mexican and Indian troops, the Spanish force was already vastly superior in size to the American expedition. But when the Pawnees declined to enlist as well, for some reason the Spanish commander turned back.

It was too late anyway. Speeding home with the current, the explorers were averaging nearly fifty miles a day. "The men ply their oars," Clark wrote, "and we descended with great velocity." They even told the captains they wanted to push on without halting to send out hunters for meat.

They began encountering boat after boat going in the opposite direction—in all, nearly 150 fur traders and other explorers headed upriver, eagerly pushing west in the Corps's wake and gladly willing to exchange whiskey, tobacco, and news from the East for any information Lewis and Clark could give them about the newest section of the United States.

September 12th. Met Mr. McC[lellan] with a large keel Boat. . . . He
was rejoiced to see us [and] gave our officers wine and the party as much
whiskey as we all could drink. Mr. McC[lellan] informed us that the
people in general in the united States were concerned about us, as they
had heard that we were all killed. Then again, they heard that the
Spanyards had us in the mines [of Mexico].

JOHN ORDWAY

September 17th. [Another] Gentleman informed us that we had been long
Since given up by the people of the U.S. . . . and almost forgotton. [But]
the President of the U. States had yet hopes of us.

WILLIAM CLARK

The captains learned of changes that had occurred in their absence. While they had been gone, a war had been declared, waged, and won against Tripoli. Jefferson had been reelected. Aaron Burr and Alexander Hamilton, two of America's most prominent political leaders, had fought a duel, and Hamilton was dead. Relations with both Spain and England were edging toward hostilities. Two Indians had recently been hanged in St. Louis for murder. And President Jefferson had already dispatched two more expeditions to explore the other sections of the Louisiana Territory: Zebulon Pike, through the middle Plains toward the Rockies of what is now Colorado, and the Freeman-Custis expedition up the Arkansas and Red rivers in the Southwest. (Both would be intercepted by Spanish patrols.)

On September 20 a shout of joy erupted from the men. They had seen their first cows in two and a half years, a clear sign they were nearing the settlements. Later that day, they reached La Charette, whose citizens, Clark wrote, seemed

On September 23, 1806, after an absence of two and a half years, the Corps of Discovery returned to St. Louis, as portrayed here in a painting by Stanley Meltzoff. "We Suffered the party to fire off their pieces as a Salute to the Town," Clark wrote. The townspeople had long since given up all hope for the expedition, and they swarmed down to greet the explorers, who appeared, one person noted excitedly, "like Robinson Crusoes."

"much astonished in seeing us return." On the twenty-first, they made it to St. Charles and were greeted again with both surprise and celebration.

September 23 was their final day as a Corps of Discovery.

Thursday, September 23rd, 1806. A wet disagreeable morning. We Set out after breakfast and proc[eeded] on. Soon arived at the Mouth of the Missourie. Entered the Mississippi River and landed at River Deboise where we wintered in 1804. . . . We delayed a Short time. About 12 oClock we arived in Site of St. Louis. Fired three Rounds as we approached . . . and landed oppocit the center of the Town. The people gathred on the Shore and Huzzared three cheers.

We unloaded the canoes and carried the baggage all up to a Store house in Town. Drew out the canoes, then the party all considerable much rejoiced that we have the Expedition Completed.

And now we look for boarding in Town and wait for our Settlement, and then we entend to return to our native homes to See our parents once more, as we have been So long from them.

JOHN ORDWAY

CHAPTER 12

Done for Posterity

The Political Observatory, *Walpole, New Hampshire.*

It is, with the sincerest pleasure, that we announce to our fellow citizens,
the arrival of Captain Lewis, with his exploring party, at St. Louis.
 The President of the United States has received a letter from him. . . .
Captain Lewis speaks of his colleague, Captain Clarke, in the most
affectionate terms, and declares his equal title to whatever merit may be
ascribed to the success of this enterprize.

*T*HE DAY the Corps of Discovery returned to St. Louis, letters went out across the nation proclaiming the news. A report to the Philadelphia *Register* noted excitedly that winters were very mild on the Pacific and that "one of the hands, an intelligent man, tells me that Indians are as numerous on the Columbia as the whites are in any part of the United States." Another paper carried the news that on the west side of the Rocky Mountains, "it is thought to be a very poor Indian indeed that did not own three hundred horses." And in an account marveling at the eighty-pound horns of a sheep that the expedition had brought back to St. Louis, a Connecticut newspaper displayed the headline "More Wonders. Rocky Mountain Sheep Beats the Horned Frog All Hollow."

> *St. Louis. September 23rd, 1806. [Mr. President], It is with pleasure that I anounce to you the safe arrival of myself and party at 12 OClk. today. . . . In obedience to your orders we have penitrated the Continent of North America to the Pacific Ocean. . . .*
>
> *I am very anxious to learn the state of my friends at Albemarle, particularly whether my mother is yet living. I am with every sentiment of esteem Your Ob[edien]t and very Humble servant,*
>
> MERIWETHER LEWIS

Lewis immediately dispatched a long letter to Jefferson. In it he praised his partner (whom he pointedly called "*Capt.* William Clark"), giving him equal credit for the success of the expedition, and predicted that, with government assistance, "in the course of ten or twelve years a tour across the Continent . . . will be undertaken by individuals with as little concern as a voyage across the Atlantic is at present."

Buried within the pages was the bad news: the fabled Northwest Passage, the half-day portage across the Continental Divide everyone had dreamed about, was instead a 340-mile overland trek. And some 140 of those miles were "over tremendious mountains which for sixty miles are covered with eternal snows." Still, Lewis quickly added, horses for transportation were plentiful and cheap, and 90 percent of the furs taken from this vast new part of the nation, "the most valuable fur country of America," could be taken over the route for trade with the Orient.

Most of Lewis's account focused instead on the rich potential for "a most lucrative trade" in furs. In the West, he proclaimed, the rivers "abound more in beaver and common otter than any other streams on earth."

Washington. I received, my dear Sir, with unspeakable joy your letter. . . . The unknown scenes in which you were engaged, & the length of time without hearing of you had begun to be felt awfully. . . . I salute you with sincere affection.

THOMAS JEFFERSON

Oct. 1, 1806.

By the last Mails.

MARYLAND.   BALTIMORE, OCT. 29, 1806.

A LETTER from *St. Louis (Upper Louisiana),* dated *Sept.* 23, 1806, announces the arrival of Captains LEWIS and CLARK, from their expedition into the interior.—They went to the *Pacific Ocean ;* have brought some of the natives and curiosities of the countries through which they passed, and only lost one man. They left the *Pacific Ocean* 23d March, 1806, where they arrived in November, 1805 ;—and where some American vessels had been just before.—They state the Indians to be as numerous on the *Columbia* river, which empties into the *Pacific,* as the whites in any part of the U. S. They brought a family of the Mandan indians with them. The winter was very mild on the *Pacific.*—They have kept an ample journal of their tour ; which will be published, and must afford much intelligence.

They had left for the West virtually as unknown as the territory they were sent to explore.

They returned as national heroes.

As they traveled east, the captains were honored at gala balls in St. Louis, Indiana, Kentucky, Virginia, and finally Washington, D.C., where one senator said it was as if they had just returned from the moon. Congress awarded the men double pay and 320 acres of land for their services; Lewis and Clark each got 1,600 acres. Poems were written in their honor. A statue was made of Lewis and placed in Independence Hall.

Exactly one year after his lonely New

Partial View of S.t Louis

Reports of Lewis and Clark's return left St. Louis (seen here in a drawing from 1817) the same day they arrived, but news traveled slowly in those days as it spread from newspaper to newspaper. This excerpt from Boston's *Columbian Centinel* (opposite) did not appear until November 5, more than a month and a half after the actual event.

Year's journal entry in Fort Clatsop at the continent's farthest reach, Lewis was once again with his patron and mentor, Thomas Jefferson, in the White House, where years earlier they had dreamed together of a Corps of Discovery reaching the Pacific. What was actually said between them is not known, although Jefferson later wrote that he spread Lewis's maps out on the floor and "examined these sheets myself minutely." The section where the myth of a Northwest Passage had died probably held his attention the longest—a disappointment, to be sure, but as a man of the Enlightenment, Jefferson always preferred fact to legend.

Interested as he was in geography, science, Indian customs, economic trade, and the potential for the future expansion of his young nation, presumably Jefferson would have been full of questions for his protégé. He was equally anxious for Lewis to get to work on publishing a formal report of the expedition—to satisfy the scientific world, but also because Jefferson knew that the rest of the country wanted answers to the same questions.

Never did a similar event excite more joy through the United States. The humblest of its citizens had taken a lively interest in the issue of this journey, and looked forward with impatience for the information it would furnish.

THOMAS JEFFERSON

John Colter left the expedition to become one of the first "mountain men" working for an American fur company. His reports of seeing boiling mud and steaming geysers during his travels were discounted and derided as "Colter's Hell." Not until the early 1870s, when William Henry Jackson showed Congress photographs like this one, did Easterners finally believe in a place that soon became the world's first national park: Yellowstone.

Private Alexander Hamilton Willard's life paralleled the events of the nation itself. Born in New Hampshire, he crossed the continent and returned with Lewis and Clark, then crossed it once more in 1852 when gold was discovered in California. He is shown here with his wife, Eleanor McDonald Willard, in one of the few existing photographs of an expedition member.

When Sergeant Patrick Gass was 60, he married 20-year-old Maria Hamilton, and they had six children. He was 90 when he volunteered to fight in the Civil War. And he was almost 99 when he died in West Virginia, the last surviving member of the Corps of Discovery.

In the years that followed, the men of the Corps of Discovery went in many directions. Little is known about most of them, except that they seemed to have died relatively young.

John Ordway returned to see his parents in New Hampshire, then got married and moved to Missouri to farm the land the government had awarded him. He died there in 1817.

Joseph Whitehouse was arrested for bad debts in 1807, rejoined the army for the War of 1812, but then deserted and drifted into obscurity.

The expedition's news of abundant beaver and wildlife in the West helped touch off a fur-trading boom, and several of the explorers followed John Colter back west to become mountain men. At least three of them were killed by Blackfeet Indians, including George Drouillard, who had been with Lewis in the first fight with the tribe.

Colter himself narrowly escaped a run-in with the Blackfeet—surviving only after crossing hundreds of miles, alone and naked, to an American fort. He wandered into places, he said, where steam rose from the ground and mud boiled in sulfur pits. "Colter's Hell," people called it, refusing to believe his stories. It would later become the world's first national park—Yellowstone.

Young George Shannon, who seemed to have a knack for getting separated from the expedition or forgetting items on the trail, went to law school and became a legislator in Kentucky, then a state senator and United States attorney in Missouri.

Alexander Willard, who was given a hundred lashes instead of death for falling asleep on sentry duty along the trail, became a government blacksmith at different agencies serving the Sauk, Fox, Delaware, and Shawnee Indians. Married and with twelve children, in 1852 he took his family across the continent in a covered wagon to California, where gold had been discovered. Born in Charlestown, New Hampshire, he died in Sacramento.

Patrick Gass outlived everyone, dying in 1870 near the age of ninety-nine. He had lost an eye in the War of 1812, published a book of his expedition journals, then settled in Wellsburg, West Virginia. He was ninety years old when the Civil War broke out; still, he volunteered for the Union.

December 10th, 1808
I did wish to do well by him [York]. But as he has got Such a notion
about freedom and his emence Services, that I do not expect he will be of
much Service to me again.

WILLIAM CLARK

A New Frontier

It was the brainchild of a President who challenged his country with a daring plan to enter an international race to explore—and perhaps control—the unknown. On the one hand, it was promoted as necessary for the advancement of science; but on the other, Congress was more impressed by the possibilities of its commercial side benefits. It drew on the expertise of the nation's leading scientists, yet ultimately relied on the armed services for the explorers who would put their lives on the line. Its members were hailed as heroes, yet some of them had difficulty readjusting to more mundane duties after their mission was completed. It even overran its original budget.

Many elements of the Lewis and Clark expedition, the nation's first official exploration, are hauntingly similar to, almost interchangeable with, the United States' race to the moon in the 1960s. Admittedly, there are differences, but the parallels exist even across the gulf of a century and a half.

The prairie dog and the antelope skeleton that the Corps of Discovery sent back were not quite moon rocks, but they attracted the public's curiosity. The new Harpers Ferry rifle that Lewis brought along hardly equals a space suit or a lunar excursion module, but it was the most advanced of its kind at the time. "Portable soup" in lead canisters is not Tang, but it was meant to solve the same problem of providing nourishment when no other source was available. A bulky keelboat is no Saturn booster rocket, but both lifted their precious cargo from the familiarity of the "civi-

Mission Control. From his bedroom study at Monticello, with its telescope, books, and scientific instruments, Thomas Jefferson launched his nation on a tradition of exploring the unknown.

lized" world to the edge of the unknown before being jettisoned, while the explorers pushed farther ahead.

"In many respects, the expedition *was* like going to the moon," according to geographer and historian John Logan Allen, "with one remarkable exception that I think a lot of people forget about, and that is that when Apollo 13 is having difficulty, those people are in constant contact with Earth. They're speaking with Houston, and they're getting advice on how to deal with problems. Lewis and Clark were on their own."

To that might be added another difference: while the Great Plains, the Rocky Mountains, and the far side of the Continental Divide may be much closer than the moon, far less was known about them at the outset of the mission. Science had not prepared Lewis and Clark for the vastness of the Plains or the height and breadth of the Rockies; instead, it had told them to expect woolly mammoths, Welsh-speaking Indians, and a half-day portage from the Missouri to the Columbia. Before Neil Armstrong landed his spacecraft on the Sea of Tranquillity in 1969, its dusty, barren terrain had been thoroughly studied and photographed.

He did not take that first giant leap for mankind expecting to walk on a moon made of cheese.

When Thomas Jefferson dispatched the Corps of Discovery toward the Pacific, he launched the nation on a trajectory of exploration that arcs all the way to the present. It began a tradition that links Lewis and Clark to Zebulon Pike and John C. Frémont and John Wesley Powell in the nineteenth century, as well as to the astronauts of the twentieth century. It connects Monticello with Mission Control. And it unites the names scratched into the bark of a tree overlooking the Pacific in 1806 with a plaque and a flag left on the lunar surface.

Lewis and Clark had the honor of being first; they would not be disappointed—or surprised—to learn that they were not the last. "I think that the nature of America, how it was born, how it grew up, sort of exemplified the idea of exploration," says James Lovell, the famous astronaut. "We were a young country, we grew, and I think this idea of being explorers is ingrained in our psyche here in this country. I think we'll always be explorers."

For York, returning from the West meant a return to a world of slavery. He asked Clark for his freedom, or at least to be hired out near Louisville to be near his wife, the slave of another owner. Both requests were initially refused, though in 1809 Clark sent him to Kentucky hoping that "perhaps if he has a Severe Master a While he may do Some Service . . . and give over that wife of his."

Finally, at least ten years after the expedition, Clark granted York his freedom. He went into the freighting business in Tennessee and Kentucky, and is believed to have died of cholera sometime before 1832. (Accounts that York returned to the Rocky Mountains to live out his years among Indians who considered him an equal are generally discounted by most historians, who think such tales mistake York for other African Americans.)

We had on board [our boat] a Frenchman named Charbon[neau], with his wife, an Indian woman of the Snake [Shoshone] nation, both of whom had

Toussaint Charbonneau, in his seventies, was the only interpreter at Fort Clark in June 1833, when Karl Bodmer and his patron, Prince Maximilian of Wied, arrived to study the Mandans and Hidatsas. In Bodmer's painting of their first meeting with the Indians, the artist himself stands at the far right, next to the Prince, with Charbonneau presumed to be the figure in the center, making the introductions.

accompanied Lewis and Clark to the Pacific, and were of good service. The woman, a good creature, of a mild and gentle disposition is greatly attached to the whites, whose manner and dress she tries to imitate, but she had become sickly and longed to revisit her native country; her husband, also, who had spent many years among the Indians, was become weary of the civilized life.

HENRY M. BRACKENRIDGE, 1811

Toussaint Charbonneau stayed among the Indians of the upper Missouri the rest of his life, interpreting for government officials, explorers, and artists. Sacagawea remained with him. In 1809 they traveled down the Missouri to St. Louis, where they entrusted their son, Baptiste, and his education to William Clark before eventually heading back upriver.

In 1812, at Fort Manuel, a fur-trading post in what is now South Dakota, Sacagawea gave birth to a daughter, Lisette. But that winter, Sacagawea grew ill with fever and died. "She was," wrote a clerk at the post the night she died, "a good and the best woman in the fort." (As with York, there are legends, also discounted by most historians, that she lived much longer, dying near the age of one hundred in 1884 on the Wind River Shoshone Reservation in Wyoming. But in a list Clark compiled reporting the status of expedition members in the 1820s, she was listed as already dead.)

True to his promise, Clark assumed custody of Sacagawea's children.

Baptiste Charbonneau, who had spent the first two years of his life on the expedition's trail, never settled down. After being educated in St. Louis, he became friends with a traveling German prince and went to Europe for five years, learning several languages. When he returned, Baptiste became a mountain man, a guide for United States troops in the war with Mexico, a magistrate of San Luis Rey Mission in California. In 1866, at age sixty-one, he heard of gold discoveries in Montana and set off with a wagon train, but died of pneumonia on his way.

Since our forefathers first beheld [Lewis and Clark], more than seven times ten winters have snowed and melted. . . . We were happy when [the white man] first came. We first thought he came from the light, but he comes like the dusk of the evening now, not like the dawn of the morning. He comes like a day that has passed, and night enters our future with him. . . .

. . . Had Heaven's Chief burned him with some mark to refuse him, we might have refused him. No; we did not refuse him in his weakness. In his poverty we fed, we cherished him—yes, befriended him. . . . [But] he has filled graves with our bones.

. . . How often does he come? You know he comes as long as he lives, and takes more and more, and dirties what he leaves.

CHARLOT, *Salish chief, 1876*

For Indian peoples of the West, the century that followed Lewis and Clark's expedition was the most chaotic and traumatic in their history.

Cameahwait of the Shoshones was killed in a battle with the Hidatsas, part of the intertribal warfare that continued unabated, despite the captains' calls for a grand peace.

The Arikara chief whom the explorers sent to meet Jefferson in Washington died of disease there, turning the tribe for a while into implacable enemies of Americans traveling up the Missouri.

The coastal village of the Clatsops, who had befriended the Corps of Discovery, was bombarded and burned to the ground over a misunderstanding with fur traders.

In 1837, smallpox—brought upriver by an American trading boat—swept through the crowded villages of Mandans and Hidatsas, who dared not disperse onto the prairies for fear of the Lakota war parties camped nearby. Nine out of ten of them died from the disease. Farther upriver, the Blackfeet were also decimated by the same sickness.

Of all the tribes in the West, the Lakotas fought the Americans the longest

A mixed legacy with Native Americans. No Horn on His Head (far left, top) was part of a small Nez Percé delegation that traveled all the way to St. Louis in 1832 to see their old friend William Clark; George Catlin painted his portrait on the way back home by riverboat. When Struck by the Ree (right), a Yankton Sioux, visited Washington in 1867, he told officials that he had been born during the expedition's stay among his people, and that Lewis had wrapped him in a United States flag and declared him "an American." Among the Nez Percé who fought a brief war with the United States in 1877 was Tzi-kal-tza (far left, bottom), who the tribe said was William Clark's half-Indian son. Wolf Calf (below), a Piegan, was an old man when he told the historian George Bird Grinnell about his part in Lewis's fight with the Blackfeet. Pe-tow-ya (near left) was 110 years old when this picture was taken, but she said she distinctly remembered being a young girl when Lewis and Clark stopped among the Cayuse on their return trip; they had a black man with them, she said, and one of the captains was kind enough to treat her father's rheumatism.

The "Writingest Explorers"

They were opened and written upon near campfires on the Great Plains. They survived a harsh winter in North Dakota and a boat accident in Montana. They were an essential part of the luggage that was hauled on a crude, jolting cart around the Great Falls of the Missouri, in saddlebags up and down the Bitterroot Mountains, and in dugout canoes catapulting through the rapids of the mighty Columbia. They were with the Corps of Discovery upon its triumphant return to St. Louis. And they were with Meriwether Lewis when he died.

Few documents in American history have endured as have the journals of the Lewis and Clark expedition. The captains and their men were, according to historian Donald Jackson, the "writingest explorers of their time. They wrote constantly and abundantly, afloat or ashore, legibly and illegibly, and always with an urgent sense of purpose." The result was the journals, which another historian, Paul Russell Cutright, has called "among the glories of American history . . . classics in the vast literature of discovery and exploration."

Most of the captains' journals can now be found at the American Philosophical Society in Philadelphia. But the Missouri Historical Society has some of Clark's journals and manuscripts, as does Yale University. The journals of other members, as well as important miscellaneous documents, are in Chicago; Charlottesville, Virginia; Louisville; Washington, D.C.; and Madison, Wisconsin. Their journey finally to reach the public's view was nearly as long and arduous as their initial trip across the continent and back.

Sergeant Patrick Gass was the first into print with an account of the expedition. His *A Journal of the Voyages and Travels of a Corps of Discovery*, published in 1807, is a heavily edited version of the expedition's story using highly imaginative drawings as illustrations. Gass's original journal, however, is missing.

Although he had issued a public prospectus in 1807 promising a map and a three-volume account of the expedition (with one volume devoted "exclusively to scientific research"), Lewis died in 1809 without having written a single word for publication. Clark tried to take over. He was painfully self-conscious about his lack of formal education (in his journals he spelled "mosquito" nineteen different ways, and he sometimes asked Lewis to draft important letters on his behalf). So Clark got an editor to compile the narrative and asked Dr. Benjamin Smith Barton to handle the daunting amount of botanical, zoological, and other scientific material. But there was confusion and delays. Two publishers went bankrupt.

A two-volume edition of the captains' journals was finally brought out in 1814. It included Clark's master map of the West, but hardly any science, since Barton had not done any of the work he had promised. (Thus it was that later naturalists garnered credit for "discovering" plants and animals that Lewis and Clark had painstakingly described years earlier.)

Not until the centennial of the expedition, in 1904, were the complete journals of Lewis and Clark finally published. Edited by Reuben Gold Thwaites, this multivolume edition also included the journals of Sergeant Charles Floyd and Private Joseph Whitehouse, which Thwaites had tracked down. By 1916 Sergeant John Ordway's journal was discovered and published. Since then, additional Lewis and Clark material has turned up, principally more letters and documents, and an up-to-date edition of all the known journals and maps, edited by Dr. Gary E. Moulton at the University of Nebraska, has recently been published.

But, like the rumors of Welsh Indians or a Northwest Passage just over the next horizon, a tantalizing prospect still clings to the Corps of Discovery: the possibility of more journals, as yet undiscovered in someone's attic trunk or collection of family papers. All the sergeants were under orders to keep diaries. Gass's, Floyd's, and Ordway's are accounted for; where is Sergeant Nathaniel Pryor's? Even more intriguing is Private Robert Frazer. Within a month of the expedition's arrival in St. Louis, Frazer announced plans to publish a four-hundred-page book containing "an accurate description of the Missouri . . . of the Columbia . . . of the face of the Country in general . . . of the several Tribes of Indians . . . [and] of the vegetable, animal and mineral productions discovered." The book was never published, and Frazer's journal has never been found.

In his last letter to Lewis, in August 1809, Thomas Jefferson expressed his eagerness for the journals to be published. "I am very often applied to know when your work will begin to appear," he wrote. "Every body is impatient for it." Jefferson, who had insisted that the expedition keep detailed records, understood the importance of the journals—for the advancement of human knowledge but also for less tangible motives. Americans were hungry to learn more about the Corps of Discovery's incredible journey across the continent and into their nation's future. Nearly two hundred years later, they still are.

On a buffalo hide he painted each winter, a Lakota named Lone Dog kept a different kind of journal. He recorded his people's history by drawing the most memorable event of the year. The spiral began in the winter of 1800 with straight lines signifying Lakotas killed in a fight with Crows. The years of the Lewis and Clark expedition are marked by pictures representing more battles and a horse-stealing raid against other tribes, but later years show trading posts, treaty ceremonies, disease, flags, and other signs of the increasing presence of white men.

and hardest. In 1876, seventy years after Black Buffalo struck his gun on the ground as a curse on Lewis and Clark and their nation, his people won the greatest Indian victory against the United States Army in the West, annihilating General George Armstrong Custer's cavalry at the Little Bighorn. Then the Lakotas, too, were conquered.

The first white men of your people who came to our country were named Lewis and Clark. They also brought many things that our people had never seen. They talked straight, and our people gave them a great feast, as a proof that their hearts were friendly. These men were very kind. They made presents to our chiefs and our people made presents to them. All the Nez Percés made friends with Lewis and Clark, and agreed to let them pass through their country, and never to make war on white men. This promise the Nez Percés have never broken. . . . It has always been the pride of the Nez Percés that they were the friends of the white men.

CHIEF JOSEPH

William Clark, shown here in a portrait by Chester Harding, lived a long and distinguished life after the expedition, before dying at the home of his eldest son, Meriwether Lewis Clark. On the St. Louis gravestone of the explorer who carved his name into a tree at the mouth of the Columbia and into a rock on the Yellowstone River are these words: "His life is written in the history of his country."

The Nez Percé always remembered the explorers fondly. A few of them visited Clark in St. Louis before he died, asking to learn more about the white man's powers. Even after their trip was misinterpreted by church newspapers as a plea for spiritual salvation, the tribe welcomed Protestant missionaries who came west to tell them they had to abandon the ways of their forefathers.

Then, in 1877, provoked by broken treaties and mistreatment into a war they didn't seek, part of the tribe headed for sanctuary in Canada. They started their odyssey by traveling the same trail over the Bitterroot Mountains that Lewis and Clark had followed. Fifteen hundred miles later, after fighting seventeen battles and coming within forty miles of the border, their leader, Chief Joseph, was forced to surrender. "From where the sun now stands," he said, "I will fight no more forever."

Among those who surrendered with Joseph was a seventy-year-old man named Tzi-kal-tza. He was, the Nez Percé told the army officers, the son of William Clark. The next year, in Oklahoma's Indian Territory, he died in captivity, far from his home.

Immediately following the expedition, William
Clark had married Julia ("Judith") Hancock of Virginia, in whose honor he had named a river in Montana. They moved to St. Louis, where he assumed his
duties as the government's Indian agent for the West.

The Indians called him "the Red-Headed Chief,"
and considered him their friend. He was sorry, he
wrote Jefferson in the 1820s, that there wasn't more he
could do for them. When Missouri achieved statehood, he lost the election for governor, in part because
of his reputation of being too "soft" on Indians.

After his triumphant return to
Washington, and before his
personal demons overtook
him at Grinder's Stand, Lewis
stood for this portrait (above)
by the artist Charles B. J. F. de
Saint-Memin. Wrapped
around his neck is an Indian
tippet, an elaborate cape made
of otter fur and more than a
hundred white weasel skins,
probably the same one that
Cameahwait had given him
during his time with the
Shoshones. In his moody
journal entry two days after his
31st birthday in 1805, Lewis
described the tippet in great
detail and called it "the most
eligant peice of Indian dress I
ever saw."

But he was successful in business and widely respected throughout his long life. Mountain men, explorers, and travelers paid him visits on their way through St. Louis. He gave them advice and incorporated their findings into an even more detailed map of the West, considered by historians to be "a cartographic masterpiece."

He was sixty-eight years old when he died on September 1, 1838, at the home of his oldest son, Meriwether Lewis Clark.

> *Governor Lewis had from early life been subject to hypochondriac affections. It was a constitutional disposition in all the nearer branches of the family. . . . During his Western Expedition, the constant exertion which that required of all the faculties of body and mind suspended these distressing affections; but after his establishment at St. Louis in sedentary occupations, they returned to him with redoubled vigor and began seriously to alarm his friends. He was in a paroxysm of one of these when his affairs rendered it necessary for him to go to Washington.*
>
> THOMAS JEFFERSON

As a reward for his role in the expedition, Meriwether Lewis was appointed governor of the Louisiana Territory. Like his partner, Clark, he, too, moved to St. Louis.

But unlike his friend, Lewis was soon overwhelmed by problems in his new life. He courted several women, but none would marry him. He speculated in land and lost money. Debts mounted up. And he found himself ill suited to the duties of governor: mounds of paperwork over land claims; disputes between Indian trading companies; incessant partisan politics; and a territorial secretary who tried to turn officials in Washington against him.

He started drinking too much, and then compounded that affliction with heavy doses of opium, originally taken to combat malaria.

Throughout it all, despite Jefferson's prodding, he did not even begin writing the report on the expedition that he had promised a publisher and that the public eagerly awaited. After a while, he stopped answering Jefferson's letters. Finally, in 1809, when a new administration questioned some of his expenditures, he decided to go to Washington to defend his name and his honor. He never made it.

After trying to disentangle his financial affairs with the help of Clark, Lewis boarded a boat to go down the Mississippi. "I have not Spent Such a day as yesterday for maney years," Clark wrote his brother about Lewis's departure. "His Crediters all flocking in near the time of his Setting out distressed him much, which he expressed to me in Such terms as to Cause a Cempothy [sympathy] which is not yet off—I do not believe there was ever an honester man in Louisiana nor one who had pureor motives. . . . [I]f his mind had been at ease, I Should have parted Cherefully."

Patrick Gass was the first expedition member to publish an account of the journey. It contained a number of fanciful illustrations, including these. Opposite, Lewis is supposedly holding an Indian council; above, an animal looking more like a friendly Newfoundland dog than a fierce grizzly bear has chased an explorer up a tree.

Along the way, Lewis wrote out a will and then twice tried to commit suicide. Officials at a river fort took him into their custody and kept him under close watch for two weeks, until he convinced them he was well enough to keep traveling, this time overland. Following a road called the Natchez Trace through Tennessee, he reached Grinder's Stand, a small inn south of Nashville, on October 10.

Lewis seemed agitated for a while, the innkeeper's wife later said, but then he sat down on the porch, faced toward the west, regained his composure, and pronounced, "Madam, this is a very pleasant evening." He declined her offer to prepare a feather bed for him. Instead, he told his servant to bring in some bearskins and a buffalo robe from the expedition and lay them on the floor. Clark knew of his difficulties, Lewis assured the servant, and was on his way to help.

Then, sometime around 3:00 a.m. on October 11, while everyone else was sleeping, Lewis loaded his pistols and shot himself twice, once in the forehead and once in the chest. Shortly after sunrise, he died. (Many years after his death, theories arose that Lewis was murdered. None of them are persuasive against the accounts of people at the scene, or in contrast to the immediate reactions of Clark and Jefferson, the two men who knew him best and who, though admittedly not at Grinder's Stand, never doubted that Lewis died by his own hand.) "I fear," Clark wrote when the news arrived, "O! I fear the weight of his mind has overcome him."

––––––––––

The work we are now doing is, I trust, done for posterity, in such a way that they need not repeat it. . . . We shall delineate with correctness the great arteries of this great country; those who come after us will . . . fill up the canvas we begin.

THOMAS JEFFERSON

By the time the last member of the Corps of Discovery died, the boundaries of the United States had pushed far beyond the Louisiana Territory.

Texas had been annexed into the Union. California and the Southwest had been won by a war with Mexico. And England had relinquished its claim to the Oregon territory, around the mouth of the Columbia River, where Lewis and Clark had once carved their names into the bark of a tree.

The Civil War had been fought and won, reuniting the nation, North and South, and a transcontinental railroad had been built, beginning the process of joining the nation, East and West, in ways never before thought possible. At the same time, the vast herds of buffalo that had so amazed Lewis and Clark were about to be hunted to near extinction, the grizzly and elk were already retreating from the Plains to the remotest mountains, and the prairies that the explorers had described as stretching "as far as the eye can reach" were being turned into cattle pastures and waving fields of wheat.

By the end of the century, all along the expedition's route states had been organized—Missouri, Kansas, Iowa, Nebraska, North and South Dakota, Montana, Idaho, Washington, and Oregon—and nearly sixteen million Americans were already living in them.

Jefferson had estimated that it would take his nation a hundred generations to inhabit the land he had sent Lewis and Clark to explore. Instead, Americans did it in less than five.

In being first, then, the Corps of Discovery was also the last. They saw the West as it was before the rest of their nation followed them across the continent—and changed it forever.

Buffalo and Elk on the Upper Missouri, **by Karl Bodmer. "This immence river," Lewis had written to his mother from Fort Mandan, "waters one of the fairest portions of the globe, nor do I believe that there is in the universe a similar extent of country."**

Rivers of change. Within a century of the Corps of Discovery's journey, steamboats crowded the St. Louis waterfront (above) and, as the following photographs show, the first railroad bridge spanning the Missouri was completed at Kansas City and a hydroelectric dam was built at the Great Falls in Montana.

WE PROCEEDED ON

DAYTON DUNCAN

ONE JANUARY AFTERNOON years ago, I found myself huddled around a fire inside an earth lodge near Stanton, North Dakota. The temperature outside had managed a high of only 3 degrees below zero. A north wind howled across the prairies. The sun was slipping below the horizon, to be followed by nearly sixteen hours of darkness. The word "cold" does not begin to express where the night was clearly headed.

Across from me, patiently feeding the fire with cottonwood logs, sat Gerard Baker, a Mandan-Hidatsa and park ranger for the National Park Service. He had built the earth lodge as a "living history" demonstration for the Knife River Indian Villages National Historic Site, where three Hidatsa villages once stood when Lewis and Clark wintered in the area. I was retracing the explorers' route, trying to connect their experience with my own over a gap of nearly two centuries, and had asked if I could spend a night in the earth lodge, which with a dusting of snow looked something like a sod igloo. Gerard had seemed bemused by my request, but he agreed to accompany me, even provided our supplies.

First he smudged the interior in all four directions with the smoke from a bundle of sweet grass. "For the spirits," he explained. Then, in an iron pot, he boiled potatoes, onions, red peppers, and buffalo tripe, the spongy membranes of a buffalo stomach—a rubbery meal that we ate with our hands. I told him tales about my trip upriver from St. Louis, about all the changes I had seen compared to what the captains had described in their journals. He shared stories of his ancestors and sang some Hidatsa chants. Outside, the northern lights began to dance while the temperature kept sinking. It was time to go to bed.

Gerard had brought along five large buffalo robes, and he advised me to place one of them, fur side up, on the dirt floor as my mattress. The other four, he said, would provide more warmth stacked on top of me, fur side down.

"But what about you?" I asked, thinking that he was taking Indian hospitality to a foolish extreme. In the back of my mind, I recalled Clark's journal entry about the two Indians who had stayed out all night on the frozen prairie and survived—proof, he wrote, that the "customs and habits of those people have inured them to bear more cold than I thought possible for a man to endure." The smudge ceremony, the meal of buffalo, the stories around the campfire, *and now this,* I thought. History was repeating itself.

"Are you sure you'll be okay?" I insisted.

Gerard smiled at me, his eyes twinkling in the firelight. "I'll be all right," he answered, and he unrolled a fancy down-filled sleeping bag next to my buffalo robes. "This one's guaranteed to twenty below."

―――――

I have been out and back across the entire Lewis and Clark trail three complete times since that evening in the earth lodge with Gerard. And more times than I can count, I have visited individual sites along their route. Yet every time my path has crossed theirs, I have wondered what the two captains would think if somehow they were magically transported back to life in the modern world and sent out as, say, a Corps of Rediscovery. What would they recognize? What would confound them? What would they regret? What would they appreciate?

Certainly, a frigid night on the northern Plains would be almost painfully familiar to them. These were two Virginia-born gentlemen, accustomed to the mildest of winters; I doubt that they could ever forget their experience at Fort Mandan, where they were exposed to one of the harshest weather extremes this continent has to offer.

I, too, have stood on the banks of the Missouri and been awestruck by its raw power as huge chunks of ice floated relentlessly downstream, only to be even more stupefied the next morning on finding the mighty river frozen solid, conquered by the cold. It's something you remember. (In my case, the memory is aided by a minor case of frostbite in my nasal passages, which still acts up whenever the mercury drops below zero.) In the column headed "Unchanged," place a big checkmark for the ferocity of winters on the upper Missouri.

Nor would the captains find anything new in a meal of buffalo, or in a Mandan's willingness to share it with a stranger. But Lewis, I imagine, would be fascinated by Gerard's sleeping bag—so lightweight, yet so warm; just the kind of scientifically advanced equipment he had scoured Philadelphia to find when outfitting his expedition. Whether the captain would appreciate the irony that in this case it was an Indian showing off the latest in technology to a white man—and poking a little good-natured fun in the bargain—depends on your own assessment of Lewis's psyche. Personally, I doubt it. In my mind's eye, I see him bristling silently as he tucked himself in between the buffalo robes. Clark's the one who might have enjoyed the joke, even if it was on him. But he would also have been the one most troubled by a story Gerard had told as the embers turned crimson.

In 1836, when an aging Clark was still Indian agent for the territory, the government sent two doctors up the Missouri with instructions to vaccinate all the tribes along the river against smallpox. They inoculated most of the tribes until winter turned them back, before they had reached the Mandans, Arikaras, and Hidatsas. For some reason, the Secretary of War did not dispatch them to finish the job the next spring (and even misled Congress into believing the project was completed). That summer, catastrophe struck.

When a fur-trading boat filled with supplies paid its annual visit, it unintentionally also brought the smallpox virus, which quickly spread among the unprotected Indians. Gerard has read all the eyewitness accounts, as well as listened to oral history passed down through the tribes' generations. Smallpox, he says, causes a "very, very ugly death"—sores that ooze and burst on the victim's skin, swelling, aching, vomiting, delirium, and finally loss of life. In the villages, people began dying at a rate of eight to ten a day. Corpses piled up; the stench of rotting bodies could be smelled for miles.

Fearing their protective spirits had abandoned them, some Mandans sought escape through suicide. After debating the bravest way to die, one warrior cut his own throat while another forced an arrow into his own lungs. Some drowned themselves in the Missouri.

Among those struck by the sickness was Four Bears, a Mandan chief of some note. As a warrior, he had killed five chiefs of other nations in hand-to-hand combat, wrested a knife from a Cheyenne warrior and used it to kill its owner, taken many prisoners, and survived an enemy arrow and six gunshot wounds. But like the rest of his people, he had always felt nothing but friendship for the white man. When the fever first hit him, he put on his ceremonial garments, mounted his horse, and rode through his village singing his sacred songs. And then, as he, too, began to succumb to the dread disease, he gave a final speech to his people. A fur trader transcribed it, and it is preserved in a book of tribal history that Gerard lent me:

Ever since I can remember, I have loved the whites. . . . To the best of my knowledge, I have never wronged a white man. On the contrary, I have always protected them from the insults of others, which they cannot deny. The Four Bears never saw a white man hungry, but what he gave them to eat, drink and a buffalo skin to sleep on in time of need. . . . And how they have repaid it! With ingratitude! I have never called a white man a dog, but today I do pronounce them to be a set of black-hearted dogs. They have deceived me. Them that I have always considered as brothers have turned out to be my worst enemies.

I have been in many battles, and often wounded, but the wounds of my enemies I exalt in. But today I am wounded, and by whom? By those same white dogs that I have always considered and treated as brothers.

I do not fear death, my friends. You know it. But to die with my face rotten, that even the wolves will shrink with horror at seeing me, and say to themselves, "That is the Four Bears, the friend of the whites."

Along with Four Bears, 90 percent of the tribe perished in the epidemic. The once prosperous nation, whose villages had constituted the biggest city on the Plains during Lewis and Clark's time, was reduced to barely a hundred inviduals, huddled together with remnants of the Arikaras and Hidatsas.

Word of the devastation would have reached Clark in St. Louis shortly before he died. He was experienced in the loss of friends, but it must have greatly saddened him, "the Red-Headed Chief," to ponder the fate of the people who had so warmly welcomed the expedition thirty years earlier. Showing up in Gerard's earth lodge nearly two centuries later would undoubtedly flood him with even stronger emotions. Outside, the three villages once teemed with life and noise, and the smoke of cook fires curled from the tops of hundreds of earth lodges, and neighbors and explorers alike shared food, music, and laughter to ward off winter's chill. Now there are only large, circular depressions in the ground marking where each lodge stood, like so many supplicating palms oustretched on the barren plain.

My guess is that Clark would have had the same trouble sleeping that I did that night, hearing

echoes of Four Bears' words whenever the night wind hissed or a cottonwood groaned as it shook in the gale. And I imagine that he, too, would have uttered a silent prayer that Gerard had adequately appeased the spirits of friendship with the smudge of his sweet grass.

———

"We proceeded on" is the most recurrent phrase in the journals of the Lewis and Clark expedition. Charles Floyd wrote it several times in the brief diary he kept before he died far from home—the first United States soldier to die west of the Mississippi, but certainly not the last. His comrades Patrick Gass, Joseph Whitehouse, and John Ordway used it all the time as well. So did the captains.

With three matter-of-fact words they could describe the act of getting up each morning, facing an unknown horizon whose only certainty was another day of hard work, and pushing forward with, if not confidence, then at least dogged determination to move at least a little farther toward that horizon before the sun went down.

"We proceeded on." It became, in effect, the Corps of Discovery's motto, a mantra that kept them going in the face of every obstacle. When I travel in their footsteps, I adopt it as my own. It reminds me that they didn't have the luxury to look backward, to pause and contemplate the past. And it helps me conjure up their spirits so that they can join me on my modern journey.

The captains in particular were Jeffersonian men, imbued with the Enlightenment notion of steady progress. "We proceeded on" could summarize their view of how the universe works. It would also influence their reactions to many of the starkest changes to be found today along their route across the continent.

Lewis, who devoted so much time to scientific descriptions, would no doubt be enthusiastic about the agricultural transformation of the Louisiana Territory. The Missouri, he had written his mother from Fort Mandan, "waters one of the fairest portions of the globe, nor do I believe that there is in the universe a similar extent of country equally fertile." He would probably nod his head, as if to say "I told you so," when he learned that the area is now the food basket for the nation and much of the world.

Clark, with his keen eye for terrain, had marked locations on his map as likely places for future forts and settlements. The mouth of the Kansas River, where the Missouri bends sharply toward the east, was such a spot. He would enjoy, I think, the vista from his old campsite. Where once two rivers met in the wilderness, now rises the skyline of Kansas City, the largest city along the Lewis and Clark route west of St. Louis. Other cities, like Omaha and Bismarck and Portland, grew up at strategic places that Clark had identified. "We proceeded on," he might say.

More changes. A series of dams, built to prevent flooding and to provide irrigation and hydroelectricity, has turned much of the Missouri into more lake than river. The "sublimely grand spectacle" of the Great Falls, which Lewis described so ecstatically, is now dominated by a concrete barrier that holds back the Missouri; except in times of unusually high water, the falls themselves are dry rocks. The same goes for the Columbia. Celilo Falls, the Long and Short Narrows, the Cascades—places that Clark noted for their "horrid appearance of this agitated gut swelling, boiling & whorling in every direction"—are now entombed under reservoirs.

What would the explorers think of the two mighty rivers now? To them, the raging cataracts were uncommonly magnificent, but they were also

Also within a century of the expedition, the towns of Lewiston, Idaho, and Clarkston, Washington, had sprung up at the confluence of the Snake and Clearwater Rivers (above), and at the mouth of the Columbia, the city of Astoria, Oregon (opposite), was a bustling seaport.

impediments. I can imagine Lewis noting ruefully at the Great Falls that their majesty had once reduced him to wishing for better words to adequately describe their beauty—and then walking excitedly into the powerhouse to see how the turbines work. On the Columbia (and its tributary, the Snake), Clark would be wide-eyed at the sight of deep-draft vessels carrying cargo toward the twin cities of Clarkston and Lewiston, now officially designated as *sea*ports though they are four hundred miles inland from the Pacific.

It would not escape their notice that the same dams that tamed the Columbia for boat traffic, and that generate electricity used as far away as Califor-

nia, have also virtually eliminated the salmon. The number of salmon, Clark wrote in 1805, was "incrediable to say." Even attempting to estimate their numbers seemed preposterous. I think he would be equally speechless today if he went with me into one of the deeper recesses of the Bonneville Dam. There one employee literally—and rather easily—counts each adult salmon that manages to swim past a window looking out on the dam's fish ladder.

Lewis and Clark would have questions about wildlife. They would remember beaching their canoes for hours as a buffalo herd forded the river; going for several months in which encountering a grizzly bear was almost a daily event; seeing enormous elk herds and packs of wolves; being kept awake at night by the slapping of beaver tails; witnessing a midday sky darkened by huge flocks of wild geese; filling their journals with description after description of animals they had never seen before, in numbers beyond imagination; passing through a landscape in which, as they wrote, "the Game is gitting so pleanty and tame in this country that Some of the party clubbed them out of their way."

Some of the species they recorded have vanished entirely; others are struggling back from the brink of extinction. Another side of the same coin upon which the nation emblazoned, "We proceeded on."

Likewise, we would encounter fewer Indians. Lewis and Clark had been the first to tell them they had a new "great father." In their speeches, the captains promised that he had "offered you the hand of unalterable friendship, which will never be withdrawn from your nation." But on the modern trail, moving from reservation to reservation, they would hear instead tales of lands lost and promises broken. For the Lakotas, the Nez Percé, the Shoshones, the Blackfeet, and the tribes along the Columbia, the offered hand turned into a fist. And even for those tribes that never experienced war with the United States—like the Salish and Hidatsas and Mandans—the handshake of friendship proved a bad bargain.

"Follow these councils," Lewis said in the conclusion to his first speech to western Indians, "and you will have nothing to fear, because the great Spirit will smile upon your nation and in future ages will make you to outnumber the trees of the forest." Even by the standards of the Virginia gentry, Lewis was acutely sensitive about matters of honor; seeing how his word was so cavalierly disregarded would probably start him sputtering, and then, perhaps,

send him into dark despair. Clark's face, I think, would turn as crimson as his hair, out of both anger and shame.

To cheer them, I'd take the captains through the White Cliffs of the Missouri in north-central Montana, protected by Congress from damming and development. This is another place where Lewis waxed rhapsodic, writing for pages about "scenes of visionary enchantment." I'd invite him to do what friends and I have done on several occasions: read passages from his journal and then look up from our campsite or canoe to see precisely what he had struggled so hard to describe. With luck, we might even see a bighorn on the cliffs.

On our journey together, the captains would learn that the western sky is still as big as it was for the Corps of Discovery, the horizons still as simultaneously intimidating and exhilarating. Nothing has changed the broiling summer heat on the Plains or the startling fury of a prairie hailstorm—not to mention the maddening persistence of mosquitoes up and down the Missouri. And the mountains? To Clark, they were the "Shineing Mountains." Lewis called them "tremendious . . . covered with eternal snows." Snow still covers their peaks in midsummer; from a distance they still shine. Farther west, winters on the Pacific coast are still sodden with rain.

It was on the coast where the Corps of Discovery got into the habit of carving their names into tree trunks. From the journal accounts, it seems few trees near the sea escaped their knife blades. I get the impression they emblazoned the date and their names and initials with particular gusto, relief, and pride, as the most tangible evidence they could think of to prove they had actually crossed the continent. But mixed in with those emotions was also a tinge of fear—fear that they might not make it back to their homes, that they would never be heard from again, that they and their remarkable achievements would be lost to history. Marking a tree was both a boast and a plea to be remembered.

The tree markings have long since disappeared. But other things now bear their names. On our hurried return toward St. Louis, I would point some of them out: towns, counties, and national forests, rivers and mountain passes, high schools and colleges, campsites and cafes, the Lewis and Clark Search and Rescue Association and the Lewis and Clark 24-Hour Wrecking Service. Where they ran out of whiskey, there is a Lewis and Clark Distillery. And where they switched from eating horses to eating dogs, there is the Lewis and Clark Animal Shelter.

Federal highway signs mark the "Lewis and Clark Trail" all the way from the Pacific to the east bank of the Mississippi, where they embarked on their epic journey. Near St. Louis, I would drive them over the Lewis Bridge and then the Clark Bridge, before dropping them off on the Illinois side, at the Lewis and Clark Motel. "We proceeded on," I would tell them on behalf of their nation, "but you weren't forgotten."

———

There would be much for them to report on to Mr. Jefferson, some of it with great pride, some of it with profound sorrow. Before we parted, I would add one more story, about what happened back in North Dakota on the morning after the cold night in the earth lodge with Gerard Baker.

Thanks to his sleeping bag, Gerard woke up warmer than I did. My feet felt like blocks of ice, and it took some time near the fire to restore them. Gerard teased me, saying that in honor of my experience he might give me an Indian name. What did I think of "Man Who Sleeps in Buffalo Robes" or "Smells Like Tripe"? Once more we shared stories over the fire. He invited me back for the summer, promising that we could visit a traditional sweat lodge he had built along the banks of the Missouri. A friendship was forming that has now lasted for a decade and a half—despite the distances between our homes and the differences of race and culture.

We have learned that we have many things in common. Among them is a passion for history, not just out of intellectual curiosity but based on a more practical belief: that the journey to a better future must include discovering the past and learning from it. And while our approach is to explore history by being clear-eyed about its darker moments, we both try to pay attention and respect to the spirits of those who came before us.

Gerard's desire to honor his ancestors and keep alive the traditions of his people had led him to the journals of Lewis and Clark, one of the best-written records about the Mandans and Hidatsas before the cataclysmic epidemic that nearly ended the tribes' very existence. My search to understand my nation, by retracing its pursuit of the next horizon, had led me to the same source. Along the trail of the Corps of Discovery, our paths had crossed, and if I could meet their spirits I would thank the two captains for bringing us together.

That morning was as cold as the morning before. The sun was rising, but the temperature was not going to reach zero. The north wind still howled. We had planned on hiking to the site of Fort Mandan, a walk guaranteed to be both bone-chilling and fatiguing. For a moment we considered staying put, near the warm comfort of our fire. But like Lewis and Clark, we were moved by the spirit of discovery. We packed up our gear and stepped out together to face the new day. And then we proceeded on.

Acknowledgments

L IKE THE TWO CAPTAINS at the heart of this story, we undertook our own "voyage of discovery" in creating this book and the documentary film upon which it is based. Like Lewis and Clark, we followed the Missouri River to its source, crossed the Rocky Mountains, and descended the Columbia to the sea. Like them, we were constantly awed by the landscape, challenged by the weather, surprised by unexpected obstacles, yet spurred on by a curiosity about what awaited us just beyond the next horizon. And like them, we returned with both our friendship and our appreciation for our country deepened by the experience.

But most important, like Lewis and Clark, we could not have completed our mission without the help and hard work of many other people.

Buddy Squires and Allen Moore—assisted by Roger Haydock—retraced the explorers' route with us, managing to capture both the exquisite details and majestic sweep of the land through their cameras' lenses. Their stunning images were augmented by the photographs and paintings compiled by Susanna Steisel and Pam Tubridy Baucom. Paul Barnes and Erik Ewers put those images together to create the film; Jennifer Bernstein and Cassandra Pappas performed the same alchemy for this book. Archie Ferguson added an elegant grace note with his jacket design.

Our own "corps" at Florentine Films made this project not only possible, but pleasurable: Brenda Heath, Susan Y. Butler, Patty Lawlor, Aaron Vega, and Craig Mellish. We are as proud of our crew as Lewis and Clark must have been of theirs.

Besides contributing book essays, Stephen E. Ambrose, William Least Heat-Moon, and Erica Funkhouser shared their enthusiasms and insights with us on-camera—as did Gerard Baker, John Logan Allen, Mylie Lawyer, and James P. Ronda, all of whom also helped guide our ultimate understanding of the story. Geoffrey C. Ward helped hone the telling of it. Gary E. Moulton, one of our consultants, provided us with more than historical guidance; his recently published edition of the expedition's journals was our bible, as it will be for generations of scholars and enthusiasts.

Hal Holbrook's superb narration took the script to new levels, just as the words of Lewis, Clark, and the other journalists were brought to life by the voices of other fine actors—Adam Arkin, Murphy Guyer, Matthew Broderick, Kevin Conway, Gene Jones, Sam Waterston, Tantoo Cardinal, Tim Clark, Daniel Von Bargen, John Trudell, and Ken Little Hawk.

236

The success of the Lewis and Clark expedition depended to a great degree on the generosity and assistance (though often overlooked or conveniently forgotten) of people already living along the route they followed. The same applies to our project. At every step along the way, local people overwhelmed us with hospitality and useful information. They are literally too many to mention, but we wish to thank a few in particular.

The Lewis and Clark Honor Guard of Great Falls, Montana; the Discovery Corps, Inc., of Omaha, Nebraska; Friends of Discovery, from Onawa, Iowa; and the Lewis and Clark Discovery Expedition of St. Charles, Missouri—these enthusiasts who preserve the spirit and look of the original expedition set up campsites for us to film, dragged a heavy canoe along a steep ridge, and patiently rowed, poled, and waded in knee-deep water to move a bulky keelboat back and forth in front of our cameras. Chairman Mike Jandreau and the members of the Lower Brulé Sioux Tribe kindly set up a village of tepees for us in South Dakota; farther upriver, the McLean County Historical Society and the North Dakota Parks and Recreation Department helped us appreciate the shelter of a fort and an earth lodge in a northern Plains blizzard; in crossing the Bitterroots, Harlan and Barb Opdahl kept us warm, dry, and well fed (three things Lewis and Clark missed); near the Pacific, Superintendent Cindy Orlando and her staff made Fort Clatsop National Memorial seem as if the explorers were still wintering there.

From the long list of boatmen who took us out on the great rivers, we especially want to thank Larry and Bonnie Cook of Missouri River Outfitters for their tours of the scenic White Cliffs; John and Stephenie Ambrose Tubbs for braving a rainstorm in the Gates of the Rocky Mountains; and Jim Peterson for taking us to spots on the middle Missouri where the current still chews at the riverbank and the snags and sawyers still await the uninitiated. Victor Bjornberg and Travel Montana made every trip to that state enjoyable.

For nearly thirty years, the Lewis and Clark Trail Heritage Foundation, Inc., has kept the remarkable story of the Corps of Discovery before the public—through its local chapters, its annual meetings along the trail, its publications, and its support of worthwhile projects. We thank them for an initial research grant to start our film, and we encourage anyone whose interest in the expedition has been stimulated by it to become members: The Lewis and Clark Trail Heritage Foundation, Inc., P.O. Box 3434, Great Falls, Montana, 59403.

We also wish to thank the American Philosophical Society, the Missouri Historical Society, and Yale University's Beinecke Library for sharing their treasure trove of expedition journals and artifacts with us. Special thanks go to Ashbel Green, our editor, who guided this book to completion, and to Gerry McCauley and Chuck Verrill, our agents, who helped conceive it.

Our film could not have been made without the generous financial support of General Motors; the Corporation for Public Broadcasting and the Public Broadcasting System; the Pew Charitable Trusts; the Arthur Vining Davis Foundations; the William T. Kemper Foundation; and the People of the State of Montana. Our good friends at WETA-TV, especially Sharon Rockefeller, David Thompson, and Phylis Geller, were equally instrumental in making it all possible.

Finally, we wish to thank our families—Sarah and Lilly Burns, and Dianne, Emmy, and Will Duncan—who reminded us that both the launching point and the final destination of every great expedition is the same place: home.

KEN BURNS
DAYTON DUNCAN
Walpole, New Hampshire

Bibliography

Allen, John Logan. *Passage Through the Garden: Lewis and Clark and the Image of the American Northwest.* University of Illinois Press, 1975.

Ambrose, Stephen E. *Undaunted Courage: Meriwether Lewis, Thomas Jefferson, and the Opening of the American West.* Simon & Schuster, 1996.

Anderson, Irving W. "A Charbonneau Family Portrait." Fort Clatsop Historical Association, 1988.

Appelman, Roy. *Lewis and Clark: Historic Places Associated with Their Transcontinental Exploration.* National Park Service, 1975.

Betts, Robert B. *In Search of York: The Slave Who Went to the Pacific with Lewis and Clark.* Colorado Associated University Press, 1985.

Chuinard, Eldon G. *Only One Man Died: Medical Aspects of the Lewis and Clark Expedition.* Arthur Clark Co., 1980.

Coues, Elliot, ed. *The History of the Lewis and Clark Expedition.* Dover reprint of 1893 Francis P. Harper 4-vol. ed., 1987.

Cutright, Paul Russell. *Lewis and Clark: Pioneering Naturalists.* University of Illinois Press, 1969.

DeVoto, Bernard. *The Course of Empire.* Houghton Mifflin, 1952.

———, ed. *The Journals of Lewis and Clark.* Houghton Mifflin, 1953.

Dillon, Richard. *Meriwether Lewis: A Biography.* Coward-McCann, 1965.

Duncan, Dayton. *Out West: An American Journey.* Viking Penguin, 1987.

Funkhouser, Erica. *Sure Shot and Other Poems.* Houghton Mifflin, 1992.

Furtwangler, Albert. *Acts of Discovery: Visions of America in the Lewis and Clark Journals.* University of Illinois Press, 1993.

Gass, Patrick. *A Journal of the Voyages and Travels of a Corps of Discovery Under the Command of Capt. Lewis and Capt. Clark.* Ross & Haines, 1958.

Holmberg, James J. " 'I Wish You to See & Know All': The Recently Discovered Letters of William Clark to Jonathan Clark." *We Proceeded On,* vol. 18, no. 4 (November 1992).

Jackson, Donald. *Among the Sleeping Giants: Occasional Pieces on Lewis and Clark.* University of Illinois Press, 1987.

———, ed. *Letters of the Lewis and Clark Expedition, with Related Documents: 1783–1854.* 2d ed. University of Illinois Press, 1978.

———. *Thomas Jefferson and the Stony Mountains: Exploring the West from Monticello.* University of Illinois Press, 1981.

———. "Call Him a Good Old Dog, but Don't Call Him Scannon." *We Proceeded On,* vol. 11, no. 3 (July 1985).

Large, Arlen. "Lewis and Clark Under Cover," *We Proceeded On,* vol. 15, no. 3 (August 1989).

Lavender, David. *The Way to the Western Sea: Lewis and Clark Across the Continent.* Harper & Row, 1988.

Moulton, Gary E., ed. *The Journals of the Lewis and Clark Expedition.* University of Nebraska Press, 1988.

Osgood, Ernest S., ed. *The Field Notes of Captain William Clark, 1803–1805.* Yale University Press, 1964.

———. "Our Dog Scannon." *Montana: The Magazine of Western History,* vol. 26, no. 3 (Summer 1976).

Quaife, Milo M., ed. *The Journals of Captain Meriwether Lewis and Sergeant John Ordway.* Historical Society of Wisconsin, 1916.

Ronda, James P. *Lewis and Clark Among the Indians.* University of Nebraska Press, 1984.

———. "A Moment in Time: The West—September 1806." *Montana: The Magazine of Western History,* vol. 44, no. 4 (Autumn 1994).

Thwaites, Reuben Gold, ed. *Original Journals of the Lewis and Clark Expedition.* Arno Press reprint, 1969.

Wheeler, Olin D. *The Trail of Lewis and Clark, 1804–1806.* 2 vols. New York, 1904.

Index

China, 5
Chinook Indians, 51, 160, 171, 172
Christmas fern, *38*
Civil War, xiii, *210*, 211, 224
Clark, Gen. George Rogers, 7, 13, 121, 138
Clark, Meriwether Lewis, 220, 222
Clark, William: during boat accident, 95; animals and plants studied by, 35–41; in Bitterroot Mountains, 140–2, 145, 191–2; compass used by, *21;* and courts-martial, 29; death of, 222; diet of, 151–3; distance traveled estimated by, 160; and Floyd's death, 31; at fork of Missouri River, 100–2, 106; friendship of Lewis and, 119–25; illness of, 113; Indians and, 47–60, 63–7, 71, 81–2, 111, 114–15, 135, 137, 143, 144, 173, 188–90, 215, *217*, 220, 228, 230, 233; Jean-Baptiste raised by, 214–15; Jefferson and, 14, 20, 207–8; journal of, xi, 23, *23*, 24, 31, 40, 41, 43, 57, 60, 73, 76, 77, *90*, 92, 99, 103, 104, 106, *125*, 141, 142, 149–51, 153–9, 161, 191, 193, 198–201, *202*, 218, 227; keelboat dispatched downriver by, 84; keelboat sketched by, *29;* and Lewis's decline, 223, 224; list of supplies by, *24;* and Louisiana Purchase, 16, 21; maps drawn by, *94*, 116, 166–7, 231; marriage of, xiv, 123, 221; naming of landmarks by, 97, 193, *194*, 195; on Pacific coast, 168–9, *170*; recruited by Lewis to lead expedition, xviii, 11, 13–14; rewarded by Congress, 208; roster of Corps by, *28;* Sacagawea and, 92–3, 95, 103, 135, 176–82, 213; sets off, 21–5; slave brought on expedition by, *see* York; Spanish plot against, 79–80; at Three Forks, 112; winter quarters of, 71–4, 76, 77, 160–1, 165, 175
Clark's Fork, *120*
Clatsop Indians, 160–1, 164, 165, *168*, 171; artifacts of, 51, *52*; burning of villages of, 215; canoe stolen from, 187; food of, 152
Clearwater River, 143, 145, 149
Clymer, John, *91*, *169*
Coastal Mountains, 167
codes, 12, *13*
Collins, John, 29
Colter, John, 199, *210*, 211
Columbia River, 5, 118, 137, 140, 150–8, *159*, 160–1, 167, 181, 213, 220, 231, *188*; damming of, 187–8; Indians along, 93, 150–1, 154, *155*, 156, 207; map of, *158*
Columbia River Gorge, *156*
Columbus, Christopher, 118
Comanche Indians, 138
condor, California, *38*
Congress, U.S., 123, *210*, 212, 234; appropriation for expedition by, *10*, 12; Lewis and Clark rewarded by, 208; and Louisiana Purchase, 64; and vaccination of Indians against smallpox, 228

Continental Divide, xiii, *116*, 118, 133–135, 182, 208, 213
Corps of Discovery, x, xiii–xvii, 8, *25*, 42, 77, 79, 85, 89, 106, 111, 116, 124, 145, 153, *158*, 165, 175, 209, 211–13, 224, 225, *226*, 231, 234–5; daily routine of, 22–3; division into four groups of, 192; dog traveling with, 26–7; expenditures of, 12; fatality suffered by, 31, 201; food for, 152; Indians and, 47, 50–1, 55, 58, 62–7, 134, 135, 143, *197*, 200, 215; keelboat of, *29;* landmarks named after members of, *94*, 97; and Madoc myth, 138; mapping by, 166; at Pacific Ocean, 157; physical evidence left by, 195, 212; plants and animals recorded by, 37, *41;* return of, x, *174*, 202, 203, 207, *209*, 218; roster of, *28;* Sacagawea and, 92, 137, 177, 179–82, 193; sets off, 21
courts-martial, 29, 58
Cree Indians, 71
Crow Indians, 53, 64, 71, 142, *178*
Cruzatte, Pierre, 22, 95–6, 179, 198
Curtis, Edward S., *53, 59, 115, 170, 172, 177, 178, 195*
Custer, Gen. George Armstrong, 67, 220
Cutright, Paul Russell, 218
cutthroat trout, 37

Delashelwilt, 172, 173
Delaware Indians, 138, 211
DeVoto, Bernard, xx
Dixon, Joseph Kossuth, *63*
Dobell, Byron, xiii
Drouillard, George, 22, 40, 47, *90*, 113, 114, 117, 195, 196, 211
Duncan, Dayton, xiii–xiv, 227–35

Eagle's Feather, 58
Ellicott, Andrew, 9
English, *see* British
Enlightenment, the, 209, 231
eulachon, *152*
Evans, John, 138

Faro, 130, 132
Field, Joseph, 28, 42, 196
Field, Reuben, 28, 66, 196
Fisher, L. Edward, *xvii*
Flathead Indians, 139, 195
flax, Lewis's, 37
Floyd, Charles, 28; death of, 30, 31, 66, 201, 231; journal of, 22–24, 28, 218, 219
food, 106, 152, 153, 212; for Christmas, 73; foraged by Sacagawea, 93, 95; hunting for, 22, 23, 43, 76–7, 89, 198; of Indians, 131–3, 143, 144, 150–3; prepared by Charbonneau, 96; shortages of, 122, 140–2, 165, 168
Fort Clatsop National Memorial, 168
fossils, 10, 36
Four Bears, 82, 229–31

Fox Indians, 211
Frazer, Robert, 219
Freeman-Custis expedition, 202
Frémont, John C., 213
French, 5, 7, 8, 40, 79; Indians and, 49, 55, 71; Louisiana purchased from, *see* Louisiana Purchase
Funkhouser, Erica, 176–83
fur traders, 5, 7, *78*, 79, 81, 166, 167, 200, 201, 208, *210*, 211, 215, 229; muskets supplied to Indians by, 131
Fur Traders Descending the Missouri (Bingham), 200

Gallatin, Albert, 112
Gass, Patrick, 28; journal of, xix, 22, 23, 31, 34, 40, 41, *42*, 50, 60, 73, 76, *81*, 98, 99, 136, 139, 141, 145, 171, 188, 192, 198, 218, 219, 231; later life of, *210*, 211; published account of expedition by, 218, *223*
Gray, Robert, 5, 153
Gray's Bay, 157
Great Plains, 34, 35, *42*, 193, 213, 218, 224–5, 228, 234; Indians of, 51, 55, 59, 81, 143 (*see also specific tribes*); Pike's expedition to, 202; plants and animals of, 37, 40–2; winter on, 72, *74*
Green, Joshua, 15
Grinnell, George Bird, *217*
grizzly bears, 90–2, 104, *223*, 224, 232

Half Man, 54
Hall, Hugh, 29
Hamilton, Alexander, 202
Hamilton, Maria, *210*
Hancock, Julia ("Judith"), 221
Harding, Chester, *220*
Harvard University, 124; Museum of Comparative Zoology, 36; Peabody Museum, 84
Haydock, Roger, xiv–xvi
Haynes, F. J., *102*
Hays, William Jacob, *xii, 41*
Henry, Alexander, the Younger, 65
Herd of Bison Crossing the Missouri River, A (Hays), *xii*
Hidatsa Indians, 58, 71, *77*, 80–82, 84, 90, 100, *102*, 137, *177*, 201, 215, 227, 233; Bodmer's paintings of, *83*, *214*; Canadian fur traders and, 79, 131; Sacagawea captured by, 78, 113, *132*, 177, 179–81; smallpox epidemic among, 228–9, 235; winter spent with, 64, 65, 80, 171
Hollow Horn Bear, *53*
House of Representatives, U.S., 8
Hood, Mount, *151*, 153
Hudson's Bay Company, 79
Hunkpapa Indians, 62–4
hunting, 22, 23, 43, 89, 90, 171, 198; by Indians, 75–6

Illustration Credits

Each credit lists source, negative or accession number (when one exists), and artist/photographer's last name (where one is known).

ARCHIVE ABBREVIATIONS

AAS	American Antiquarian Society
AHC	American Heritage Center, University of Wyoming
ALFP	The American Lives Film Project, Inc.
ANS	Academy of Natural Sciences of Philadelphia
APS	American Philosophical Society Library
BL	Beinecke Rare Book and Manuscript Library, Yale Collection of Western Americana
DCL	Dartmouth College Library
Gilcrease	Gilcrease Museum, Tulsa, Oklahoma
Joslyn	Joslyn Art Museum
Lautman	Robert Lautman Photography
LOC	Library of Congress
MHS	Missouri Historical Society, St. Louis
MTHS	Montana Historical Society
NA	National Archives
NAA	National Anthropological Archives, Smithsonian Institution
NMAA/AR	National Museum of American Art, Washington, D.C./Art Resource, N.Y.
OrHiS	Oregon Historical Society

ARTISTS AND PHOTOGRAPHERS

Anderson, John A.; **Bingham,** George Caleb; **Bodmer,** Karl; **Burns,** Ken; **Catlin,** George; **Clark,** William; **Clymer,** John; **Curtis,** Asahel; **Curtis,** Edward Sheriff; **Dixon,** Joseph Kossuth; **Duncan,** Dayton; **Fisher,** Edward; **Grand,** William; **Harding,** Chester; **Haynes,** F. Jay; **Hays,** William Jacob; **Hooker,** William Jackson; **Huffman,** Layton Alton; **Jackson,** William Henry; **Jefferson,** Thomas; **Kane,** Paul; **King,** Charles Bird; **Lampert,** Harold; **Lautman,** Robert; **Lewis,** Meriwether; **Lewis,** Samuel; **Lukens,** Isaiah; **McClintock,** Walter; **Meltzoff,** Stanley; **Miller,** Alfred Jacob; **Moore,** Allen; **Morganthaler,** Charles; **Morrill,** Justin E.; **Orduño,** Robert; **Peale,** Charles Willson; **Peale,** Rembrandt; **Pursh,** Frederick; **Reeves,** Enoch; **Reid,** Russell; **Russell,** Charles M.; **Seltzer,** Olaf; **Shindler,** A. Zeno; **Soulard,** Antoine; **Squires,** Buddy; **St. Memin,** Charles B. J. F.; **Stanley,** John Mix; **Throssel,** Richard; **Watkins,** Carleton E.; **Wilson,** Alexander; **Wimar,** Charles

ENDPAPERS: front APS, 917.3 L58 Codex E, pp. 132–3, Clark; **back** APS, 705 sketch file 3, Codex H, Clark.
ii–iii: BL, Tableau 41, Bodmer.

KEN BURNS
Preface: Come Up Me

viii: ALFP, Moore. **xii:** Buffalo Bill Historical Center, Cody, WY, Gertrude Vanderbilt Whitney Trust Fund, 3.60, Hays. **xvii:** Missouri Bankers Association, Fisher.

Introduction
xx: ALFP, Squires.

CHAPTER I
Look Forward to Distant Times

2–3: Lautman, Lautman. **4:** White House Historical Association, R. Peale. **6:** Lautman, Lautman. **7:** BL, WA MSS 303 Vol. 1 #2, Soulard. **9:** Independence National Historical Park, C. W. Peale. **10: left** NA, M. Lewis; **right** NA, M. Lewis. **11: top** H. M. Stewart Collection, Virginia Military Institute, 88.083, Lukens; **middle** Buffalo Bill Historical Center, Cody, WY, 1988.8. 1584; **bottom** NA, M. Lewis. **13: top left** LOC, 27748-203 (code), Jefferson; **bottom left** LOC, 27748-204 (key), Jefferson; **top right** MHS, Clark papers, Jefferson. **14:** Independence

National Historical Park, C. W. Peale. **15: right** Historical Society of Cheshire County, NH, May 26, 1804; **bottom** AAS, July 13, 1803. **17:** GeoSystems Global Corporation, Morrill.

CHAPTER 2
Floyd's Bluff

18–19: Joslyn, VIGXXXI, Bodmer. **21:** National Museum of American History, Smithsonian Institution, 95-3550. **23:** MHS, Clark papers, 26 Oct. 1805, Clark. **24: top** BL, WA MSS 303-#4, Clark; **bottom** St. Charles County Historical Society, Morganthaler. **25:** Joslyn, NA 5, Bodmer. **26:** Culver Pictures, AN1016 CP015 003. **28:** BL, WA MSS 304, Clark. **29:** BL, WA MSS S-897 Folder 3 p. 7, Clark. **30: top** Gilcrease, 0176.2129, Catlin; **bottom** NMAA/AR, 1985.66.376, Catlin.

CHAPTER 3
Land of Plenty

32–33: Amon Carter Museum, Fort Worth, TX, 1964.58, Stanley, *Herd of Bison, Near Lake Jessie* (detail). **36:** ANS, Coll.79 Lawson Vol. 2:12, Wilson. **37:** Joslyn, NA204, Bodmer. **38: left top** APS, 917.31 L58 Codex J, p. 80, M. Lewis; **left upper middle** APS, 917.3 L58 Codex J, p. 83, M. Lewis; **left lower middle** APS, 917.3 L58 Codex J, p. 71, M. Lewis; **left bottom** APS, 917.3 L58 Codex J, p. 66, M. Lewis; **right** MHS, Voorhis #2, March 2, 1806, Clark. **39: top left** ANS, Pursh; **top right** ANS, Pursh; **bottom left** ANS, Pursh; **bottom right** ANS, Hooker. **41:** National Museum of Wildlife Art, 989.64, Hays. **42:** ALFP, Burns.

CHAPTER 4
Children

44–45: BL, F805, McClintock. **48: top** NMAA/AR, 1985.66.384,22, King; **left** American Numismatic Society, CT93164. **49:** NA, M. Lewis. **52: left** APS, 917.3 L58 Codex J, p. 1, M. Lewis; **right** APS, 917.3 L58 Codex F, p. 147, M. Lewis. **53: left** DCL, Vol. 3, plate 82, E. S. Curtis; **middle** DCL, Vol. 5, plate 150, E. S. Curtis; **right** DCL, Vol. 5, plate 16, E. S. Curtis. **54:** NMAA/AR, 1985.66.438B, Catlin. **56:** Nebraska State Historical Society, A547:1-27, Anderson. **57:** AAS, Jackson. **59:** LOC, LC USZ62 46989, E. S. Curtis.

WILLIAM LEAST HEAT-MOON
Vision Quest

63: NAA, 83-751, Dixon. **66:** Western History Collections, University of Oklahoma Library, Phillips #436.

CHAPTER 5
Perfect Harmony

68–69: NMAA/AR, NMAA 1985.66.502, Catlin. **72:** APS, 917.3 L58 Codex J, M. Lewis. **74:** ALFP, Moore. **75:** Joslyn, Tableau 18, Bodmer. **77:** AHC, Throssel #8 (TP #6), Throssel. **78:** Joslyn, 1963.612, Miller. **80:** Gilcrease, 0126.2179, Catlin. **81:** BL, Tableau 19, Bodmer. **82:** Joslyn, NA117, Bodmer. **83: top** MTHS, Russel; **bottom left** Joslyn, R23, Bodmer; **bottom right** Joslyn, NA133, Bodmer. **84:** Peabody Museum, Harvard University, T1908, Mandan Indians.

CHAPTER 6
Scenes of Visionary Enchantment

86–87: Joslyn, Tableau 29, Bodmer. **90: top** Joslyn, NA 208, Bodmer; **bottom** MHS, Voorhis #1, May 25, 1805, M. Clark. **91:** John F. Clymer, courtesy Mrs. Doris Clymer, Clymer. **92:** State Historical Society of North Dakota, A-4264, R. Reid (photographer). **94: left** APS, Codex D, p. 131, M. Lewis; **right** Joslyn, Sheet 34, Clark. **95:** Joslyn, NA64, Bodmer. **99:** BL, Tableau 35, Bodmer. **101:** BL, Thwaites #25, Clark. **102:** Haynes Foundation Collection, MTHS, H326, Haynes. **104–105:** Portage Route Chapter, Lewis and Clark Trail Heritage Foundation, Inc., Great Falls, MT, Orduño.

CHAPTER 7
The Most Distant Fountain of the Mighty Missouri

108–109: ALFP, Moore. **112:** MTHS, 947-567. **114:** ALFP, Squires. **115:** DCL, Vol. 8, p. 44, E. S. Curtis. **116:** Lautman, Lautman. **117:** ALFP, Squires. **118:** Gilcrease, 0137.756, Seltzer.

STEPHEN E. AMBROSE
Friends

120: APS, Codex H, p. 33, Clark. **125: top** APS, Codex K, p. 105, M. Lewis; **bottom** APS, Codex N, p. 28, Clark. **126–127:** GeoSystems Global Corporation, Morrill.

CHAPTER 8
Hungry Creek

128–129: ALFP, Squires. **132:** AAS, Jackson. **133:** Idaho Forest Industry, Coeur d'Alene, ID, Russell. **134:** Denver Public Library, Western History Collection, F26714. **136:** APS, 917.3 L58 Codex F, p. 130, M. Lewis. **139:** MTHS, 952-797, Russell. **140:** ALFP, Squires. **143:** Idaho State Historical Society, 2715. **144:** OrHiS, 95017. **145:** ALFP, Squires.

CHAPTER 9
O! The Joy

146–147: Stark Museum of Art, Orange, TX, 31.78/216 WOP19, Kane. **150:** DCL, Vol. 8, plate 274, E. S. Curtis. **151:** ALFP, Squires. **152:** APS, Codex J, p. 93, M. Lewis. **154:** OrHiS, 21099, Watkins. **155: top** Stark Museum of Art, Orange, TX, 31.78/210 WOP13, Kane; **bottom left** MHS, Voorhis Collections, Clark; **bottom right** Montreal Museum of Fine Arts, purchase, William Gilman Cheney Bequest, 1947.991, Kane. **156:** Historical Photograph Collection, Washington State University Libraries, PC2, Lampert. **157:** APS, 917.3 L58 Codex H, p. 147, Clark. **158:** APS, Codex I, p. 152, Clark. **159:** APS, 917.3 L58 Codex H, p. 148, Clark. **160:** J. Paul Getty Museum, Los Angeles, CA, 84.XM.493.1, Watkins.

CHAPTER 10
Wet and Disagreeable

162–163: DCL, Vol. 8, plate 287, E. S. Curtis. **166:** LOC, US West 1806, S. Lewis (after Clark). **168:** ALFP, Squires. **169:** John F. Clymer, courtesy Mrs. Doris Clymer, Clymer. **170: top** DCL, Supp. II, plate 396, E. S. Curtis; **bottom** BL, WA MSS 303#32110, Vol. 2, Clark. **171:** APS, Vol. 6, Weather Diary, Lewis. **172:** DCL, Vol. 11, plate 366, E. S. Curtis. **173:** DCL, Vol. 9, facing page 4, E. S. Curtis. **174:** OrHiS, 50130 #944A, Grand.

ERICA FUNKHOUSER
Finding Sacagawea

177: left DCL, Vol. 8, plate 266, E. S. Curtis; **right** DCL, Vol. 4, facing page 142, E. S. Curtis. **178:** DCL, Vol. 4, facing page 178, E. S. Curtis. **181:** DCL, Vol. 3, facing page 18, E. S. Curtis.

CHAPTER 11
See Our Parents Once More

184–185: DCL, Vol. 6, plate 184, E. S. Curtis. 188: DCL, Vol. 8, facing page 106, E. S. Curtis. 189: AHC, 18571, Throssel. 191: Nez Perce National Historical Park, 1037, Reeves. 194: **top** MTHS, 981-376, Huffman; **bottom** ALFP, Moore. 195: DCL, Vol. 6, plate 208, E. S. Curtis. 196: **top** Joslyn, NA145, Bodmer; **middle** Joslyn, NA144, Bodmer; **bottom** Joslyn, NA142, Bodmer. 197: Duncan. 199: AHC, 2394 box 4 file 1 TP 204-9, Throssel. 200: Metropolitan Museum of Art, 33.61, Bingham. 202: Exxon Co., USA, courtesy MHS, order 5142, Meltzoff.

CHAPTER 12
Done for Posterity

204–205: Gilcrease, 0126.1598, Wimar. 208: AAS, Nov. 5, 1806. 209: Eric P. Newman, Mercantile Money Museum, courtsey MHS. 210: **top** Denver Public Library, Western History Collection, F19851, Jackson; **bottom left** Willard Family Association; **bottom right** Jeanette Taranik. 212: Lautman, Lautman. 214: Joslyn, Vignette XXVI, Bodmer. 216: **top left** NMAA/AR, 1985.66.146, Catlin; **bottom left** NAA, 2962-b, Jackson; **right** Olin D. Wheeler, *The Trail of Lewis and Clark, 1804–1806*. 217: **top** NAA, 3545-A, Shindler; **bottom** Olin D. Wheeler, *The Trail of Lewis and Clark, 1804–1806*. 219: National Museum of the American Indian, Smithsonian Institution, Lone Dog. 220: Mercantile Library of St. Louis, Harding. 221: **top** The New-York Historical Society, 1971.125, St. Memin; **bottom** ALFP, Moore. 222: BL, Zc10 807 gac. 223: BL, Zc10 807 gac. 225: Joslyn, Tableau 47, Bodmer.

DAYTON DUNCAN
We Proceeded On

226: NA, 77-H-10580P-1. 229: Special Collections, Kansas City Public Library, V-675 Bridges Hannibal #3. 230: Montana Power Company. 232: Washington State Historical Society, Tacoma, p35 #36553, A. Curtis. 233: OrHiS, 36611 #54B.

Film Credits

Lewis & Clark
*The Journey of the Corps
of Discovery*

A Film by
KEN BURNS

Written by
DAYTON DUNCAN

Produced by
DAYTON DUNCAN
KEN BURNS

Edited by
PAUL BARNES
ERIK EWERS

Cinematography by
BUDDY SQUIRES
KEN BURNS
ALLEN MOORE

Narrated by
HAL HOLBROOK

Voices
ADAM ARKIN
Meriwether Lewis

MURPHY GUYER
William Clark

SAM WATERSTON
Thomas Jefferson

MATTHEW BRODERICK
John Ordway

KEVIN CONWAY
Patrick Gass

GENE JONES
Joseph Whitehouse

with
TANTOO CARDINAL
TIM CLARK
KEN LITTLE HAWK
JOHN TRUDELL
DANIEL VON BARGEN

Associate Producer
SUSANNA STEISEL

Coordinating Producer
PAM TUBRIDY BAUCOM

Assistant Editor
AARON VEGA

Senior Creative Consultant
GEOFFREY C. WARD

Program Advisers
JOHN LOGAN ALLEN
STEPHEN E. AMBROSE
WILLIAM LEAST HEAT-MOON
GARY E. MOULTON
FRANK MUHLY
LYNN NOVICK
JAMES P. RONDA

Chief Financial Officer
Brenda Heath

Administrative Assistants
Susan Y. Butler
Patty Lawlor

Supervising Sound Editor
Ira Spiegel

Dialog Editor
Marlena Grzaslewicz

Music Editor
Jennifer Dunnington

Assistant Sound Editor
Renee Taylor

*Sound Post-Production and
Sound Effects*
Sound One

Re-Recording Mixers
Dominick Tavella
Lee Dichter

Assistant Camera
Roger Haydock
Kevin Kertscher

Production Assistant
Steve Szymanski

Animation Stand Photography
The Frame Shop
Edward Joyce and
Edward Searles

Maps
GeoSystems Global
Corporation
Justin E. Morrill

Archival Still Photography
Stephen Petegorsky

Voice-Over Recording
Lou Verrico
A&J Recording Studios

Other Voice-Over Recording
Third Street Sound,
Hollywood
Bad Animals, Seattle
Waves Sound Recorders Inc.,
Hollywood

Sound Department Management
Erik Ewers
Craig Mellish

Sound Recording
Erik Ewers
Richard H. Kuschel

Post-Production Assistant
Craig Mellish

Post-Production Interns
Regina Lehman
Christine Lyon
Dave Mast
Bettina Anne Carpenter
Christopher Ohlson
Carrie Spring
Xantha Bruso
Kara Mickley
Skyler Casey
Marius Glabinski

Kine Camera Operator
Christopher Ohlson

Negative Matching
Noelle Penraat

Title Design
James Madden

Color
Duart Film Labs

Spirit Data Cine Film Transfer
The Tape House
John J. Dowdell III

Expedition Members
Lewis and Clark Honor
Guard, Great Falls, Montana

The Discovery Corps, Inc.,
Omaha, Nebraska
Friends of Discovery,
Onawa, Iowa
Lewis and Clark Discovery
Expedition,
St. Charles, Missouri

Boatmen
Larry and Bonnie Cook,
Missouri River Outfitters
Marty Smith,
Three Rivers Rafting
John and Stephenie Tubbs
Hugh Ambrose
Dave Parchen
Steve Szymanski
John Adams
Doyle Meeker
Walt Marten
John Voorhis
Jerry Farenthold
Glen Bishop
Harry Fry
Ivan Larsen
Mike McGillivary,
North West Guide Service
Jim and Pete Peterson

Helicopter Service
Minuteman Aviation, Inc.

Stock Footage
Energy Productions Inc.
Fabulous Footage Inc.
National Geographic

Legal Services
Robert N. Gold

*Instrumentalist and
Studio Arrangements*
Bobby Horton

Traditional Music
Jacqueline Schwab, piano
Jay Ungar, violin
Molly Mason, guitar
Matt Glaser, violin
L. E. McCullough, tin whistle

Native American Music
Dennis Yerry
Ken Little Hawk
Dane Lebeau
Jimmy Fall
Bernard Cottonwood
Butch Brown
Melvin Youngbear

Music Recorded at
Soundesign,
Brattleboro, Vermont

Music Engineers
Billy Shaw
Alan Stockwell

Songs
"Heart of the Heartland"
Written and performed by
Peter Ostroushko
Courtesy of Red House Records
"Buffalo Hump"
Written and performed by Skip
Gorman
Courtesy of Rounder Records
"When Summer Ends"
Written by Phil Cunningham
Performed by Silly Wizard
Courtesy of Green Linnet Records
"Cheyenne Eyes"
Written and performed by
Gary Stroutsos, Epamindondas
Trimis, Joseph Fire Crow
From "Winds of Honor"
Courtesy of Makoche Music/BMI
"Along the River"
Performed by Gary Stroutsos
From "Winds of Honor"
Courtesy of Makoche Music/BMI
"Woman Comes First"
Written and performed by
Joseph Fire Crow
From "Fire Crow"
Courtesy of Makoche Music/BMI
"Song of Departure"
From "Spirit of Song"
Courtesy of Makoche Music/BMI
"Original Grass Song"
Performed by the
Mandaree Singers
Courtesy of Sweetgrass Records
"Simple Majesty"
Written and performed by
Bobby Horton
"Brown Adam the Smith"
Arranged and performed by
Bobby Horton
"Sacagawea's Lullaby"
Written by Emmy Duncan
*Original Soundtrack Album
available on RCA Records
Cassettes and CDs*

Locations
Fort Clatsop National Memorial
Lewis and Clark State Park,
Onawa, Iowa
McLean County Historical
Society, North Dakota
Beaverhead National Forest
Bitterroot National Forest
Charles M. Russell National
Wildlife Refuge
Clearwater National Forest

Ecola State Park, Oregon
Fort Abraham Lincoln State
Park, North Dakota
Fort Canby State Park,
Washington
Helena National Forest
Lower Brule Sioux Tribe,
South Dakota
Meriwether Lewis Site,
Natchez Trace Parkway
Nez Perce National Forest
Niobrara State Park, Nebraska
Rossow Buffalo Ranch,
North Dakota
Salmon National Forest
Sherwood Outfitting,
Columbus, Montana
Triple U Ranch, Pierre,
South Dakota
Dan Wicklander Ranch,
North Dakota
U.S. Bureau of Land
Management

Archival Material
American Antiquarian Society
American Heritage Center,
University of Wyoming
American Philosophical Society
Amon Carter Museum
Beinecke Rare Book and
Manuscript Library,
Yale University
Brown Brothers
Church of Jesus Christ of
Latter-Day Saints Archives
Division
John F. Clymer, courtesy
Mrs. Doris Clymer
Colorado Historical Society
Dartmouth College Library
Robert Drummond
Exxon Company, U.S.A.
The Filson Club
Gilcrease Museum,
Tulsa, Oklahoma
Historical Society of
Pennsylvania
Idaho Forest Industries
Idaho State Historical Society
Independence National
Historical Park
Joslyn Art Museum
Library of Congress
Metropolitan Museum of Art
Missouri Historical Society
Montana Historical Society
Montreal Museum of Fine Arts
Museum of Fine Arts, Boston
National Anthropological
Archives

National Archives
National Gallery of Art
National Museum of American
Art/Art Resource
Nebraska State Historical
Society
New Bedford Free Public
Library
New-York Historical Society
New York Public Library
Nez Perce National
Historical Park
Oregon Historical Society
David Palmquist
Royal Ontario Museum
St. Louis Art Museum
St. Louis Mercantile Library
Stanford University Library,
Special Collections
Stark Museum of Art
State Historical Society of
North Dakota
United States Army Military
History Institute
Washington State University
Libraries
White House Historical
Association
George S. Whiteley IV
Willard Family Association
of America, Inc.
Winterthur Museum
Wyoming State Archives

Extra Special Thanks
The Lewis and Clark Trail
Heritage Foundation, Inc.
Travel Montana

Special Thanks
Lower Brule Sioux Tribe
Nez Perce Tribal
Executive Committee
American Philosophical Society
Missouri Historical Society
Adams National Historical Site
City of Astoria, Oregon
Greater Falls Travel
Greater St. Charles Conven-
tion and Visitors Bureau
Keene State College,
Mason Library
Missouri Film Office
Montana Power Company
North Dakota Film
Commission
North Dakota Parks and
Recreation Department
Oregon State Parks
The Park Hyatt,
Washington, DC
South Dakota Public
Television

Film Credits

South Dakota Department
of Tourism
The Thomas Jefferson
Memorial Foundation
Triple "O" Outfitters,
Pierce, Idaho
University of Nebraska Press
U.S. Department of the Interior,
National Park Service
U.S. Department of Agriculture,
National Forest Service
U.S. Department of the Interior,
Bureau of Land Management
Walpole Public Library
Washington State Parks and
Recreation Commission
The People of Walpole,
New Hampshire

Michael Alderman, Anne
Ames, Cheri Anderson,
Kate Arnold-Schuck,
Georgia Barnhill, Joe Blake,
Jerome Boeckman, Stanley
Brown, John Cameron,
Christopher Cardozo,
Elizabeth Carroll-Horrocks,
Dr. Edward C. Carter II,
John Carter, Philip N.
Cronenwett, Debra Dearborn,
Rita Dockery, Julie Dunfey,
Tom DuRant, Rudy Eiler,
Jeff Eslinger, Charlie Farren,
Dick Gannon, Victoria Gohl,
Sherlee and Leo Graybill, Jan
Grenci, Diane Hamann,

Sandra Hilderbrand,
Strode Hinds, Steve Holen,
Richard Hunt, Mike Jandreau,
Curt Johnson, the David and
Dorothy Jones family,
Stephen Jones, J. Brooks
Joyner, Dianne Keller, Hedi
Kyle, Courtney Little, Mylie
Lawyer, Larry Mensching,
Bonnie Morgan,
Joseph A. Murgalo, Jr.,
Carol Murray, Harlan and Barb
Opdahl, Cynthia Orlando,
Ricardo Perez, Hadley B.
Roberts, Sheila Robinson,
Duane Sneddeker, Angela
Spann, Marcia Staigmiller,
Steve Szymanski, Jeanette
Taranik, John Taylor, Ellen
Thomasson, Mikki Tint, John
Toenyes, Shelley Welsch,
Ruth H. Willard, Tom, Brian,
and Ira Ziegler

Special Thanks (Book)
Academy of Natural Sciences
American Numismatic Society
Buffalo Bill Historical Center
Culver Pictures
Denver Public Library
Detroit Institute of Art
Historical Society of
Cheshire County
J. Paul Getty Museum
Mercantile Library of St. Louis
Kansas City Public Library

Missouri Bankers Association
Montreal Museum of
Fine Arts Collection
National Museum of
American History
National Museum of
American Indians
National Museum of
Wildlife Art
Peabody Museum,
Harvard University
St. Charles Savings and
Loan Association
University of Oklahoma,
Western History Collection
University of Wyoming,
American Heritage Center
Virginia Military Institute
Washington State Historical
Society Research Center
Lt. Col. Keith Gibson
Ned Gray
Michael Labriola
Robert Lautman
Carol Lichtenberg
Robert Orduño
Donald Peterson
Michael Shoup
Carol M. Spawn

National Publicity
OWEN COMORA ASSOCIATES

*Produced in Association
with* WETA-TV,
Washington

*Executive in Charge of
Production for WETA*
PHYLIS GELLER

Project Director for WETA
DAVID S. THOMPSON

Associate Producer for WETA
KAREN KENTON

Publicity for WETA
MARY SCHULTZ

SHARON ROCKEFELLER,
President and CEO

A PRODUCTION OF
FLORENTINE FILMS

Executive Producer
KEN BURNS

*Copyright © 1997,
The American Lives Film
Project, Inc.*

All Rights Reserved

Funding Provided by
General Motors Corporation
The Pew Charitable Trusts
Corporation for
Public Broadcasting
Public Broadcasting Service
The Arthur Vining
Davis Foundations
William T. Kemper Foundation
The People of
the State of Montana